RICHARD BARNFIELD, COLIN'S CHILD

Florida State University Studies

Number Thirty-Eight

RICHARD BARNFIELD, COLIN'S CHILD

by

HARRY MORRIS

THE FLORIDA STATE UNIVERSITY

1963

Copyright 1963 by Florida State University
Library of Congress Catalogue Card Number 63-63443.

Printed and bound in the United States of America
by the Hillsboro Printing & Lithographing Company, Tampa, Fla.

Published under the Auspices
of
THE RESEARCH COUNCIL
The Florida State University

vii

CONTENTS

the best for pastorall: . . . sir *Philip Sidney,* master
Challener, Spencer, Stephen Gosson, Abraham Fraunce
and *Barnefield.*

Francis Meres, Palladis Tamia

Dowland to thee is deare . . .
Spenser to mee; whose deepe Conceit is such,
As passing all Conceit, needs no defence.

Barnfield, To his friend
Maister R. L.

I should like to dedicate this work
to my mother
GERTRUDE A. MORRIS

PREFACE

The debts I have incurred in writing this book are many, some of such a kind that I cannot acknowledge them here. But I should like especially to record my gratitude to the Folger Shakespeare Library and Tulane University. The former provided me with a fellowship, giving me full access to its superb facilities and Renaissance holdings, without which I could never have written this book; the latter provided me with a summer grant, making it possible for me to stop thinking about my stomach long enough to get to work at my typewriter.

I should like also to thank the reference librarians at the Howard Tilton library of Tulane University, Mrs. Dorothy Whittemore and Miss Betty Mailhes, for their uncomplaining and untiring labors in procuring books for me through interlibrary loan.

My greatest academic debts are to Professors Irving Ribner, Dick Taylor Jr., and Max Schulz, all of Tulane University, who kept me often from grave errors, directed my feet on proper paths, and read parts of my work at various stages. I must thank also Miss Mary Lynn Johnson and Mr. James Whitman for innumerable aids of all kinds, as well as Mrs. Sarah Kost for invaluable secretarial assistance.

Chapter II of the present work appeared in altered form in TULANE STUDIES IN ENGLISH, the editors of which I should like to thank for permission to reprint here. An essay on Barnfield which I published in *PMLA* along with a subsequent controversy with Prof. Walter F. Staton Jr. helped form some of my ideas, but I have not reproduced substantial parts of these works here.

HARRY MORRIS

Tallahassee, Florida
October 1, 1962

CHAPTER I

INTRODUCTION

Richard Barnfield has his place in the history of Elizabethan poetry. He has written at least one fine ode, good enough for several critics of the nineteenth century to claim for Shakespeare, as well as a graceful sonnet similarly misappropriated. The freshness of his pastoral poetry receives praise still in the accounts of that genre; and his sonnet sequence to Ganimede, while deplored for its unnatural sentiments, is somewhat more original than many performances in that difficult and demanding medium which became popular in the last decade of the sixteenth century. But despite almost unvarying praise for those things which Barnfield does well, almost no critic or scholar has felt it necessary to write an extended study of his poetry. The Rev. Alexander B. Grosart was the first to edit the complete poems,[1] although editions of individual quartos preceded his work. Boswell the younger printed *The Encomion of Lady Pecunia* for the Roxburghe Club in 1816, and John Payne Collier published the same volume again in 1866 in his *Illustrations of Old English Literature*. E. V. Utterson printed a bowdlerized edition of *Cynthia* in 1841, and J. O. Halliwell-Phillipps prepared *The Affectionate Shepheard* for the Percy Society in 1842. But none of these forerunners of Grosart provided either a life of the poet or a critical evaluation of the poems. In fact before Grosart's labors almost no biographical information had come to light. One sentence in H. C.'s *Piers Plainnes Seauen Yeres Prentiship* (1595) shows that Barnfield had early recognition: "Young Daphnis hath giuen his verdict of *The Shepheards Content*: duely praising it, as it meriteth";[2] and Meres' affectionate tribute three years later establishes Barnfield's contemporary reputation as resting upon pastoral verse:

As *Theocritus* in Greeke, *Virgil* and *Mantuā* in Latine,

---

[1] *The Complete Poems of Richard Barnfield*, ed. A. B. Grosart, printed for the Roxburghe Club (London, 1876).

[2] Ed. H. Varnhagen (Erlangen, 1900), p. 37. H. C. is thought by most scholars to be Henry Chettle. In support of this identification is the possibility that the friendship for Robert Greene displayed by both Barnfield and Chettle at the time of the unfortunate Greene's death may have developed kindliness between them.

Sanazar in Italian, and the Authour of *Amyntae Gaudia* and *Wasinghams Meliboeus* are the best for pastorall: so amongst vs the best in this kind are sir *Philip Sidney,* master *Challener, Spencer, Stephen Gosson, Abraham Fraunce* and *Barnefield.*

· · · · · · · · · · · · · · ·

As noble *Mecaenas* that sprung from the *Hetruscan* Kinges not onely graced Poets by his bounty, but also by beeing a Poet himselfe; and as *Iames the 6.* nowe king of Scotland is not only a fauorer of Poets, but a Poet, as my friend master *Richard Barnefielde* hath in this Disticke passing well recorded:
     The King of Scots now liuing is a Poet,
          As his Lepanto, and his furies show it:
so *Elizabeth* . . . .[3]

All mention of Barnfield ceases with these remarks until, approximately three-quarters of a century later, Edward Phillips links him to others who by 1675 were perhaps remembered best also for their pastoral works: "Richard Barnfeild, one of the same Rank in Poetry with Doctor *Lodge, Robert Green, Nicholas Breton,* and other Contemporaries already mention'd in the foregoing Treatise of the Moderns."[4] I do not know through what channels or by what processes of criticism Phillips arrived at his opinion, but it is clear that he owes nothing to Meres since none of the names connected with Barnfield in *Theatrum Poetarum* correspond to the representatives of pastoral in *Palladis Tamia.* Barnfield's inclusion in a work in 1675 implies that he was still read, still known, and that some of his volumes were still available at least to an interested few.

After Phillips, a whole century passes before further comment on Barnfield. Thomas Warton's *History of English Poetry,* in a comment on Fraunce's translation of Virgil's second eclogue, defends Barnfield from a charge of homosexuality. Expressing surprise that Fraunce should select the second eclogue rather than any of the other nine, Warton continues:

Such at least is our observance of external propriety, and so strong the principles of a general decorum, that a writer of the present age who was to reprint love-verses in this style, would be severely reproached and universally proscribed. I will instance only in the *Affectionate Shepherd* of Richard Barnfeilde, printed in 1595. Here, through the course of twenty sonnets, not inelegant, and which were exceedingly popular,

---

[3]*Palladis Tamia,* ed. D. C. Allen (New York, 1938), pp. 284ʳ-284ᵛ.
[4]*Theatrum Poetarum* (London, 1675), p. 231.

the poet bewails his unsuccessful love for a beautiful youth,
by the name of Ganimede, in a strain of the most tender passion,
yet with professions of the chastest affection.

Warton has confused *The Affectionate Shepheard* (1594) with
the sonnets in *Cynthia* (1595), and his dates are hopelessly mud-
dled, unless he refers to editions now lost to us.[5] Biographically
this comment is worth little, since the preface to *Cynthia* shows
that even at first publication *The Affectionate Shepheard* was
objectionable to the "tolerant age" of Elizabeth. Warton's claim
that the sonnets were exceedingly popular cannot be given much
attention, for he seems to believe that *The Affectionate Shepheard*
was a sonnet sequence which received republication at least twice
more in the two editions of *Cynthia*.

Only in 1813 do we get the first documentary facts of the
poet's pre-literary life. Although Wood had omitted Barnfield,
Bliss's revised edition of *Athenae Oxonienses* repairs the oversight.
Working from a record of his matriculation at Brasenose College
—"1589, Noũeb 27⁰ Richard Barefield Stafford. gen. fil. aetat.
15"—Bliss concluded that the poet had been born in 1574 and
had come of gentle parents, residing in Staffordshire. To this,
Bliss added very little, embarrassed at his inadequacy:

> [Barnfield] took the batchellor of arts, Feb. 5, 1591-2, and
> in the following Lent performed the exercise for his master's
> gown, to which, however, I cannot find that he was ever ad-
> mitted. Certain it is, that he did not take this degree previous
> to the year 1600, as his name does not occur in the register of
> congregation, which is very perfect and regular about that
> period. I am not able to offer any other particulars of the life
> of Barnfield, and can now only mention him as a writer, in
> which capacity he seems to have been much esteemed by his
> contemporaries.[6]

---

[5] *The History of English Poetry*, a full reprint—Texts and Notes—of
Edition, London 1778 & 1781 (London, 1870), p. 887. In a footnote to
this passage Warton cites Lownes as printer of *The Affectionate Shepheard*
when in fact it was Danter. The dates he gives there for *Cynthia* correspond neither to that he gives in the text nor to any known editions.
In reading the Stationers' Register he forgets that January, 1594, would
be January, 1595, new calendar.

[6] Anthony A. Wood, *Athenae Oxonienses*, ed. Philip Bliss (London,
1813), I, 683-684. Malone had noticed the record of Barnfield's matriculation at Brasenose and gave the information to the younger Boswell,
who edited *The Encomion of Lady Pecunia* for the Roxburghe Club in
1816.

Since neither Barnfield nor his publisher blazoned "M. A. Oxford" on the title page of the 1598 or 1605 editions of *Lady Pecunia* but rather the simple legend "Graduate in *Oxford*," Bliss's findings for the years up to 1600 are probably correct for the years thereafter as well. The phrase "much esteemed by his contemporaries" must, like Warton's "exceedingly popular," be received with caution. From Bliss's documentation, it is clear that the statement derives from the notices given by Meres and Phillips.

Joseph Hunter, in *Chorus Vatum* (c. 1852), collected some tentative and uncertain notes: "Several Richard Barnfields of the poet's time appear in a pedigree of a family of the name seated in Shropshire at Newport and Edgemund . . . . At a Court for the manor of Fulham in the reign of James I a Richard Barnfield takes a cottage and acre of land, garden and orchard in Old Brentford by surrender of John Stamford and Ann his wife."[7] As Grosart stated later, the pedigree was the poet's and through it Hunter might have ascertained eventually all that Grosart discovered through this clue in 1876. The names of Fulham, Brentwood, and Stamford suggest that the second item has no relationship to the poet since they are all common to Middlesex but alien to either Shropshire or Staffordshire at the end of the sixteenth century.

Five years before Grosart's work, W. Carew Hazlitt made some ill-advised guesses about the origins and associates of Barnfield, for which Grosart takes him to task. Since the initials R. B. were appended to some commendatory verses prefacing Richard Verstegan's *Restitution of Decayed Intelligence*, Hazlitt toyed with the idea that Barnfield was a Dutch or Flemish name:

> Verstegan himself came from Flanders; possibly the two were brought into acquaintance in that way. But in Barnfield's case, the change of residence must have been less immediate, for surely no author, whom we could name, has fairer pretensions to be regarded as a writer of genuine, untainted vernacular English.[8]

Grosart made these speculations look ridiculous, but he remains

---

[7] From a typescript of Hunter's *Chorus Vatum*, British Museum Add. MS. 21487 in the Folger Shakespeare Library, Vol. II, p. 3. The entry under each name is paginated anew.

[8] *The History of English Poetry*, ed. W. Carew Hazlitt (London, 1871), IV, 439-440.

indebted to Hazlitt for the assertion that "a collected edition of Barnfield's surviving works is a want in English literature, and would only form an appropriate and deserved tribute to the genius of so graceful and so neglected a poet."[9]

With the exception of Bliss's work in the various registers at Oxford, Barnfield biography proper begins with Grosart in 1876. Led by Hunter's note to Harleian MS. 1241 in the British Museum, Grosart published the Barnfield pedigree[10] along with a commentary—sometimes quite unnecessary and sometimes excessively detailed and far afield—that can hardly be added to. I give the main branches of the genealogy as printed in the Harleian Society Visitation of Shropshire, since Grosart's contains some errors:[11]

Barnfeld of Edgmond and Newport
Harl. 1396, fo. 23; Harl. 1241, fo. 105; S., fo. 27.
Arms: Harl. 1396.—Or, on a bend gules three mullets argent, an annulet for difference, sable.
Crest: A lion's head erased sable, ducally crowned gules.
[These arms and crest were confirmed, 18 May 1604, to Robert Bamfield or Barnfield, of Edgmond, co. Salop, a kinsman of Sir Amyas Barnfeld of Poultemore, co. Devon.—(Guillim, 1724, p. 102.)

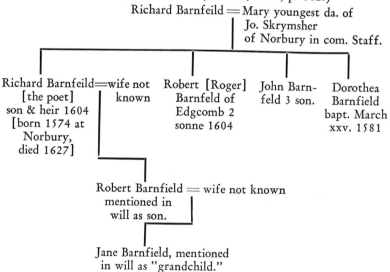

Richard Barnfeild = Mary youngest da. of
Jo. Skrymsher
of Norbury in com. Staff.

Richard Barnfeild = wife not known [the poet] son & heir 1604 [born 1574 at Norbury, died 1627]

Robert [Roger] Barnfeld of Edgcomb 2 sonne 1604

John Barnfeld 3 son.

Dorothea Barnfield bapt. March xxv. 1581

Robert Barnfield = wife not known mentioned in will as son.

Jane Barnfield, mentioned in will as "grandchild."

─────────

[9]Hazlitt's *Warton*, IV, 439.
[10]Since published with additions from Harleian MS. 1396 by the Harleian Society, eds. George Grazebrook and John Paul Rylands (London, 1889), I, 34.
[11]Grosart seems unaware that a coat of arms was confirmed for the

This pedigree sent Grosart next to the Visitation of Staffordshire for the family history of the poet's mother. The Skrymshers came from York before settling in Staffordshire, Thomas Skrymsher, Barnfield's great-grandfather, being the first to settle in the county. Seventeenth-century Skrymshers traced their ancestry back to the Scrymgeours, the hereditary standard-bearers of Scotland.[12] Thomas Skrymsher, a prothonotary of the Common Pleas, upon bringing his family to Norbury, purchased the manor house and other estates nearby, founding the Staffordshire branch of the family. His eldest son, John, was the father of Mary, the poet's mother:[13]

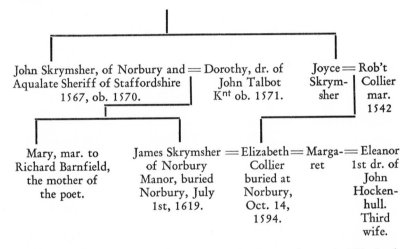

John Skrymsher, of Norbury and = Dorothy, dr. of
Aqualate Sheriff of Staffordshire   John Talbot
    1567, ob. 1570.   K^{nt} ob. 1571.

Joyce = Rob't
Skrym-   Collier
sher   mar.
         1542

Mary, mar. to
Richard Barnfield,
the mother of
the poet.

James Skrymsher = Elizabeth = Marga- = Eleanor
of Norbury   Collier   ret   1st dr. of
Manor, buried   buried at   John
Norbury, July   Norbury,   Hocken-
1st, 1619.   Oct. 14,   hull.
                   1594.   Third
                                          wife.

Of great importance in the Skrymsher pedigree is Elizabeth Collier, the first wife of James Skrymsher, the poet's uncle; she is commemorated in Barnfield's "Epitaph vpon the Death of His Aunt" which appeared in the 1598 edition of *The Encomion of Lady Pecunia*. Her burial in October, 1594, throws light not only upon the date of the epitaph but also upon the makeup of the 1598 volume. Apparently unable to satisfy his publisher with newly written pieces, Barnfield filled out the quarto with work

family in 1604. He errs also in calling the poet's great-grandfather James instead of Thomas. However, I add from Grosart what is lacking in the Harleian Society publication. All brackets are either Grosart's or Grazebrook and Ryland's.

[12]Grosart, *The Complete Poems*, p. vii.

[13]Pedigree is taken from Grosart, *The Complete Poems*, p. xlv.

from the bottom of his trunk. The Collier family were prominent in and around Stone, James, Elizabeth's grandfather, having bought "Darlaston and almost all of Stone."[14] Through Robert Collier's marriage to Joyce Skrymsher, Elizabeth was first cousin to her husband.

The Norbury register corroborates these pedigrees. An entry for 1572 records the marriage of the poet's parents:

Richardus Barnefield et Maria Skrimsher matri. cōtraxere
Aprillis xvi.

Baptism of their first child took place two years later:

Richardus Barnfield baptizatus fuit mensis [June] xiii. 1574.

Remaining entries in the Norbury register date the baptism of his sister and the burial of his mother, one following close upon the other:

Dorothea Barnefield filia Ricardi Barnfield baptizata fuit
Martii xxv. [1581].
Maria Barnefield sepulta fuit die mēsis p[rae] d[icto] xxvii°.[15]

Apparently Mary died of complications resulting from the birth of her second child.

Nothing is known about Barnfield from the time of his baptism until his matriculation at Brasenose in 1589; and after his performance for the degree of Master of Arts in Lent of 1592, no further mention of him occurs until his appearance on the London scene, where, from the testimony of the dedication of *The Affectionate Shepheard*, we may assume him to have been taken into the literary circle surrounding the fascinating and learned Mary Herbert, Countess of Pembroke. Barnfield's entré to this scintillating group may have come through the offices of Abraham Fraunce, one of its mainstays. Several poetic productions and literary entanglements, dating from Barnfield's earliest adventures in London, reveal prominently the name of Fraunce. Robert Greene's death on September 3, 1592, did not put an end to quarrels and controversies occasioned by that unfortunate man's career. Gabriel Harvey continued his attacks, although his adversary was unable to reply. Thomas Nashe took up the defense of his dead friend, and an anonymous supporter penned a tribute to Greene's memory which, under the title of *Greenes Funeralls*, was also a counter-attack upon his ill-wishers. The authorship of

[14]Grosart, *The Complete Poems*, pp. xvii-xviii.
[15]*The Complete Poems*, p. x.

this pamphlet, which was not entered in the Stationers' Register until February 1, 1593/4, has been vigorously debated.[16] Later the same year, probably in November, *The Affectionate Shepheard* appeared also anonymously. But in January, 1595, Barnfield acknowledged his authorship of *The Affectionate Shepheard* in an address to the "Gentlemen Readers" of his new volume, *Cynthia*. Although he did not claim *Greenes Funeralls*, there are excellent reasons to believe that he was its author. Both *Greenes Funeralls* and *The Affectionate Shepheard* pay glowing tribute to a writer who appears to be a close and helpful friend of the author and who is presented under the pastoral name of Amyntas. I suspect that this person may be Abraham Fraunce, although with the exception of Charles Edmonds[17] all students of Barnfield have identified Amyntas as Thomas Watson.

Abraham Fraunce was born in Shrewsbury between 1558 and 1560.[18] He attended Shrewsbury school, his name appearing in the register of scholars for 1571. G. C. Moore Smith suggests that this was a date of re-entry and that Fraunce probably attended first some years earlier. Sir Henry Sidney, Lord President of the Marches of Wales since 1559, sent his son Philip to Shrewsbury school from 1564 to 1568. It is quite possible that Fraunce began before Philip left. In any case, by 1576 Philip was paying the expenses of Fraunce's education at St. John's College, Cambridge. After taking the M. A. degree in 1583, Fraunce entered Gray's Inn and was called to the bar in 1588. In the meantime, Sir Philip had died on October 17, 1586, but Fraunce never forgot his debt to the family, and in 1587 he dedicated *The Lamentations of Amyntas for the Death of Phillis* and in 1588 *The Arcadian*

---

[16]See Charles Crawford, *"Greenes Funeralls,* 1594, and Nicholas Breton," *SP,* Extra Series, I (1929), 1-39; R. B. McKerrow, ed. *Greenes News both from Heauen and Hell By B. R. 1593 and Greenes Funeralls By R. B. 1594* (Stratford-upon-Avon, 1922); Warren B. Austin, "A Supposed Contemporary Allusion to Shakespeare as a Plagiarist," *SQ,* VI (1955), 373-380; Harry Morris, "Richard Barnfield, 'Amyntas,' and the Sidney Circle," *PMLA,* LXXIV (1959), 318-324; and Chapter V below.

[17]*Shakespeare's Venus and Adonis,* The Isham Reprints, ed. Charles Edmonds (London, 1870), "Preface" to *The Passionate Pilgrim,* p. xxiii, paginated separately.

[18]For the material on Fraunce's life, I have gone to G. C. Moore Smith's introduction to the edition of *Victoria* in Bang's *Materialien,* Vol. XIV (Louvain, 1906), still the best account.

Rhetorike to "the Ladie Mary, Countesse of Penbroke"; in 1588 the Latin prose work entitled *Insignium, Armorum, Emblematum, Hieroglyphicorum, et Symbolorum* was dedicated to Sir Robert Sidney, Sir Philip's brother; and also in 1588 *The Lawiers Logike* was dedicated to Henry Herbert, Earl of Pembroke, the dead Philip's brother-in-law. All other printed works of Fraunce—the *Emanuel* of 1591 and the two parts of *Yuychurch* in 1591 and 1592—were dedicated to Mary Herbert, her title gracing the names given to the works in imitation of Sir Philip's *The Countess of Pembrokes Arcadia*. Fraunce possibly returned to Shropshire in 1588, to practice law at the Court of the Marches in Ludlow, where his patron Henry Herbert served as Lord President of the Marches of Wales, replacing Henry Sidney, Mary's father.

The relationship of these facts to Barnfield's known biography should not be overlooked. Born and undoubtedly raised at Norbury in Staffordshire, Barnfield was only about five miles from Newport and six from Edgmond, both just over the county line in Shropshire and both locations of older and larger branches of the poet's family. Even at his death, his will, indicating that he spent the latter part of his life at Darlaston, near Stone in Staffordshire, shows that his country life was centered never farther than twelve miles from family ties and acquaintanceships in Shropshire. Therefore, when in his earliest productions, he several times addresses an Amyntas, dedicates *The Affectionate Shepheard* to Penelope Rich, Sidney's Stella, and commemorates lyrically within the work Sir Philip himself, it is not strange to seek for contacts with Abraham Fraunce. Between Barnfield and the older writer from Shrewsbury seems to have existed the classic relationship of the youth sent to the city with letters of introduction from home which contain expressions of gratitude for whatever help a former neighbor might give to the bearer. Such a hypothesis satisfies the implications of Barnfield's lines to Amyntas in "The Shepheards Content" better than the theory that a deep, strong, and selfless friendship on the part of an older and well-established literary figure like Thomas Watson should develop almost immediately after Barnfield's arrival in London:

> And thou my sweete *Amintas* vertuous minde,
> Should I forget thy Learning or thy Loue;
> Well might I be accounted but vnkinde,
> Whose pure affection I so oft did proue.
>
> (E4ᵛ)

It would seem that Fraunce not only received him kindly but also suggested that he try an entry to the old Sidney group through Penelope Rich. A difficulty arises in the following stanza, which states clearly that Amyntas is dead: "But sleepe his soule in sweet Elysium" (F^r). Joseph Hunter believed Fraunce to be alive as late as 1633. But Hunter may have erred and Fraunce have died not later than 1595.[19] Not to be forgotten either are Barnfield's dedications in the 1598 *Lady Pecunia* to Edward Leigh and Nicholas Blackleech, both of Gray's Inn. Grosart and Arber sensed a connection with the Inn of Court, but no search has ever turned up Barnfield's name in connection with Gray's. Still, it is not unreasonable to suppose that Barnfield first went to London, from the university, as Fraunce before him, with the intention of entering Gray's. Fraunce, as a resident therein from 1583 to 1588, might have been the link to Leigh and Blackleech. Also in the 1598 volume is a dedication to John Steventon of Dothill, a very small town in Shropshire, not far from Newport and Edgmond. The appeal to Steventon suggests that the poet had not severed completely his ties with his father's people, even though the elder Barnfield had left Shropshire to live with his wife's people in Staffordshire.

Barnfield could not have remained in the aura of the Penshurst gathering long. His second acknowledged work was dedicated nominally to William Stanley, Sixth Earl of Darby; figures such as Amyntas, Sir Philip Sidney, and Penelope Rich, who had appeared so importantly in *The Affectionate Shepheard,* are missing altogether from *Cynthia.* The real dedicatee is Queen Elizabeth, although the sonnet sequence perpetuates Barnfield's relationship with Ganimede, the object of his affections in the first volume, and pays continued tribute to Spenser and Drayton. A probable explanation for the shift in Barnfield's poetic loyalties is the disappearance from the scene of Abraham Fraunce. Whether or not Fraunce had died by 1595, as I suspect, at least he stopped publishing. If not dead, he ceased his perennial dedications to the Sidney family either because he had returned to Shropshire to practice law or because he simply did not care to write any longer, and after 1594, Barnfield alludes never again to Amyntas.

---

[19]See Harry Morris, "Richard Barnfield, 'Amyntas,' " etc., 318-324; Harry Morris, "Thomas Watson and Abraham Fraunce," *PMLA*, LXXVI (1961), 152-153; and Chapters II and VI below.

The volume published in 1598 indicates that the poet had severed almost all personal relationships with writers in London. Dedications are either to men from Gray's Inn or to an acquaintance from Shropshire. If the 1605 edition of the same volume was indeed dedicated to Sir John Spencer of London, as Grosart claims, then this isolation remains unchanged. The praises of Sidney, Spenser, Daniel, Drayton, and Shakespeare, sung in poems collected for these publishing ventures, do not imply friendship. The only figure whom Barnfield addresses with warmth is the rather mysterious R. L., sometimes identified as Richard Lynche but not on very good evidence.

Precisely when Barnfield left London it is impossible to determine. He could have gone at any time. Not only the 1605 edition of *Lady Pecunia* could have been written from the country but also the 1598 edition and even *Cynthia* as well. It is evident that Fraunce wrote much of his work at the Court of the Marches in Wales and sent or brought it down to London for publication. Barnfield could have done the same, but I doubt that he left London before the 1598 *Lady Pecunia*. It bears the signs of having been seen through the press by the author, and the dedication to John Steventon of Dothill, Salop, reads as though written by a person in the city to a friend in the country. As difficult to determine as the date of his going is the place in which he settled. His will, in the District Probate Court at Lichfield, opens with the simple statement, "I Richard Barnfield of Dorlestone in the Countie of Stafford Esquire." He was buried at St. Michael's in Stone, less than two miles south of the site of Darlaston, a village to be identified with Barnfield's Dorlestone, but apparently no longer an active community. Present road maps indicate that Darlaston Hall still stands, but it appears to be the only remnant of the village. The old Darlaston is not to be confused with the thriving modern community in the southeast corner of the county. Grosart and Arber have speculated that Barnfield retired to the country early, and "in all likelihood leased some part of their farmland from the Colliers, if indeed his aunt (of the epitaph) did not herself provide for his settlement there."[20] Wherever he went and whatever he did after leaving London are relative mysteries. The only documents Grosart turned up for the period between the publication of *Lady Pecunia* in 1605 and the poet's

---

[20]Grosart, *The Complete Poems*, p. xviii.

death were the will and burial notice in St. Michael's register and an incidental piece of information that, before James Skrymsher died in 1619, he appointed the poet's father, Richard Barnfield, one of the executors of his estate. However, in a record of Final Concords, published by the William Salt Archaeological Society under the title of *Collections for a History of Staffordshire*[21] there is the following entry:

> On the Octaves of St. Hillary .7 James I [January 20, 1611] Between Richard Barnefilde, armiger, and John Coyney, gentleman, complainants, and James Skrimshaw, armiger, and Eleanor, his wife, deforciants of a messuage, a garden, 20 acres of land, 20 acres of meadow, and 60 acres of pasture in *Hales*.
>
> James and Eleanor remitted all right to Richard and John and to the heirs of Richard, for which, Richard and John gave them £100.

James Skrimshaw can be only the poet's uncle, who was living at Norbury and had been Sheriff of Staffordshire in 1608 and who had married Eleanor Hockenhull, making her the third mistress of Norbury manor, the first having been the Elizabeth of Barnfield's epitaph to his aunt. John Coyney is undoubtedly the father of the George Coyney of Chipnal who had married Winifred, sister to James Skrymsher and aunt to the poet. The Richard Barnefilde can be either the poet or his father. The relationship with John Coyney suggests that it is the poet's father who, according to the Shropshire Visitation, being there designated as "of Edgmond," had returned to Shropshire after sojourning with his wife Mary at Norbury manor at least until after their son Richard was born. Everything about the elder Richard from 1611 on indicates a marked rise in fortunes. Apparently so poorly established at the time of his marriage to Mary Skrymsher in 1572 that he had to live with his wife's family at Norbury, by 1619 he is stable enough to be named by his wealthy brother-in-law James as one of the executors of the Norbury estate. Furthermore he is referred to in the Concords as armiger, pointing to the confirmation in 1604 to Robert Barnfield of Edgmond, the poet's brother, of family arms and crest. Now at Edgmond, the elder Richard would be only some six miles from Chipnal, the probable residence of John Coyney. Hales is a scant three miles from Chipnal just over into Staffordshire, and it is quite plausible that two such close

---

[21] (London, 1900), III, 37.

neighbors would go into a farming or livestock venture together on new property so close to the holdings of one.

The poet's life came to a close in March, 1627, and he was buried in the churchyard of St. Michael's in Stone, some two and a half miles from the Darlaston of his will, on the 6th of the month. The will and accompanying inventory of goods show that Barnfield died in worldly security if not precisely in the affluence scholars often claim. Although he had a son and granddaughter to inherit him, no land was passed on, and his worldly goods were appraised by his auditors at "Some lxvi $\underline{l}$., xv^s, 11^d."[22] Except for these few frail documents in time, Richard Barnfield defies our attempts to know more about him other than what he himself has made testimony to in the three or four volumes of his verse. In general his was the life of an elder son, whose family was able to indulge him in a good education and an extended sojourn in London. Possibly a career in law was intended for him, but he never pursued it. Choosing instead to retire to the country, he lived there a life so quiet that he was not heard from again, either in the verse that he loved apparently to write or in the documents that attend merely living, until the notice of his death:

> Richardus Barnefeild generosus sepultus
> fuit Sexto Die Martij.[23]

---

[22]Grosart, *The Complete Poems*, p. xvii. Something might be said here about the biographies that came after Grosart's. Arber's brief notes are taken from his predecessor and add nothing except perhaps to increase the belief that Barnfield was a rich man. Edmund Gosse's account in the *DNB* errs in claiming the poet's birthplace as Norbury in Shropshire, a mistake perpetuated in many another dictionary of biography, and adds to the picture of the wealthy country squire by housing our man in a "mansion" at Darlaston. The highly fanciful reconstruction by Montague Summers (*The Poems of Richard Barnfield*, [London, 1936], pp. vii-xxx), seems more interested in establishing Barnfield as a homosexual than in any judicial reappraisal of facts.

[23]Grosart, *The Complete Poems*, p. xvii.

CHAPTER II

THE AFFECTIONATE SHEPHEARD

Richard Barnfield was only twenty when in 1594 a slim quarto issued from the press of John Danter for sale at the shop of T. G[ubbin] and E. N[ewman] in Saint Dunstone's Churchyard in Fleet Street.[1] Entitled *The Affectionate Shepheard*, it was dedicated to Penelope Rich but carried no author's name. Of its five poems two were long and three relatively short. The full name of the title piece was "The Teares of an affectionate Shepheard sicke for Loue. OR The Complaint of *Daphnis* for the Loue of *Ganimede*"; divided into two parts, called lamentations, it was the longest work in the volume. It was followed by a second major piece: "The Shepheards Content. OR The happines of a harmles life." The shorter poems, in order of inclusion, were a sonnet beginning "Loe here behold these tributarie Teares"; "The Complaint of Chastitie"; and "Hellens Rape."

Although *The Affectionate Shepheard* appeared anonymously, Barnfield claimed it the following year in the preface to *Cynthia*:

> Gentlemen; the last Tearme there came furth a little toy
> of myne, intit'led, *The affectionate Shepheard*.
> (A.^{r})

Upon this book, the poet's contemporary reputation rested, since it is for pastoral verse that Barnfield was praised by the author of *Piers Plainnes*, by Meres, and perhaps by Phillips. Yet no modern scholar has done more than to mention this volume. Barnfield's work is neither insignificant nor unattractive. "The Shepheards Content" is a very pleasant poem, and all the pastoral verse deserves closer examination, wider reading than it has received up to now.

Pastoral in England broadened into two great streams—one of poetry, the other of prose—at the appearance of Spenser's *Shepheardes Calender* (1579) and Sidney's *Arcadia* (1590). Preceded by Barclay's eclogues (1515), Googe's (1563), and Turberville's translations of Mantuan (1567), *The Shepheardes Calender* marked a departure in style and accomplishment and so

---

[1] At present only two copies are known to exist: one in Sion College Library and the other in The Folger Shakespeare Library.

instituted a vogue. Even then the pastoral remained purely a poetic function until Sidney's MS. of the *Arcadia* began to circulate. In the minds and practices of the lesser writers who came after, the prose work merged with the poetic into one great confluence and source for their labors. From Spenser came the eclogue, from Sidney the lyric, spread in profusion throughout the prose pages of the *Arcadia*.

The earliest imitator of Spenser is Michael Drayton, whose *Shepheards Garland* (1593) so much resembles *The Shepheardes Calender* that no other English source need be sought to explain its form and general content; but not far behind Drayton is Richard Barnfield, a life-long admirer and imitator of Spenser, who establishes in his first acknowledged work an immense debt to this great master of pastoral and who never ceases to increase that debt until he stops publishing altogether. But the publication of *The Affectionate Shepheard* requires in explanation of its composition additional observance of the pastoral scene. The title poem is not a series of eclogues nor is it a string of lyrics; it is a stanzaic poem of some length, divided into "Tears" or lamentations, each dirge encompassing one day. To locate the sources for Barnfield's structural divisions is not only to account for the poem's divergence from the example of Sidney and Spenser but also to fill in the background of pastoral poetry of the 1580's and 1590's.

In 1585 Thomas Watson published his Latin pastoral *Amyntas*. Abraham Fraunce's *The Lamentations of Amyntas for the death of Phillis*, "paraphrastically translated out of Latine into English Hexameters" followed two years later. Although Fraunce failed to acknowledge his original until 1591 when he republished *The Lamentations* as the second part of *The Countesse of Pembrokes Yuychurch*, the work was a close translation of Watson's *Amyntas*. Fraunce's poem, both by Elizabethan standards and modern, is a pedestrian affair. Yet, strangely enough, it was widely popular, for three new editions of the 1587 version appeared in 1588, 1589, and 1596. Both Watson's poem and Fraunce's may be called pastoral laments; Watson's Latin is divided into eleven "querelae," Fraunce's translation into eleven days' lamentations in the 1587 version, twelve in that of 1591. *The Arte of English Poesie* (1589) indicates that the genre was important by devoting chapter XXIIII to "The forme of Poeticall lamentations"; but it gives no illustrations from English verse, as its author is accustomed to do for other genres, nor does it mention any English poets practicing the pastoral lament. Nevertheless, Watson may be considered its English innovator and Fraunce its popularizer.[2] Theirs are the works that provide Barnfield with the basic structure of "The Teares." It is the more likely that Barnfield became familiar with the poems of these two men first through *The Countesse of Pembrokes Yuychurch* since earlier editions of Fraunce's translation of *Amyntas* contained only the lament, whereas *Yuychurch* included also "The Lamentation of Corydon for the loue of Alexis," a close translation of Virgil's second eclogue and the very poem which Barnfield claimed he was imitating:

> Some there were, that did interpret *The affectionate Shepheard*, otherwise then (in truth) I ment, touching the subiect thereof: to wit, the loue of a Shepheard to a boy; a fault, the which I will not excuse, because I neuer made. Onely this, I will vnshaddow my conceipt: being nothing else, but an imitation of *Virgill*, in yᵉ second Eglogue of *Alexis*.
>
> (*Cynthia*, Aᵈʳ-Aᵈᵛ)

The importance of *Yuychurch* should not be underestimated; it must stand alongside *The Shepheardes Calender* as a shaping influ-

---

[2]In *The Countesse of Pembrokes Yuychurch* Fraunce translates also the second eclogue of Virgil and entitles it "The Lamentation of Corydon for the loue of Alexis," a work he had published earlier in *The Lawiers Logike* (1588). He did not then give any title to the poem nor did Webbe, who translated the second eclogue two years before Fraunce in his *Discourse of English Poetrie* (1586). But Webbe does not precede Fraunce as the first man to produce an English pastoral lament, nor does Fraunce's earlier production move the date of the first appearance forward from 1591 to 1588, for it would seem to be the appearance of the word *lamentation* in the title that creates the genre. Undoubtedly Fraunce's own labors on the translation of Watson's *Amyntas* gave him the idea of adding the word to the title of the 1591 eclogue. I have not seen any student of pastoral poetry—not those great workers at the turn of the century, E. K. Chambers in his seminal essay *English Pastorals* (1895) and W. W. Greg in his massively erudite book *Pastoral Poetry and Pastoral Drama* (1906), nor any other—who discusses a pastoral lament tradition such as the one in question. Walter F. Staton (*Studies in the Renaissance,* VI [1959], 243-250) attempts, mistakenly it seems to me, to attach Elizabethan Ovidian-erotic-myth poetry to Watson's beginnings in the lament genre. On the basis of the chapter in *The Arte of English Poesie* and on the *Amyntas* of Watson, followed by the translations of Fraunce and imitations of Barnfield, a new chapter in the history of English pastoral poetry might be written.

ence on *The Affectionate Shepheard*. *Yuychurch* appeared three years before Barnfield's volume, and two of its components figure importantly in "The Teares." By Barnfield's own admission, Virgil's second eclogue informed his work; the division of *Amyntas* into days of lamentation was the structural source. Although Watson wrote an *Amyntas*, it is not known that he translated Virgil; furthermore, Watson's poem deals with the normal love and grief which Amyntas displays for Phillis, lost to him through her death; Fraunce's translation, as it had to, renders Virgil's story of unnatural love, in which Corydon laments the scornful rejection he suffers at the hands of a boy. Barnfield's Daphnis, in mourning the youth Ganimede's icy disdain, imitates Corydon rather than Amyntas. There is a strong possibility that it was Spenser's *Shepheardes Calender* that sent Barnfield in search of a full treatment of Virgil's poem. Line 57 of the January eclogue refers to Hobbinol's "clownish gifts," and E. K. glosses the phrase as an imitation of "Virgils verse.

'Rusticus es Corydon, nec munera curat Alexis.'

. . . . In thys place seemeth to be some sauour of disorderly loue, which the learned call *pæderastice*."[3] Virgil's line is from Eclogue II, 56.

Fraunce's translation from Virgil seems also to be the source for Barnfield's pastoral name for himself. Daphnis, which occurs on L3v of *Yuychurch*, is the name undersigned to the dedication to Penelope Rich as well as that assumed by the shepherd-lover of *The Affectionate Shepheard*. Barnfield uses it again in the sonnet sequence in *Cynthia*. The name is common in pastoral poetry, but its appearance in a poem which has other points of similarity to "The Teares" helps to identify Fraunce's Daphnis as Barnfield's original. Still, these matters remain slight in the way of establishing literary antecedents.

More important is Barnfield's indebtedness to Fraunce's *Alexis* eclogue in a sixteen-stanza defense in "The second Dayes Lamentation" of the virtues of black as opposed to the worthlessness of white. The "affectionate shepherd" concludes, "Oh then be not so proud because th'art fayre" (D2v). Without doubt, the suggestion for the passage came from Fraunce's translation:

---

[3]*The Works of Edmund Spenser*, A Variorum Edition, eds. C. G. Osgood, H. G. Lotspeich, and Dorothy Mason (Baltimore, 1943), VII, Part I, 18. All quotations from Spenser will come from this edition.

Wast not farr better t'haue borne with surly *Menalcas,*
And sore displeased, disdaigneful, prowd *Amaryllis,*
Although thou white were, although but swarty
   Menalcas?
O thou fayre white Boy, trust not too much to thy
   whytenes:
Fayre white flow'rs fall downe, black fruyts are duely
   reserued.

(L$_3$^{r})

Barnfield's attempts at being different, at seeking the strange and
the rare, so evident in the address "To the Gentlemen Readers"
in *The Encomion of Lady Pecunia* (1598) where the poet writes,
"At length I bethought myselfe of a Subiect, both new (as hauing
neuer beene written vpon before) and pleasing" (A$_3$^{r}), cannot
account for the coincidence. For the combined reasons then of
similarity of form and of content, of similarity in the names of
characters and of sources, of similarity in imagery and in concept,
it is safe to assume that Barnfield was influenced greatly by
Fraunce's volume of 1591.

Closely connected with "The Teares" is the second poem,
"The Shepheards Content," "Written vpon the Occasion of the
former Subiect." It differs from "The Teares" both in intention
and in structure but contains several references to a shepherd's
love for a boy. The sonnet which follows "The Content" is devoted entirely to this love and helps to draw the two preceding
poems even more closely together. "The Teares" is composed of
113 six-line stanzas, and "The Content" of 43 seven-line stanzas.
The first poem is primarily a lament, whereas the second eulogizes
pastoral life. Nevertheless they are linked together, and the things
they hold in common illustrate some of the additional forces at
work upon the composition of both.

The structural source of the title poem may have been
Fraunce's *Amyntas,* and its content may have been derived ultimately from Virgil's *Alexis* eclogue, but the tone and spirit of
much throughout Barnfield's entire first volume come from Spenser. No poet of merit was ever so closely allied to another as Barnfield was to Spenser. Not Drayton among the early imitators nor
the brothers Fletcher among the later owe quite so much to their
common master. Yet Barnfield's work is neither any more slavish
nor any less his own. Many poets of the age worked as with an
alembic into which they poured the works of their contemporaries

and then added their own to produce an entirely new substance. Barnfield worked pre-eminently in this fashion. A major ingredient—in all his books—came from Spenser, but to it was added matter from others such as Fraunce; still his own unique talent made all his volumes uniquely his own. No critic, scholar, or reader can say, "This part sounds like Spenser, this like Watson, this like Fraunce." Especially is Spenser's considerable contribution to *The Affectionate Shepheard* lost under the larger elements borrowed from Fraunce; but it is pervasive, found in every corner of the work. The second stanza of "The Teares" expresses the poet's awareness of the guilty nature of his love:

> If it be sinne to loue a sweet-fac'd Boy,
> . . . .
> If it be sinne to loue a louely Lad;
> Oh then sinne I, for whom my soule is sad.
> (A8ʳ)

In the light of the influence of *The Shepheardes Calender*, everywhere evident, Barnfield's lines should be understood perhaps in terms of E. K.'s vigorous expostulation in the January gloss: "let no man thinke, that herein I stand with Lucian or hys deuelish disciple Vnico Aretino, in defense of execrable and horrible sinnes of forbidden and vnlawful fleshlinesse" (p. 18).[4]

An image that both Barnfield and Spenser liked, since both used it more than once (see *Aff. Shep.*, C2ʳ and *F. Q.*, II.iii.22), is that of the sharply contrasting colors of red and white flowers:

> But as the Lillie and the blushing Rose,
> So white and red on him in order growes.
> (A8ᵛ)
>
> The Redde rose medled with the White yfere,
> In either cheeke depeincten liuely chere.
> (p. 38)

----

[4]But compare Barnfield's stanza also with Sidney's *Astrophel and Stella*, XIV, 9-14:

> If that be sinne which doth the manners frame,
> . . . .
> If it be sin which in fixt hart dooth breede,
> A lothing of all loost true chastitie;
> Then love is sin, and let me sinfull bee.

The Complete Works of Sir Philip Sidney, ed. A. Feuillerat (Cambridge, England, 1922), II, 248.

But in the image is a commonplace of the age. A debt of larger consequence may be found in the Guendolena episode, which owes its origin possibly to these two stanzas from April; Hobbinol, who loves Colin, speaks:

> *Colin* thou kenst, the Southerne shepheardes boye:
> Him Loue hath wounded with a deadly darte.
> Whilome on him was all my care and ioye,
> Forcing with gyfts to winne his wanton heart.
>
> But now from me hys madding mynd is starte,
> And woes the Widdowes daughter of the glenne:
> So naowe fayre *Rosalind* hath bredde hys smart,
> So now his frend is chaunged for a frenne.
> (p. 37)

Of course Barnfield's boy is disdainful both of Daphnis and of Guendolena, and Spenser's Colin only disdains Hobbinol while he pursues Rosalind; but the comparison is significant for the introduction of the lady, in each case, who makes the boy-lover Hobbinol or Daphnis, unhappy merely by her existence.

Barnfield's garden owes undoubtedly as much to Spenser's as to any other poet's:

> The Pinke, the Primrose, Cowslip and Daffadilly,
> The Hare-bell blue, the crimson Cullumbine,
> Sage, Lettis, Parsley, and the milke-white Lilly,
> The Rose, and speckled flowre cald Sops in wine,
>   Fine pretie King-cups, and the yellow Bootes,
>   That growes by Riuers, and by shallow Brookes.
> (B8^r)
>
> Bring hether the Pincke and purple Cullambine,
>   With Gelliflowres:
> Bring Coronations, and Sops in wine,
>   worne of Paramoures.
> Strowe me the ground with Daffadowndillies
> And Cowslips, and Kingcups, and loued Lillies.
> (p. 40)

Only six stanzas later, Barnfield introduces a calendar of the months and names December, January, April, and May, suggested to him without doubt either by conscious or unconscious remembrances of Spenser. The first day's lamentation ends with a Latin tag—*Plus fellis quam mellis Amor*—that is, in effect, a loose rendering of Thomalin's emblem at the close of the March eclogue:

Of Hony and of Gaule in loue there is store:
The Honye is much, but the Gaule is more.
(p. 33)

In the second stanza of "The second Dayes Lamentation"
four lines raise the question of whether Barnfield went straight to
Spenser for them or whether he got them transmuted through a
poem by the unfortunate Babington accomplice, Chidiock Tichbourne:

Why is my Summer season almost done?
My Spring-time past, and Ages Autumne gone?
My Haruest's come, and yet I reapt no corne:
My loue is great, and yet I am forlorne.
(*Aff. Shep.*, B₄ʳ)

In the January eclogue, Spenser writes,

And yet alas, but now my spring begonne
And yet alas, yt is already donne.
(p. 16)

In December, the image recurs:

Thus is my sommer worne away and wasted,
Thus is my haruest hastened all to rathe:
The eare that budded faire, is burnt and blasted,
And all my hoped gaine is turnd to scathe.
Of all the seede, that in my youth was sowne,
Was nought but brakes and brambles to be mowne.
(p. 116)

To my ear, the poem of Tichbourne stands between Barnfield's
lines and Spenser's:

My prime of youth is but a frost of cares,
My feast of joy is but a dish of pain,
My crop of corn is but a field of tares,
And all my good is but vain hope of gain;
The day is past, and yet I saw no sun,
And now I live, and now my life is done.

It is interesting in itself to think that Tichbourne's language and
imagery must have come from Spenser, that the poor fellow with
only imminent death before him could recall at such a time the
"recreational" eclogues that belong in a make-believe world of
pastoral; but it is more interesting to the student of Barnfield to
consider how the single brief stanza of Tichbourne got between
the author of *The Affectionate Shepheard* and the otherwise over-

whelming influence of his master Spenser. For surely the cadence of Barnfield's lines is traceable more to Tichbourne's caesura, the corn more to Tichbourne's image than to anything in Spenser's eclogues.

The case for Spenser's influence over *The Affectionate Shepheard* can be concluded with the following list of parallels:

Winter hath snow'd vpon my hoarie head,
(*Aff. Shep.*, D₄ᵛ)

My head besprent with hoary frost I fynd,
(p. 117)

My Teares the Marble Stones to ruth haue moued;
(Eʳ)

Thy teares would make the hardest flint to flowe.
(p. 63)

Nipt with the fresh of thy Wraths winter, dyes,
(Gʳ)

Thou barrein ground, whome winters wrath hath wasted.
(p. 16)

In addition to specific lines, Spenser's epitaph for Tityrus (Chaucer) in the June eclogue may have suggested Barnfield's tribute to Sidney and Amyntas in "The Shepheards Content" (E₄ᵛ), and Thomalin's story of Cupid in the March eclogue may have supplied some of the material for stanzas 35-37 of the same work. The idea of an aging shepherd, which is so common to a great deal of amatory verse of all kinds, may nevertheless have come to Barnfield from the December eclogue.

With this considerable mass of evidence for the influence of *The Shepheardes Calender,* no serious investigator can leave Spenser out of the picture. But we have seen how the young Barnfield blended into his work also the structural and conceptual materials of Fraunce, and there is no reason to stop with these two poets. In one way or another, *The Affectionate Shepheard* makes its levy on almost every well-known pastoralist of the age. In the 1590's the love-invitation was one of the more popular forms of pastoral poetry, and in large measure the love-invitation unites "The Teares" to "The Shepheards Content." In "The Teares," sixteen stanzas of the first day's lament offer the boy Ganimede various simple gifts and country pastimes. Twelve stanzas of the second day's song continue the seduction. In one sense the entire "Shep-

heards Content" is a love invitation; for after elaborating upon
the delights of country pleasures, Barnfield makes clear his intention to attract the boy Ganimede to bucolic pastimes:

> Thus haue I showed in my Countrey vaine
> The sweet Content that Shepheards still inioy;
> The mickle pleasure, and the little paine
> That euer doth awayte the *Shepheards Boy.*
> (F₄ʳ, my italics)

The poem most influential in establishing this fashion of the
1590's was Marlowe's "Passionate Shepherd."[5] That Barnfield knew
Marlowe personally has been suggested by Michel Poirier[6] on the
basis of the close association between Watson and Marlowe.[7] But
personal acquaintanceship is not required to show that the older
man exerted a considerable influence on the younger. Poirier believes that Barnfield "shared Marlowe's partiality for handsome
youths."[8] Possibly the opening of *Dido* supplied Barnfield with
the name Ganimede for the boy in *The Affectionate Shepheard*
and the sonnets in *Cynthia,* although it is an obvious pastoral guise
for such a lad and appears frequently in the literature of pederasty.
But more impressive evidence of Marlowe's influence comes from
Barnfield's echoes of "The Passionate Shepherd":

> If thou wilt come and dwell with me at home;
> (B₂ᵛ)
> All these, and more, Ile giue thee for thy loue;
> If these, and more, may tyce thy loue away:
> (B₃ʳ)
> If thou wilt loue me, thou shalt be my Boy,
> (B₄ᵛ)
> If thou wilt be my Boy, or els my Bride.[9]
> (Cᵛ)

The relationship of Barnfield to Watson and Marlowe remains still

---

[5]See R. S. Forsythe, "The Passionate Shepherd; [*sic*] and English
Poetry," *PMLA,* XL (1925), 692-742. Forsythe traces the absorption
of elements of "The Passionate Shepherd" into a great number of pastoral
poems of the end of the sixteenth century.

[6]*Christopher Marlowe* (London, 1951), p. 21.

[7]For the details of this relationship see Mark Eccles, *Christopher
Marlowe in London* (Cambridge, Mass., 1934), *passim.*

[8]*Christopher Marlowe,* p. 21.

[9]See Charles Crawford, *Collectanea* (Stratford, 1906), pp. 2-9.
Crawford lists imitations of *Dido* and *Edward II* in "The Teares" of

to be settled unquestionably, but there can be no doubt of the
literary ties between *The Affectionate Shepheard* and "Come liue
with mee, and be my loue."

Another poet active often as a writer of pastoral lyric verse
was Robert Greene. Personal connection between Barnfield and
Greene must remain also in the realm of speculation. If Barnfield
came to London early enough to be an intimate of Watson, as
almost all modern scholars believe, then he was early enough to
have known Greene, who died, at the most, two months earlier
than Watson and possibly only three weeks.[10] Since it seems as
certain as anything can be at this distance that Barnfield wrote
Greenes Funeralls, a personal friendship between the two men is
not unlikely. But as with Marlowe, proof of friendship is not
necessary to demonstrate literary influence. The mark of Greene is
not great upon Barnfield, primarily because Greene's tremendous

---

Barnfield and claims that the poem in general borrows largely from and
is in the style of a now lost poem of Marlowe's, which was an elaboration
of "The Passionate Shepherd." Crawford calls attention to Barnfield's
use of Ganimede as well as to the imitations of Marlowe's "Passionate
Shepherd" on C^v of *The Affectionate Shepheard.* But he either missed
or ignored the other lines cited above. R. S. Forsythe fails to mention
Barnfield's indebtedness to "The Passionate Shepherd" although he seems
to have found every other imitator in the Elizabethan age.

[10]Greene died on September 3, 1592. Watson is thought by John
Payne Collier to have been buried on September 26, of the same year:
"In the register of St. Bartholomew the Less . . . we meet with the
following entry of a burial, the date of which accords with the period
when it is likely that our poet expired:—'26 Sept. 1592. Thomas Watson
gent, was buried." It has never been anywhere cited, but we have little
doubt that it applies to our poet." *A Bibliographical and Critical Account
of the Rarest Books in the English Language* (New York, 1866), IV,
221. Collier has little justification for identifying the Thomas Watson
of the St. Bartholomew register as the poet, since the name, surname
and Christian together, was extremely common. Mark Eccles (*Christopher
Marlowe in London*) found four Thomas Watsons residing in London
at the appropriate dates, any one of whom may have been the poet (pp.
145-158). In any case Watson was almost certainly dead by November
10, 1592, the date of entry into the Stationers' Register of *Amintae
Gaudia.* When published, *Amintae Gaudia* carried a Latin dedication,
written probably by Marlowe, which indicated that Watson was dead:
"Dignare Posthumo huic Amyntae, vt tuo adoptiuo filio patrocinari:
Eoque magis quòd moribundus pater, illius tutelam humillimè tibi
legauerat" (A$_2$^{r}-A$_2$^{v}). Marlowe himself died June 1, 1593.

output was chiefly prosaic and dramatic, and Barnfield's slight
Muse was poetic only. But on the common ground of the lyric, a
field Greene trod only as the vagaries of his prose romances led him
there, Barnfield followed at least once.

The dominating conceit of "The Shepheards Content" is the
metaphor of the shepherd-king. It begins in the fourth stanza,
appears frequently throughout the poem, and concludes one stanza
from the end. Barnfield enthrones the shepherd as king of his
sheepcote and pastures and occasionally elevates him above rulers
of empire:

> What though with simple cheere he homely fares?
> He liues content, A King can doo no more;
> Nay not so much, for Kings haue manie cares:
> (F_2^v)
>
> Who would not then a simple Shepheard bee,
> Rather then be a mightie Monarch made?
> (F_4^v)

Against these lines might be placed a stanza from Greene's "Shepherd's wife's song":

> Ah what is loue? It is a pretty thing,
> As sweet vnto a shepheard as a king,
>   And sweeter too:
> For kings haue cares that waite vpon a Crowne,
> And cares can make the sweetest loue to frowne:
>   Ah then, ah then,
> If country loues such sweet desires do gaine,
> What Lady would not loue a Shepheard Swaine?[11]

Epanorthosis, the rhetorical device by which Greene contradicts
the equality of king and shepherd, giving precedence to the rustic,
is caught in Barnfield's "Nay not so much," just as the cadence
and meaning of "What Lady would not loue a Shepheard Swaine?"
is caught in "Who would not then a simple Shepheard bee."
Greene's influence on the pastoral writers, like Sidney's, is hard
to delineate. Most often it manifests itself in just such nebulous
ways as we see here.

Most of the interest of these fugitive influences yields in
excitement to Barnfield's citation in "The Shepheards Content" of
several contemporaries. Sidney receives highest praise:

---

[11]*The Plays and Poems of Robert Greene*, ed. J. Churton Collins
(Oxford, 1905), II, 273.

> SYDNEY, The Syren of this latter Age;
> SYDNEY, The Blasing-starre of Englands glory;
> SYDNEY, The Wonder of the wise and sage;
> SYDNEY, The Subiect of true Vertues story:
>   This Syren, Starre, this Wonder, and this Subiect;
>   Is dumbe, dim, gone, and mard by Fortunes Obiect.
>   (E₄ᵛ)

Spenser and Drayton are mentioned both once under their familiar pastoral names:

> By thee [Love] great *Collin* lost his libertie,
> . . . .
> By thee good *Rowland* liu'd in great annoy.
>   (F₃ʳ mispaginated E₃ʳ)

The influence of Spenser has been shown; the influence of Sidney and Drayton upon "The Teares" and "The Content" is slight compared with that of Greene and Marlowe. At best only isolated lines and images, and not many of those, are traceable to them. As much or more might be shown to come from poets like Dyer (or is the author Fulke Greville?). Compare the lines on Sidney above with the familiar elegy beginning "Silence augmenteth griefe" and containing the line, "Stald are my thoughts, which lou'd & lost, the wonder of our age." As much or more has been shown to come from Tichbourne. Similarly, I have been able to find only one clear echo from Sidney (See footnote 4 above). Sir Philip's influence is therefore negligible. He is mentioned more perhaps for his probable relationship with the dedicatee of the volume, Penelope Rich, than for his contributions to the poem; more for his place as acknowledged prince of pastoral writers than for his store of usable phrases.

The influence of Drayton is equally ghostlike. Familiar with his works, Barnfield, in "The Complaint of Chastitie," admits that the story of Matilda "is at large written by *Michael Dreyton*" (Gᵛ). But I would limit Drayton's influence in the first two poems to a formal one: the six-line stanza of "The Teares" and the seven-line stanza of "The Content." Drayton employs the six-line stanza more often in *The Shepheards Garland* than Spenser does in *The Calender*.[12] The seven-line stanza, which is a strange

---

[12]Drayton uses the six-line stanza in his first, seventh, and ninth eglogs and in the elegy in the second eglog. The sixth eglog is merely a slight variation of the form. Spenser uses it in the January and December eclogues only, although the October eclogue is a variation.

choice for "The Content," is more appropriate to "The Complaint of Chastitie." Rime royal is the form most used in poems of *The Mirror for Magistrates*, of which Drayton's *Matilda* is an imitation. Several scholars have suggested *Venus and Adonis* as the source for the "Teares" stanza and *Lucrece* for that of "The Content." Although many echoes from these two Shakespearean poems have been found in Barnfield's first volume, I do not think that its author was as yet consciously accepting Shakespeare as a model. "The Teares" is much closer to *The Shepheards Garland* than to *Venus and Adonis*, both in style and content. Drayton is named in "The Content" as well as in "The Complaint of Chastitie." Shakespeare is named first by Barnfield in "A Remembrance of some English Poets" (1598), a poem that could not have been written before 1597, even though it praises those works of Shakespeare published in 1593 and 1594.[13]

A fourth poet in "The Content" is hidden behind the pastoral name Amyntas. His identification is not so simple as Grosart and Arber have made it,[14] although all writers since these two great nineteenth-century editors have accepted their findings without question. Barnfield alludes to Amyntas twice:

> And thou my sweete *Amintas* vertuous minde,
> Should I forget thy Learning or thy Loue;
> Well might I be accounted but vnkinde,
> Whose pure affection I so oft did proue:
> Might my poore Plaints hard stones to pitty moue;
>   His losse should be lamented of each Creature,
>   So great his Name, so gentle was his Nature.
>
> But sleepe his soule in sweet Elysium,
> (The happy Hauen of eternall rest).
>   (E₄ᵛ-Fʳ)
>
> By thee [Love] *Amyntas* wept incessantly.
>   (F₈ʳ mispaginated E₈ʳ)

From these two quotations several things are apparent. Amyntas was dead in 1594. He was a man whose learning was noteworthy.

---

[13]Included also in the poem is praise of Drayton's "wel-written Tragedies,/ And sweete Epistles," none of which appeared before 1597.

[14]*The Complete Poems of Richard Barnfield*, ed. A. B. Grosart for the Roxburghe Club (London, 1876), pp. xxxvi-xxxvii; *Richard Barnfield: Poems: 1594-1598*, ed. Edward Arber (Westminster, 1896), p. xii; and *Thomas Watson: Poems*, ed. Edward Arber (London, 1870), p. 4.

Barnfield knew him well enough to make claim upon his affection often. Either in his life or in his verse he lamented over love not infrequently.

Grosart and Arber claimed that the figure behind the pastoral mask was Thomas Watson, but in 1870, before these two writers appeared in print, Charles Edmonds identified Amyntas with Abraham Fraunce. It was the first attempt to discover the historical man buried under the fictional shepherd:

> [Barnfield] alludes, thus feelingly, to his poetical friend, Abraham Fraunce, whose poem, "The Lamentations of Amyntas for the death of Phillis" . . . was published in 1587 . . . .
>
> The date of Fraunce's death has not been ascertained; but the above lines prove that it must have occurred previous to 1594.[15]

Edmonds was apparently in ignorance of Joseph Hunter's unpublished *Chorus Vatum* which stated that there was in existence

> An Apitolamium [*sic*] presented to Sir Gervase of Stainborough in Yorkshire on his marriage with Lady Magdaline Egerton the daughter of John Earl of Bridgewater, Lord President of the Marches of Wales in 1633 . . . . [Fraunce] becomes thus connected with Comus . . . . No one as far as I find has represented him as alive so late as 1633.[16]

Hunter (1783-1861) compiled the *Chorus Vatum* over many years; but there is no reason why Edmonds should have known about it even though it was available in the British Museum (Add. MSS. 24487-24492) where Grosart used it when he edited Barnfield six years later. Still, Edmonds, naming as the dead Amyntas a man who appears to have lived until 1633, would appear to be wrong. Also in 1870, Arber, in his edition of Thomas Watson, failing to cite the longer, more informative allusion, says out of hand that Barnfield refers to Watson in the shorter: "By thee *Amyntas* wept incessantly." Arber could not have known of Edmonds' claim for Fraunce, since he felt no compulsion to argue

---

[15]*Shakespeare's Venus and Adonis*, The Isham Reprints, ed. Charles Edmonds (London, 1870), pp. xxiii-xxiv of the Introduction to *The Passionate Pilgrim*, paginated separately.

[16]From a typescript in the Folger Shakespeare library of *Chorus Vatum Anglicanorum*, B. M. Add. MSS. 24487-24492, Vol. 5, p. 2. Each entry is paginated anew.

his point. It was Grosart, in 1876, who called Edmonds to task, although on very shaky grounds. Though he used the *Chorus Vatum* in connection with another matter,[17] Grosart failed to present the evidence that Fraunce was alive in 1633. He writes only that

> It is the more important to reclaim 'Amyntas' for Thomas Watson and not Abraham Fraunce, who merely translated (and very badly) Watson, in that Mr. Charles Edmonds . . . has assigned this tribute to Fraunce. Beyond all doubt this is an error, as the whole allusions prove.
>
> (p. xxxvi)

For Grosart, the "whole allusions" establish that " 'Amintas' refers to [Watson's] *'Amyntae* Gaudia' [*sic*] (1592), and his 'Loue' as celebrated in his 'Teares of Fancie, or Loue Disdained' (1593)" [pp. xxxvi-xxxvii]. It would seem that had Grosart brought Hunter's statement about the epithalamion to bear, his argument would have been well-nigh irrefutable.

But there is something disturbing about Grosart's attribution, especially since the ghost of Fraunce hovers over every part of *The Affectionate Shepheard*. Fraunce was born about 1558-1560. He would therefore be from seventy-three to seventy-five in 1633, a goodly age for any Elizabethan, but especially for one who in 1587 could write to his patron, Mary Sidney, that "Mine afflicted mind and crased bodie, together with other external calamities haue wrought such sorrowfull and lamentable effects in me, that for this whole yeare I haue wholy giuen ouer myselfe to mournfull meditations" (*The Lamentations of Amyntas* ¶2r). Certainly it is an interesting age for the author of an epithalamion. Of course, it is not an impossible age. But it is significant that a man who was rather a prolific writer and publisher gave nothing to the presses after 1592, the date of *The Third part of the Countesse of Pembrokes Yuychurch*. Furthermore the *Chorus Vatum* is full of so many errors that it would be difficult to catalogue them all. Hunter, it seems apparent from the nature of his notes, worked frequently from memory, and it proved faulty far too often. If Hunter is mistaken about the epithalamion he professes to have seen,[18] the latest evidence we have of a living Fraunce, aside from

[17]See *The Complete Poems*, p. iv.

[18]No one else has ever seen it. Hunter claims that the poem and a prose epistle were "Among Dr Nathl Johnston's papers at Campsall."

Yuychurch III, is a letter from Lord Pembroke to Lord Burghley, dated April 28, 1591, supporting Fraunce for the position of Queen's solicitor at the Court of the Marches.[19]

The considerable influence of Fraunce upon Barnfield is not confined to form and content. Throughout *The Affectionate Shepheard* may be found certain features of style that are studied best in "Hellens Rape," features that may be traced as clearly to Fraunce as anything else in the work of Barnfield. The seventy-five lines of English hexameters that make up "Hellens Rape" mark it as one of the most surprising productions in that measure in all English literature. Alliteration is extreme; repetition is plen-

---

[19]See the Introduction to Abraham Fraunce's *Victoria,* ed. G. C. Moore Smith (Louvain, 1906), p. xxxiv and especially pp. xxxix-xl. If Spenser's Corydon (*Colin Clovts Come home againe,* 382-383) is an allusion to Fraunce then possibly Fraunce was alive in 1595, although parts of *Colin Clovts* were written in 1591 and never revised. However Corydon is better identified with Edward Dyer as Fleay suggests (*Guide to Chaucer and Spenser,* p. 118) and Sidney's verses in the *Arcadia* support: "To worthy *Coriden* he [Lanquet] gave me ore" (ed. Feuillerat, I, 133). Actually if Spenser wrote the allusion in 1591, Corydon could be Thomas Watson, an identification never before suggested. Watson labels himself in *Meliboeus* (1590): "I figure Englande in *Arcadia* . . . and myself in *Corydon*" (Arber, p. 147); and in that poem pays elaborate tribute to Spenser:

> Yet lest my homespun verse obscure hir worth,
>   sweet *Spencer* let me leaue this taske to thee,
> Whose neuerstooping quill can best set forth
>   such things of state, as passe my Muse, and me.
>
> Thou *Spencer* art the alderliefest swaine,
>   or haply if that word be all to base,
> Thou art *Apollo* whose sweet hunnie vaine
>   amongst the Muses hath a chiefest place.
>   (Arber, p. 173)

Spenser alludes to Watson's work in the *Faerie Queene* (III.6.xlv.7-9) and to the man himself in *The Ruines of Time* (1591): "Good *Melibae,* that hath a Poet got,/ To sing his liuing praises being dead" (436-437). The publication date of *The Ruines of Time* coincides exactly with the date of the letter to Ralegh that prefaces *Colin Clovts,* a date when Spenser possibly wrote the first draft or various parts of the poem. In addition, the reference in *The Ruines of Time* shows that Spenser had read *Meliboeus,* was aware of the tribute paid him there, and must have thought of Watson as Corydon, despite the fact that other writers were referring to him always as Amyntas. He fits well the terms of the *Colin Clovts* allusion: "though meanly waged,/ Yet hablest wit of most I know this day" (382-383).

tiful; punning is adept. "Hellens Rape" is light verse. Its mode
is to use freely the devices of rhetoric to achieve a comic cast.

In 1588, Abraham Fraunce published *The Arcadian Rhetorike*,
a writers' source book, containing an imbalance of definitions and
illustrations of rhetoric that play upon the sounds of words. More
than preceptor merely, Fraunce was practitioner of his own lessons.
As early as 1587, Fraunce's *Lamentations of Amyntas for the
death of Phillis* shows his preference for alliteration and other
devices of repetition such as anaphora, antithesis, epistrophe, and
epanalepsis. In later works Fraunce went to absurd lengths to illustrate in verse the interests he exhibited in *The Arcadian Rhetorike*.
The first four lines of *The Countesse of Pembrokes Emanuel*
(1591) are a fair example of the entire poem:

> Christe euer-lyuing, once dying, only triumpher
> Ouer death by death; Christe Iesus mighty redeemer
> Of forelorne mankynde, which led captyuyty captiue,
> And made thraldome thrall.
> (A8^r)

These lines from near the beginning of *Yuychurch III* (1592),
Fraunce's last printed work, are evidence of the depths to which
Fraunce could plummet by not observing moderation in the use
of his favorite devices:

> When noe fyre, noe ayre, noe earth, noe water apeared,
> Confused fyre, rude ayre, vast earth, dull water abyded.
> Water, th'earth and ayre and fyre extreamely defaced,
> And fyre, th'earth and ayre and water fowly deformed.
> For where water or earth, where ayre or fyre was abyding,
> Fyre, ayre, earth, water were also ioyntly remaynyng.
> Fyre and ayre and earth with a shapeles water abounded,
> And earth ayre and fyre, that shapeles water aforded,
> Euery one was in all, and all was in euery one thing,
> Soe each one made all, made this rude All, to be nothing,
> Nothing els but a heape, but a masse, but a lump, but a cluster;
> Cluster, lump, masse, heape, where seedes of things disagreeing
> Fyre, ayre, earth, water lay all confusd in a corner.
> (A8^r-A8^v)

In these two passages appear almost all the figures of repetition
illustrated in The *Arcadian Rhetorike*.[20] A comparison of Fraunce's
lines with the following from "Hellens Rape" is illuminating:

---

[20]Ed. Ethel Seaton (Oxford, 1950), pp. 34-63.

Louely a Lasse, so loued a Lasse, and (alas) such a louing
Lasse, for a while (but a while) was none such a sweet
    bonny Loue-Lasse
As *Helen, Maenelaus* louing, lou'd, louelie a loue-lasse,
Till spightfull Fortune from a loue-lasse made her a
    loue-lesse
Wife.   (G₈ᵛ)

All remaining lines continue in this manner. But Barnfield used
these devices of rhetoric in a comic poem; Fraunce was only too
serious in their application. Several possibilities suggest themselves
from an examination of this obvious imitation. First, Barnfield
was Fraunce's student and admiring emulator. Second, Barnfield
was Fraunce's student but also his ridiculer. Third, Barnfield was
Watson's student and admirer; as such he disliked Fraunce who
battened on Watson's Latin poems. "Hellens Rape" would then
be satire upon a poet who overused classical rhetoric.

    Watson himself succumbed occasionally to some of these de-
vices, but he did so sparingly, never really approving of them.
The argument to poem XLI of *The Hecatompathia* (1582) shows
a mild distaste for his own performance: "This passion is framed
vpon a somewhat tedious or too much affected continuation of that
figure in Rhethorique, whiche of the Grekes is called παλιλογία
or ἀναδίπλωσις, of the Latines *Reduplicatio*" (Fʳ); and preceding
poem XLVII, Watson comments: "This passion conteineth a relation through out from line to line; as, from euery line of the first
staffe as it standeth in order, vnto euery line of the second staffe:
and from the second staffe vnto the third. The oftener it is read
of him that is no great clarke, the more pleasure he shall haue in
it" (F₄ʳ). As no admirer of rhetorical tricks, Watson becomes a
poor choice for Barnfield's master in this early book.

    A playfulness of repetition appears throughout the poetry of
Barnfield. *Greenes Funeralls*,[21] which I take to be his, follows the
examples of Fraunce in a serious temper, but the author, at
Greene's death, was only eighteen and still but twenty when the
work was finally published in 1594. By the time he wrote *The
Affectionate Shepheard* he employed extreme repetition only in
"Hellens Rape," a light poem, and possibly a satire on another
writer's style. After *The Affectionate Shepheard* he continued to
use repetition in many of its rhetorical figures but never to the
point where it intrudes its presence or becomes tedious.

_____

[21] See Chapter VI.

Although authorship of *Greenes Funeralls* suggests strongly that Barnfield was a serious student of Fraunce in 1592-1594, Amyntas need not be identified with Watson's translator. The "appeale to the pen of pierelesse Poet *Amyntas*" (*Greenes Funeralls*, B4r), though modeled upon Fraunce's hexameters, may be calling upon Watson as the greater poet to come to Greene's defense. Yet the pervasive influence of Fraunce's verse throughout *Greenes Funeralls* as well as throughout *The Affectionate Shepheard* cannot be ignored. Even Grosart's evidence in favor of Watson — the strongest thus far advanced — can be enlisted in the cause of Fraunce. If I have given reason to suspect that Fraunce may actually have been sleeping in "sweet Elysium" by 1594, then the pertinent lines used by Grosart are reduced to these:

> And thou my sweete *Amintas* vertuous minde,
> Should I forget thy Learning or thy Loue;
> Well might I be accounted but vnkinde,
> Whose pure affection I so oft did proue.
>
> (E4v)

Amintas, which Grosart associates with *Amintae Gaudia* (1592) and which he might have linked more profitably with *Amyntas* (1585), can be claimed to refer to Fraunce through his translations of Watson, especially since in the popular mind Fraunce was more closely identified with Amyntas poems. Watson's two separate pastorals were both written in Latin and, as far as we know, had but one edition apiece. Fraunce wrote three Amyntas poems —*The Lamentations of Amyntas for the death of Phillis,* the translation of Watson; the first part of *The Countesse of Pembrokes Yuychurch,* a translation of Tasso's *Aminta;* and *Amintas Dale.* The first of these had five separate publications. Watson's statement of pique in *Meliboeus* (1590) shows clearly that too many people gave Fraunce credit that belonged to Watson: "I interpret [translate] myself, lest Melibaeus in speaking English by an other mans labour, should leese my name in his chaunge, as my *Amyntas* did" (K2r). We need not assume that Watson's annoyance is directed at Fraunce. He may be setting straight only the public record. Few authors should like their most notable works to be attributed to others.

Grosart's association of "Loue" with *The Tears of Fancie or Loue Disdained* is somewhat far-fetched; yet if topical allusion was intended, Fraunce's "Lamentation of Corydon for the *Loue* [my italics] of Alexis" may be cited. Probably the word means simply affection as in line four of the quotation. But we may go further than Grosart in order to point out that Barnfield was close to Amyntas. It would be unnatural (vnkinde), Barnfield says, if he forgot the teaching (Learning) Amyntas lavished upon him or if he forgot the love which he "so oft did proue." Barnfield's indebtedness to the works of Fraunce makes it clear that the younger man learned from the older; and, apparently, the lessons were frequent and tutorial, giving rise to the personal affection. Other help may have been of the practical kind, since the publishers of Fraunce's *Amyntas* were the same Gubbin and Newman who had *The Affectionate Shepheard* put into print. But Barnfield could have been close to Watson also. It is highly probable that Watson and Fraunce were themselves good friends, as several references by contemporaries indicate.[22]

Strongest evidence in favor of Watson comes from the second, the shorter evocaton of Amyntas: "By thee [Love] *Amyntas* wept incessantly." Both Watson's *Hecatompathia* and his *Tears of Fancie* are sonnet sequences concerning love, mostly disappointed. Several of the lyrics in Watson's *first sett, of Italian Madrigalls Englished* (1590) celebrate unhappy love also. None of Fraunce's known poems are love laments, unless *Amyntas* itself or perhaps the *Alexis* eclogue be considered, but both these are translations and have no element of personal despair in them.

Perhaps the final materials in this argument should be a series of parallel passages from Barnfield, Watson, and Fraunce in order to allow the reader himself to make some independent judgments. I shall present in each comparison the lines of Barnfield first, then Fraunce's, then Watson's. Only the *Amyntas* poems of Fraunce and Watson will be used. Passages from Barnfield will come from various poems and volumes, to be indicated after each quotation:

---

[22]Most pertinent is Lodge's: "the fore-bred brothers . . . / (Who in theyr Swan-like songes *Amintas* wept)," *Phillis*, (1593), (A₄ʳ). Other references to Fraunce and Watson which may be construed as establishing their close friendship can be found in Nashe, Harvey, Peele, and Meres. These lines of Lodge might indicate also that both Fraunce and Watson were dead in 1595 since *Amintas* was their swan song. Such reasoning would increase the possibility that Fraunce is the Amyntas of *The Affectionate Shepheard*. For a different interpretation of Lodge's lines see H. Littledale, "Did Thomas Lodge Write a Poem about Amintas?" *Athenaeum*, No. 3717 (1899), pp. 82-83, and N. B. Paradise, *Thomas Lodge, The History of an Elizabethan* (New Haven, 1931), pp. 112-113.

Siluanus Chappel-Clarkes shall chaunt a Lay,
And play thee hunts-vp in thy resting place:
(Aff. Shep., B^v)

With *Cyparissus* selfe thou shalt compare,
(Aff. Shep., C^r)

And yet (alas) *Apollo* lou'd a boy,
And *Cyparissus* was *Siluanus* ioy.
(Cynthia, C^r)

And thou Syluanus, Siluanus good to the mountains,
And flocks on mountains, ...
. . . .
For thine own boyes sake, for loue of sweet Cyparissus,
(Fraunce, B^v)

  Aruorum, ô, pecorisque Deus Syluane, Deorum
Summe mihi . . . .
. . . .
. . . . . . Ego te per quae tibi sacra dicaui
Plurima, perquetuos animos ergà Cyparissum
Formosum puerum.
(Watson, A^r-A^v)

It is necessary to quote from the address to Love at some length:

O! who can vanquish Loue,
That conquers Kingdomes, and the Gods aboue?

Deepe-wounding Arrow, hart-consuming Fire;
Ruler of Reason, slaue to tyrant Beautie;
Monarch of harts, Fuell of fond desire,
Prentice to Folly, foe to fained Duetie,
Pledge of true Zeale, Affections moitie;
  If thou kilst where thou wilt, and whom it list thee,
  (Alas) how can a silly Soule resist thee?

By thee great *Collin* lost his libertie,
By thee sweet *Astrophel* forwent his ioy.
By thee *Amyntas* wept incessantly,
By thee good *Rowland* liu'd in great annoy;
O cruell, peeuish, vylde, blind-seeing Boy:
  How canst thou hit their harts, and yet not see?
  (If thou be blinde, as thou art faind to bee).

A Shepheard loues no ill, but onely thee;
He hath no care, but onely by thy causing;
Why doost thou shoot thy cruell shafts at mee?
Giue me some respite, some short time of pausing:
Still my sweet Loue with bitter lucke th'art sawcing:
  Oh, if thou hast a minde to shew thy might;
  Kill mightie Kings, and not a wretched wight.

Yet (O Enthraller of infranchizd harts)
At my poore hart if thou wilt needs be ayming,
Doo me this fauour show me both thy Darts,
That I may chuse the best for my harts mayming,
(A free consent is priuiledgd from blaming:
   Then pierce his hard hart with thy golden Arrow,
   That thou my wrong, that he may rue my sorrow.

But let mee feele the force of thy lead Pyle,
What should I doo with loue when I am old?
I know not how to flatter, fawne, or smyle;
Then stay thy hand, O cruell Bow-man hold:
For if thou strik'st me with thy dart of gold,
   I sweare to thee (by *Ioues* immortall curse)
   I haue more in my hart, than in my purse.

The more I weepe, the more he bends his Brow; [*sic*]
For in my hart a golden Shaft I finde:
(Cruell, vnkinde) and wilt thou leaue me so?
Can no remorce nor pittie moue thy minde?
Is Mercie in the Heauens so hard to finde?
   Oh, then it is no meruaile that on earth,
   Of kinde Remorce there is so great a dearth,

How happie were a harmles Shepheards life,
If he had neuer knowen what Loue did meane:
But now fond Loue in euery place is rife,
Staining the purest Soule with spots vncleane,
Making thicke purses, thin; fat bodies, leane:
   Loue is a fiend, a fire, a heauen, a hell;
   Where pleasure, paine, and sad repentance dwell.
         (*Aff. Shep.*, F₂ᵛ-F₄ʳ)

This man knows not, alas, that loue is dailie triumphant,
This man knowes not, alas, that loue can worke manie wonders,
Loue can abide no law, loue alwaies lous to be lawles,
Loue altreth nature, rules reason, maistreth Olimpus
Lawes, edicts, decrees; contemns Ioue mightilie thundring,
Ioue that rules and raigns, that with beck bendeth Olimpus.
Loue caus'de Hippolitus with bry'rs and thorns to be mangled,
For that he had foule loue of lusting Phaedra refused.
Loue made Absyrtus with sisters hands to be murdred,
And in peeces torne, and here and there to be scattred.
Loue forc'd Pasiphae mans companie long to be loathing,
And for a white buls flesh, buls companie long to be lusting.
Loue and luring lookes of louelie Polixena caused
Greekish Achilles death, when he came to the Church to be
   wedded.
  . . . .

But what neede I to shew this blindboyes surly behauiour,
Lewd pranks, false policies, slye shifts, and wily deuises,
Murdring minde, hardhart, dead hand, bent bow, readie arrowes?
No body knows better what bitter griefe is abounding
In loues lewd kingdome, then luckles louer Amintas.
                                                    (Fraunce, B₄ᵛ-Cʳ)

"Illum communis naturae regula claudit,
"Alma nec astringit Ratio, non altus Olympus
"Legibus aetherijs illum, non Iuppiter ipse
Continet imperio, qui nutu nubila cogit.
Illius impulsu priuigno Phaedra pudico
Mentitis laethum inuexit crudele tabellis.
Illius hortatu fratrem temeraria Colchis
In frusta abscissum vento commisit inani.
Illius inuento thalami pertaesa virilis
Impia Pasiphaë tauro se miscuit albo.
Illius admonitu perijt Chironis alumnus
Troiugenae blanda deceptus fraude puellae.
. . . .

    Cur autèm caeci pueri crudelia gesta
Consiliumque nocens memoro, caedesque nefandas,
Cuius fine caret nimis importuna tyrannis?
Non misero quisquam magis est expertus Amyntae
Quantas ille habeat vires, qualesque sagittas.
                                                    (Watson, B₃ᵛ-B₄ʳ)

In this apostrophe to Love, Barnfield alters the catalogues of
Watson and Fraunce from a list of classical figures to one of contemporary poets. An interesting sidelight to these passages involves
the poem sometimes attributed to Ralegh, "Now what is love? I
pray thee tell." The cadence and language of Barnfield's

Still my sweet Loue with bitter lucke th'art sawcing:
. . . .
Loue is a fiend, a fire, a heauen, a hell;
Where pleasure, paine, and sad repentance dwell

recall to the reader's mind

        It is that fountain and that well
        Where pleasure and repentance dwell.
        It is perhaps that sauncing bell
        That tolls all into heaven or hell.

Since these stanzas of Barnfield are also those which employ
Greene's metaphor of the shepherd-king comparison, which, incidentally, is another "What is love?" poem, perhaps we get some

insight into the way the young poet worked. It is almost as if he had before him all the contemporary poems of this genre and drew from them as each fit his need. But Barnfield's lines, despite their heavy draft upon all these poets, remain his own and cannot be said to be any more imitative than perhaps Greene's poem was of Peele's "What thing is love?" or Ralegh's was of either. But to continue the comparison of Barnfield to Watson and Fraunce:

> Seemelie a Boy, so seemelie a youth, so seemelie a Younker,
> That on *Ide* was not such a Boy, such a youth, such a Younker.
> (*Aff. Shep.*, G$_3$^{v})

> Making way to the sunne, taking her way to the yonker,
> *Braue* yonker Cephalus, whome faire Aurora desired.
> (Fraunce, D$_2$^{v})

> Et Cephali cupidis se submissura lacertis.
> Aeolus, Aurorae qui demulceret amores.
> (Watson, C$_4$^{r} mispaginated C$_3$^{r})

No doubt other parallels can be cited, especially if we consider other works by Watson and Fraunce. Yet when all the evidence is in, sifted, and commented upon, it seems all the harder to decide either for Watson or for Fraunce. The terms of the Amyntas allusions fit Watson best, but all the weight of influence and association favors Fraunce. The entire question of the identity of Amyntas, for my part, remains open. Directly or indirectly both men contributed to *The Affectionate Shepheard*, but then so too did many another of the most notable pastoralists of the day: Spenser, Sidney, Marlowe, Greene, Shakespeare, and Drayton.

II

The achievement of Barnfield's first acknowledged volume[23] equals that of his other works. Nothing written later is any better than "The Teares" or "The Shepheards Content" unless it be the two well-known odes: "Nights were short" and "As it fell vpon a Day." Barnfield does not improve from volume to volume; neither does he decline. He writes as well at twenty as he does at twenty-four or thirty; especially is this true if "As it fell vpon a Day"

---

[23]I have no doubt that Barnfield wrote the earlier *Greenes Funeralls,* and assuredly, *The Affectionate Shepheard* exhibits considerable improvement over this slender, juvenile attempt. But *Greenes Funeralls,* we must remember, was unclaimed by its author, perhaps for the very reason that he deemed it nothing more than journalism.

was composed somewhat earlier than the year of its appearance, as there is some reason to believe.[24]

The Affectionate Shepheard attempts several things. Apart from the pastoral verse of the first two poems, there is a sonnet in the English form, a complaint poem in the *Mirror for Magistrates* tradition, and a venture at English hexameters. These are the experimental essays of a beginning poet, for Barnfield was never anything other than an apprentice, though one must allow, an apprentice of marvelous promise. In his three volumes he tried his hand at a large proportion of the verse forms popular in his age: the two-line epigram, the common six-line stanza, rime royal, the English hexameter, the Spenserian stanza, the sonnet, and the ode. He dabbles with every genre: the pastoral lament, the *Mirror* complaint, light verse, the panegyric, the sonnet sequence, the Ovidian-myth poem, the debate, the elegy, and the epitaph. He seldom does the same thing twice; he appears always to have looked for the "subiect . . . new." Most of his work is of an unfinished quality, most at a beginner's level.

The freshness that one finds in "The Teares" comes from a quality of personal immediacy that is fused into the poem. Barnfield was writing possibly to a living youth. If so, the charge of pederasty rises, and I hardly think the perversion can be denied. Not only is much of the diction convincing, but Barnfield's own disclaimer in the preface to *Cynthia* is not very overpowering when we find in that very work the sonnet sequence to Ganimede, with language and imagery as blatant in its homosexuality as anything in the so-called "imitation of *Virgill*."

"The Teares" is a peculiar mixture of the coldest conventionality:

> His Iuory-white and Alablaster skin
> Is staind throughout with rare Vermillion red,
> Whose twinckling starrie lights doe neuer blin
> To shine on louely *Venus* (Beauties bed:)
>   But as the Lillie and the blushing Rose,
>   So white and red on him in order growes,
>   (A3ᵛ)

---

[24] The ode was published in 1598 among *Poems in diuers humors* as part of the volume entitled *The Encomion of Lady Pecunia*. In a verse dedication to "Maister Nicholas Blackleech," Barnfield calls the poems "fruits of vnriper yeares" (Eᵛ). There are eight pieces in *Poems in diuers humors*, four of which contain datable references. With the exception of "A Remembrance of some English Poets," all could have been written by 1594.

and the warmest particularity:

> O would to God (so I might haue my fee)
> My lips were honey, and thy mouth a Bee.

> Then shouldst thou sucke my sweete and my faire flower
> That now is ripe, and full of honey-berries:
> Then would I leade thee to my pleasant Bower
> Fild full of Grapes, of Mulberries, and Cherries;
>   Then shouldst thou be my Waspe or else my Bee,
>   I would thy hiue, and thou my honey bee.
>   (B^r)

The full force of this sexual imagery is unmistakable.

"The Teares" seems to me to be unfinished, as is so much of Barnfield's work; and what we have of it is put together from fragments that at one time, I feel, belonged to other poems. There are only two days' lamentations, a number far short of the twelve of Fraunce's *Amyntas*. Barnfield barely gets started into his lament. The second day is very much a repetition of the first, an extension of the love-invitation, love-gift offering, as though the poet planned to write several more days' lamentations and was in no hurry to introduce new developments. Even the *Alexis* eclogue produces more change in its relatively few lines than does the considerably longer "Teares." More characters in their relation to Alexis, in their threat to Corydon are employed by Virgil. "The Teares" introduces only Guendolena, and she is dropped altogether in the first day's lament. The entire poem is brought abruptly to a close by two conventional stanzas after the poet promises to record Ganimede's cruelty:

> But thou (more hard than Steele or Marble is)
> Doost scorne my Teares, and my true loue disdaine;
>   Which for thy sake shall euerlasting bee,
>   Wrote in the Annalls of Eternitie.
>   (E^r)

These annals are not forthcoming.

To recognize the pastiche quality of the poem, one need only pick out these sections which are unmistakable units in themselves, hardly fitting the poem, sometimes fitting so badly as to confuse the reader, and joined ineptly in almost every case. After an opening, convincing in its freshness and truth—"If it be sinne to loue a louely Lad;/ Oh then sinne I, for whom my soule is sad" (A$_3$^{r})—Barnfield works in, before the poem is fairly begun, the fable of Death and Cupid exchanging arrows. The episode is tacked on with the bald conjunction, "And thus it hapned"; it has little, if any, relationship to the rest of the poem. The concept of Cupid mixing his arrows of disdain (leaden) with his arrows of desire (golden) was a commonplace, and even Barnfield's variation of Death's arrow (black steel) was not new.[25] The entire passage, including the Guendolena material, is self-contained and can be omitted without disrupting the poem's continuity.

H. H. Hudson sees topical allegory in the episode.[26] Guendolena represents Penelope Devereux; the dead youth is Sidney. The doting old fool stands for Lord Rich; Ganimede is Mountjoy. Hudson does not press the case for allegorical reading, but he maintains that it is a clear possibility: "Whatever Barnfield intended readers put some construction upon his work which caused discussion and scandal; we know this because in his next book, *Cynthia* (1595), the poet . . . had to tell his 'curteous Gentlemen Readers' that they had misinterpreted *The Affectionate Shepheard* and that he had intended only a story of homosexual love" (p. 94).

The Love-Death passage does read as though it carries personal allegory, but Hudson's interpretation is weak. Guendolena is mistreated badly by Daphnis, who warns Ganimede that

> though she be faire
> Yet is she light; not light in vertue shining:
> But light in her behauiour, to impaire
> Her honour in her Chastities declining.
>
> (B₂ᵛ)

As correctly as this may describe Penelope Devereux, Barnfield would hardly be the one to point it out since the book was dedicated to Lady Rich. To identify Ganimede with Charles Blount is to make that Lord the object of Daphnis' affections, a situation of extreme unlikelihood. Even Hudson's use of Barnfield's apology

---

[25]See Geffrey Whitney, *A Choice of Emblems* (1586), R₂ᵛ-R₃ʳ. Whitney's poem is in the verse form and stanza of "The Teares." It is dedicated to Edward Dyer, Sidney's intimate friend. Dyer himself wrote a poem containing an exchange of arrows in "Amarillis." Barnfield, close to many members of the Sidney circle, dedicating *The Affectionate Shepheard* to Penelope Rich, surely found his source in Whitney rather than in Shakespeare's, *Venus and Adonis* (945-948), as Pooler claims in The Arden Shakespeare (1911), p. ix.

[26]"Penelope Devereux as Sidney's Stella," *Huntington Library Bulletin*, VII (April, 1935), 93-95.

in the preface to *Cynthia* is an obvious misconstruction. The explicit charge against which the poet defends himself is homosexuality ("to wit, the loue of a Shepheard to a boy"). Hudson claims that Barnfield admits to the perverted love in order to cover up some other scandal. Such misreading of Barnfield's open intention is difficult to understand. Nevertheless, the inescapable digressive quality of the passage, its almost certain allegorical nature, so different from the mode of the rest of the poem, illustrate further the patchwork character of "The Teares."

Evidence of a more serious flaw in Barnfield's workmanship is the digression at the end of the second day's lament which itself separates into two diverging directions. At stanza thirty-seven, Barnfield begins an amusing championship of black over white and continues for sixteen stanzas. Immediately following, and continuing to the end of the poem, is a moral tract of complete seriousness and considerable weight, perfectly worthy of Polonius, in which Daphnis, after urging Ganimede to return an unnatural love, belabors him to be virtuous in such matters as avoiding evil company, praying daily, foregoing oaths and lies, and in this particularity:

> Embrace thy Wife, liue not in lecherie;
> Content thy selfe with what Fates haue assignde.
>
> (D₄ᵛ)

The poem then describes Daphnis, looking and sounding somewhat like Chaucer's Reeve as described in the prologue to his tale:

> This leare I learned of a Bel-dame Trot,
> (When I was yong and wylde as now thou art):
> But her good counsell I regarded not;
> I markt it with my eares, not with my hart:
>   But now I finde it too-too true (my Sonne)
>   When my Age-withered Spring is almost done.
>
> Behold my gray head, full of siluer haires,
> My wrinckled skin, deepe furrowes in my face:
> Cares bring Old-Age, Old-Age increaseth cares;
> My Time is come, and I haue run my Race:
>   Winter hath snow'd vpon my hoarie head,
>   And with my Winter all my ioyes are dead.
>
> (D₄ᵛ)

Pointed out often as an illustration of the convention which makes the lover in pastoral verse complain of his advancing age, though the poet be quite young actually, as Shakespeare in the sonnets, the passage is part, really, of what I take to be another poem. For Daphnis, as a lover, to call Ganimede "my Sonne" is most inappropriate; for him to display his age after ridiculing the wantonness of the old man of the Guendolena episode is foolhardy. In an earlier stanza Daphnis is young and physically attractive still:

> Why doo thy Corall Lips disdaine to kisse,
> And sucke that Sweete, which manie haue desired?
>
> (C_2^r)

The youthful seducer of the first three-fourths of "The Teares" is inconsistent with the ancient moralist of the conclusion, so much so that tone, logic, and coherence break down in a way which suggests that the poet tried to weld together two completely disparate poems.

The sonnet which follows "The Shepheards Content" is, to my mind, intended as an envoy to "The Teares." It is placed after "Content" instead in order to imply that "Teares" and "Content" together are basically one poem, thus swelling in bulk a work that proved shorter than the poet had envisioned. The first line of the sonnet, "Loe here behold these tributarie Teares," refers directly to the first two days' laments, which are called "Teares." The reference can hardly include "The Content," the subtitle of which is "The happines of a harmles life" and the subject matter of which, except for two very brief digressions, can only with some difficulty be termed tearful. Barnfield is a careless poet, as Grosart and C. S. Lewis have observed,[27] but the nature of the workmanship in *The Affectionate Shepheard* indicates more than carelessness; it shows also that Barnfield was pasting poems together in order to get out a first volume.

Taken by itself, "The Shepheards Content" is the finest poem in *The Affectionate Shepheard*. Much of its success comes from its relative singleness of purpose, the poet's ability to stick, for once, to the point. Apparently Barnfield's contemporaries pre-

---

[27]Grosart asks "How did he manage to proceed homeward 'by the Moon shine light' when Cynthia had taken 'conge' of the sable Night?" *The Complete Poems*, p. 230. C. S. Lewis finds amusement in "Cassandra," which "gives a good many delights unintended by the poet . . . no one 'seemed more fair' than this god on an occasion when he 'invisibly did glide,' " *English Literature in the Sixteenth Century* (Oxford, 1954), p. 497.

ferred it also. The preface to *Cynthia* tells us that the "Coūtry *Content* found such friendly fauor, yᵗ it hath incouraged me to publish my second fruits" (Aᵈʳ). It is Barnfield's only poem singled out by name for mention by a contemporary, H. C. in *Piers Plainnes Seauen Yeres Prentiship* (1595).[28]

The dominating shepherd-king metaphor which holds the poem together has already been mentioned. This image leads comfortably into a recitation of bucolic delights, which include, inevitably, the bitter-sweet pangs of love. But first a brief digression is made, not unreasonably, to praise two dead masters of pastoral encomium: Sidney and Amyntas. When the love passage is reached, these two are invoked again, along with Spenser and Drayton, as a sort of catalogue of Cupid's saints, here canonized for suffering. This bypath gives Barnfield opportunity to return momentarily to the theme of "The Teares" in what constitutes the second brief side excursion:

> Why doost thou shoot thy cruel shafts at mee?
> Giue me some respite, some short time of pausing:
> Still my sweet Loue with bitter lucke th'art sawcing:
> . . . .
> Then pierce his hard hart with thy golden Arrow,
> That thou my wrong, that he may rue my sorrow.
> (Fₐʳ-Fₐᵛ, mispaginated Eₐʳ-Eₐᵛ)

With this note in "The Content" we may say that the first three poems—"The Teares," "The Shepheards Content," and the sonnet —celebrate to some degree Daphnis' unnatural love for Ganimede. It is the major burden of the first of Barnfield's volumes and is to be picked up again in the second. Any denial by the poet rings untrue when he ends a poem not covered by his apology with these lines:

> Now must I leaue (awhile) my rurall noate,
> To thinke on him whom my soule loueth best;
> He that can make the most vnhappie blest:
> In whose sweete lap Ile lay me downe to sleepe,
> And neuer wake till Marble-stones shall weepe.
> (Fₐᵛ)

It may not be stretching too far to read "stones" in the sense

---

[28]"Young Daphnis hath giuen his verdict of *The Shepheards Content*: duely praising it, as it meriteth," ed. H. Varnhagen, p. 37. In the nineteenth century, John Payne Collier approved of its charm by quoting a stanza in *A Bibliographical Account*, III, 203.

Harry Bailly employs, bawdily praising Chaucer's nun's priest: "I-blessed be thy breche, and every stoon"; or in the sense that the boys of Venice used upon Shylock, "Crying—his stones, his daughter, and his ducats" (II.vii.24). The pun was extremely common, Shakespeare using it at almost every opportunity throughout his plays. Thus it is perversion that removes these poems from the merely facile melodious woodnotes they are sometimes termed, and the so-called literary exercises take on pervasive tones of living accents, the confessions and pleadings of a man actually in love.

"The Complaint of Chastitie" is an ambiguous poem, difficult to classify. From its title we should include it with those pieces that complain about the vices, a prototype of which might be Philip Stubbes's prose *Anatomy of Abuses* or Lodge's *Alarum against Usurers*. But Barnfield is avowedly imitating Drayton's *Matilda*, a tragedy-complaint of the *Mirror for Magistrates* genre. "The Complaint of Chastitie" uses the prescribed seven-line *Mirror* stanza and a subject already approved by Drayton, but as a *Mirror*-complaint it never gets started. The conventional *Mirror*-poem introduces invariably the tragic victim, returned from the grave, to tell of his error, his downfall, and his lesson learned. "The Complaint of Chastitie" fails to introduce Matilda at all. In the poem's nine stanzas Matilda is spoken of only in three, and the piece concludes at a point at which the traditional *Mirror*-complaint begins.

The real nature of the poem almost defies description. In the second stanza Barnfield, through the voice of Chastity, apostrophizes and harangues some personified vice, which, after four stanzas of vituperation, he never names. We suppose that Chastity is lashing her opposite number, lechery perhaps or promiscuity; but whenever we attempt to label the vice, we find that Barnfield has employed the name in description of it. And this description alone uses fully four of the poem's total of nine stanzas. Again, in this extremely poor production can be seen the unfinished quality of Barnfield's work. He starts some lengthy project, grows tired of it quickly, and abandons it—first tacking on a hasty conclusion—before it gets fairly underway. Thus we speculated with "The Teares"; so it appears to be with "The Complaint of Chastitie."[29] The performance is somewhat less than the intention.

---

[29]Crawford may have been correct in citing Shakespeare's *Rape of Lucrece* as Barnfield's model. The purpose of "The Complaint" is to

Some attention has been given previously to formal matters in "Hellens Rape," but mostly in terms of figures of rhetoric. Its six-foot line requires comment also, and it is best examined in relation to other English hexameters. If "Hellens Rape" were meant to be serious, it is a very bad poem, as several of its critics have claimed; if it was intended to be comic—and its subtitle insists that it was—it is an entertaining if not a good poem. Admitting the theme to be humorous, we take no great risk to assume that the verse form is satiric. The sober experiments in hexameters of Spenser and Sidney were long over. Only Fraunce and Stanyhurst continued to use the six-foot line as their chief medium, while some writers like Nashe were lampooning many of its practitioners.[30] Watson leaves behind him no English hexameters,[31] although he was one of the most devoted classicists of his day, composing most of his Latin poems in the long line, but translating his own *Meliboeus* into rimed English pentameters. Barnfield, it cannot be denied, began his career in *Greenes Funeralls* as a dedicated hexametrist; but before publication of *The Affectionate Shepheard* he matured poetically, owing much perhaps to the example of Watson as well as to the failures of Fraunce. For if I am correct about the satiric element in the metrics of "Hellens

---

praise that virtue for which Lucrece was a byname. Also, Barnfield evokes *Lucrece* in "A Remembrance of some English Poets." Crawford finds in "The Complaint" four separate imitations of various lines from *Venus and Adonis;* and John Munro, since proved to be wrong, in *The Shakespeare Allusion Book* (London, 1909), p. 18, claimed these to be the earliest references (by imitation) to *Venus and Adonis* that we have. If *Lucrece* were Barnfield's model and Matilda his subject, a poem was contemplated considerably more ambitious than the one we find in *The Affectionate Shepheard.*

[30]Nashe's blasts at Harvey's hexameters ("the Doctor had some ierking hexameters or other" in *Haue with you to Saffron-walden* (1596) are too numerous to list; his attack on Stanyhurst is in the "Preface" to Greene's *Menaphon* (1589): "For so terrible was his stile to all milde eares, as would haue affrighted our peaceable Poets from intermedling hereafter with that quarrelling kind of verse." See McKerrow, *Nashe*, III, 73, 320.

[31]I ignore the couplet with which, as Nashe tells us, Watson scourged Harvey's hexameters: *"But, o what newes of that good* Gabriell Haruey,/ *Knowne to the world for a foole and clapt in the Fleet for a Rimer"* (McKerrow, *Nashe*, III, 127)? Writing in hexameters himself, Watson provides an illustration of ridicule through purposely inept imitation, exactly the method I claim for Barnfield above.

Rape," then Barnfield was satirizing his old master's measures as well as his rhetorical ornaments by using the objects scorned so ludicrously that the folly of the practice was self-apparent. Paradoxically, however, "Hellens Rape" is a rather delightful poem, with a swift pace, a subtle wit, some accomplished verse, and a gay humor despite the fact that several of its formal elements were meant to be inept:

> Embassage ended, a Banquet braue was appointed:
> Sweet Repast for a Prince, fine Iunkets fit for a Kings sonne.
> Biskets and Carawayes, Comfets, Tart, Plate, Ielly, Ginge-bread,
> Lymons and Medlars: and Dishes moe by a thousand.
> First they fell to the feast, and after fall to a Dauncing,
> And from a Dance to a Trance, from a Trance they fell to a
>   fallïng
> Either in others armes, and either in armes of another.
> Pastime ouer-past, and Banquet duely prepared,
> Deuoutly pared: Each one hies home to his owne home,
> Saue Lord and Ladies: Young Lad, but yet such an old Lad,
> In such a Ladies lappe, 'at such a slipperie by-blow,
> That in a world so wide, could not be found such a wilie
> Lad: in an Age so old, could not be found such an old lad:
> Old lad, and bold lad, such a Boy, such a lustie Iuuentus.
> Well to their worke they goe, and both they iumble in one Bed:
> Worke so well they like, that they still like to be working:
> For *Aurora* mounts before he leaues to be mounting:
> And *Astraea* fades before she faints to be falling:
> (*Helen* a light Huswife, now a lightsome starre in *Olympus*).
>   (G₄ᵛ)

Tucker Brooke wrote of Barnfield that "He came at an idle moment and was the idlest poet in it,"[32] an evaluation both acute and true. He never labored hard at any of his poems; some were abandoned before they were finished according to his original plan. When he achieved unity and concluded a poem in the spirit in which it was begun—"The Shepheards Content" and "Hellens Rape" for instance—the results were charming and delightful. His evocation of "the garden of the world" is among the finest of its kind:

---

[32]C. F. Tucker Brooke, "The Renaissance," *A Literary History of England*, ed. A. C. Baugh (New York, 1948), p. 407.

I haue a Garden-plot,
Wherein there wants nor hearbs, nor roots, nor flowers;
(Flowers to smell, roots to eate, hearbs for the pot,)
And dainty Shelters when the Welkin lowers:
Sweet-smelling Beds of Lillies and of Roses,
Which Rosemary banks and Lauender incloses.

There growes the Gilliflowre, the Mynt, the Dayzie
(Both red and white,) the blew-veynd-Violet:
The purple Hyacinth, the Spyke to please thee,
The scarlet dyde Carnation bleeding yet;
The Sage, the Sauery, and sweet Margerum,
Isop, Tyme, & Eye-bright, good for the blinde & dumbe.

The Pinke, the Primrose, Cowslip, and Daffadilly,
The Hare-bell blue, the crimson Cullumbine,
Sage, Lettis, Parsley, and the milke-white Lilly,
The Rose, and speckled flowre cald Sops in wine,
Fine pretie King-cups, and the yellow Bootes,
That growes by Riuers, and by shallow Brookes.
(B₂ᵛ-B₃ʳ)

Pastoral is the mode of *The Affectionate Shepheard,* and this is the book undoubtedly that moved Francis Meres to include his "friend master Richard Barnfielde" with Sidney, Challoner, Spenser, Gosson, and Fraunce as "amongst vs the best in this kind."[33]

---

[33]*Palladis Tamia,* ed. D. C. Allen (New York, 1938), pp. 284ʳ-284ᵛ.

CHAPTER III

CYNTHIA

The first volume that Barnfield claimed as his own by putting his name on the title page was *Cynthia. with certaine Sonnets, and the Legend of Cassandra,* printed for Humfrey Lownes in 1595. It followed very quickly his previous book, which had appeared anonymously but was acknowledged to be his in the address "To the curteous Gentlemen Readers" of *Cynthia*: "Gentlemen; the last Tearme there came furth a little toy of myne, intit'led, *The affectionate Shepheard*" (A⁴ʳ). Since *Cynthia* was entered in the Stationers' Register on January 17, 1595, and published no doubt during the Hillary term, which ran from January 11 to the Wednesday before Easter, the previous *Tearme* to which Barnfield refers was Michaelmas of 1594. Even though Michaelmas runs from November 2 to December 21, the printers completed their new issuances traditionally before December began, and, as Arber indicates,[1] it is safe to date the appearance of *The Affectionate Shepheard* in November, 1594. *Cynthia* appeared, then, no more than two-and-a-half months later, a prompt second venture, urged, as Barnfield tells us, by the success of the first: "Coūtry *Content* found such friendly fauor, yᵗ it hath incouraged me to publish my second fruits" (A⁴ʳ).

Cynthia had two editions, both issued in 1595.[2] Spelling is altered throughout, indicating that the entire book had been reset; but the only change in the text, other than pointing, is in the concluding stanza to the title poem. In one edition "Cynthia" concludes with a six-line stanza, riming ababcc, and entitled "To Her Sacred Maiestie." In the other, the last stanza is composed of

---

[1] *Richard Barnfield: Poems,* pp. vii, 44.

[2] There are extant at present five copies of the two editions. According to the *STC* and Bishop's Checklist, four of these are identical, being listed under STC # 1483 and reposing in the Bodleian, the Huntington, and the Folger Shakespeare Libraries and the British Museum. The Huntington Library is recorded as having the unique alternate, listed under STC # 1484. One of the Huntington volumes appears to be dated 1598, but careful scrutiny shows that some early owner has altered the second 5 with the stroke of a pen. *Book Auction Records,* XIX (1922), p. 225 corroborates this fact in the entry recording the sale of the volume to Rosenbach on Feb. 6, 1922.

ten lines of iambic pentameter couplets, entitled "The Conclusion." The unchanged contents of both editions comprise a dedication to William Stanley, the sixth Earl of Derby; an address "To the curteous Gentlemen Readers"; four stanzas in rime royal in commendation "of the Authour his worke" by T. T.; a three-stanza verse dedication "To his Mistresse" by Barnfield, also in rime royal; and the four major poems of the volume: "Cynthia," nineteen stanzas in the verse form of Spenser's *Faerie Queene*, concluding with either the ten-line or six-line envoi mentioned before; twenty "Sonnets" in a loose sequence; "An Ode" in ninety-six lines, beginning "Nights were short, and daies were long"; and "Cassandra," seventy-eight stanzas in the familiar six-line ababcc.

The dedicatory epistle to Stanley is conventional in its terms of praise and its understated promise and expectation. Only the reference to Barnfield's tender years are of a personal nature. Why Barnfield chose to address himself to the Earl of Derby is difficult to fathom. From the evidence adduced in the previous chapter, it is most probable that Barnfield was on the periphery of the Penshurst circle, as presided over by Mary Herbert. *The Affectionate Shepheard* had been dedicated to Penelope Rich, and one wonders why Barnfield did not offer his second volume to the Countess of Pembroke in imitation of his early master, Abraham Fraunce, who presented several to that lady. Of course, Fraunce may have been dead or outside the charmed circle by 1595, leaving Barnfield without any ingress to it.

Of Barnfield's earlier models only Greene and Spenser dedicated works to the Stanley family or praised its members in verse. But both Greene and Spenser were devoted only to Ferdinando, William's elder brother, or to Ferdinando's wife, Alice. Nashe too, possibly unknown to Barnfield, though the two of them were Greene's only posthumous defenders, praised Ferdinando excessively. Thomas Lodge, with whom I have not been able to associate Barnfield, either personally or poetically, dedicated *A Fig for Momus* to William Stanley in 1595; but Lodge was indebted considerably to the Stanley family for life-long benefactions as well as drawn to them strongly by his serious Roman persuasions, for the Stanleys were looked upon as one of the nation's leading Catholic families. *A Fig for Momus* was presented in honor of William Stanley's marriage to Elizabeth Vere, daughter of the Earl of Oxford. Possibly it was this marriage that led Barnfield to turn to Stanley, for him an otherwise unlikely patron. Barnfield's attempts at obtaining a patron were only half-hearted at best. The twelve lines to Sidney's Stella which preface *The Affectionate Shepheard* seem only to be offering a gift, warmly tendered and asking nothing in return. The 1598 edition of *The Encomion of Lady Pecunia* has no dedication at all, and the 1605 edition is prefaced by a flippant eight-line stanza, possibly to John Spencer, which is more insulting than panegyrical and could never have been expected to reap any beneficence. Only the dedication to Stanley is recognizable as following the contemporary methods of obtaining a patron, and therefore it is possible to hear the fine voice of the publisher behind Barnfield's letter, demanding that the poet attach the work to some great name, caught up at the moment in an undertaking of some significance, such as the union of two great houses, like those of Stanley and Vere.

The address "To the curteous Gentlemen Readers" encompasses several knotty problems, providing us indirectly with as much knowledge about Barnfield as has yet come from anywhere other than the documents of his birth, pedigree, education, will, and death. In addition to informing us that he wrote *The Affectionate Shepheard*, it denies that he was "the authour of two Bookes heretofore":

> I neede not to name them, because they are two-well knowne already: nor will I deny them, because they are dislik't; but because they are not mine.
> (A₄ʳ)

Several critics have identified these works as *Greenes Funeralls*, by R. B. Gent. (1594) and *Orpheus his Journey to Hell, R. B. Gent.* (1595).[3] I believe Barnfield to be the author of *Greenes Funeralls*,[4] but it has been demonstrated by Arber[5] that the poet cannot be referring to *Orpheus his Journey to Hell* since it was not entered in the Stationers' Register until August 26, 1595, almost seven months after *Cynthia* was entered. If Barnfield is the author

---

[3]Joseph Ritson, *Bibliographica Poetica* (1802), pp. 124-125, was the first to identify Barnfield with *Greenes Funeralls*, supposing him to be the author; Collier, Grosart, Charles Crawford, and others, coming upon Barnfield's disclaimer in the preface to *Cynthia*, rejected Ritson's attribution. Collier seems to have been the earliest to suggest that *Orpheus his Journey to Hell* was the other book which Barnfield was repudiating, *Bibliographical Account*, I, 62.

[4]See Chapter VI.

[5]*Poems*, p. xx.

of *Greenes Funeralls*, the book can yet be one of the two he denies as his, thus we are seeking to identify only the remaining book. Despite his claim that both are well known, we may never learn the identity of the second. No other work listed in the *Short Title Catalogue* under either the initials R. B. or the reversed B. R. could possibly be by Barnfield, and no anonymous work has yet turned up that suggests through style or subject matter that he is its author.

Barnfield's unnatural interest in a young boy figured under the pastoral name of Ganimede in *The Affectionate Shepheard* is recalled by the address to the readers. Apparently the explicitness of Daphnis' love was too great even for the strong tastes of Elizabethans. Barnfield feels compelled to make some explanations: "Some there were, that did interpret *The affectionate Shepheard*, otherwise then (in truth) I ment, touching the subiect thereof: to wit, the loue of a Shepheard to a boy; a fault, the which I will not excuse, because I neuer made" (A₄ʳ). He states that he was imitating merely Virgil's second eclogue. But the appearance in the sonnet sequence following "Cynthia" and in the ode "Nights were short" of an aberrant love more extreme than any in *The Affectionate Shepheard* discounts completely the poet's defense.

The epigram in the address to the reader raises other interesting speculations about Barnfield's affections. The six-line stanza is introduced as an explanation of the allegorical pieces:

> In one or two places (in this Booke) I vse the name of *Eliza* pastorally: wherein, least any one should misconster my meaning (as I hope none will) I haue heare breifly discouered my harmeles cōceipt as concerning that name: whereof once (in a simple Shepheards deuice) I wrot this Epigramme.

> *One name there is, which name aboue all other*
> *I most esteeme as tyme and place shall proue:*
> *The one is* Vesta, *th' other* Cvpids *Mother,*
> *The first my Goddesse is, the last my loue;*
> *Subiect to Both I am: to that by birth;*
> *To this for beautie; fairest on the earth.*
> (A₄ʳ)

Grosart is entranced with the verses in which he sees "a veiled reference to a lady who held supreme love-authority, who bore the same name with the great queen—Elizabeth; and of whom

we wish in vain to know more."[6] In Sonnet LXXIV of *Amoretti,*
Spenser plays with a coincidence of Elizabeths: his mother, his
prospective bride, and his queen all carried the same Christian
name:

> Most happy letters fram'd by skilfull trade,
>   with guifts of body, fortune and of mind.
>   the which three times thrise happy hath me made,
>   with guifts of body, fortune and of mind.
> The first my being to me gaue by kind,
>   from mothers womb deriu'd by dew descent,
>   the second is my souereigne Queene most kind,
>   that honour and large richesse to me lent.
> The third, my loue, my liues last ornament,
>   by whom my spirit out of dust was raysed:
>   to speake her prayse and glory excellent,
>   of all aliue most worthy to be praysed.
> Ye three Elizabeths for euer liue,
>   that three such graces vnto me giue.[7]

Amoretti was entered in the Stationers' Register for November
19, 1594, and published in 1595. *Cynthia* was not entered until
January 17, 1595, but was published the same year. Barnfield
might easily have seen Spenser's poem before writing his own. He
could even have seen it in print if it was published in the first
seventeen days of 1595, but Barnfield tells us that he wrote the
epigram at another time. Several possibilities exist to explain these
facts. Barnfield may have seen Sonnet LXXIV in manuscript. He
may not have seen it at all, and there is no interplay between the
two poems. There is also the bare chance that Spenser saw Barnfield's poem in manuscript before he wrote his sonnet, which
could hardly have been composed before 1592. I am inclined to
believe that there is no relationship between the poems other than
some similarity of thought and reference which may well have
been commonplace, being brought about by the accident of the
nation's having a virgin queen.

A theory most intriguing to me is the belief that Barnfield
is not writing about two women, but only about the Queen. In
all his three books Barnfield does not write one love poem to a
woman. The ode, "Nights were short," may seem such a poem,
but it is not. The ode, like the epigram, makes the Queen both his

---

[6]*The Complete Poems,* p. xii.
[7]*Spenser,* Variorum, VIII, Part II, 226.

goddess and his beloved, the last in the sense that so many of the courtly poets used to flatter Elizabeth. Nothing in the epigram precludes construing Vesta and Venus as standing both for the Queen. What Elizabethan poet, intending his work to be seen by her, would dare to claim some other lady "fairest on the earth." In "Cynthia" Barnfield emulates the conventional flattery that presents Elizabeth as containing within herself the virtue of Pallas as well as the beauty of Venus; something similar I believe him to be doing in the epigram. As for any other woman in Barnfield's life, we do not know the name of even his wife, nor do we know the date of his marriage, although it would seem that it was solemnized only after the poet retired to Staffordshire, probably sometime after 1598. If her name is ever obtained, it may prove to be Elizabeth; and we may learn also that a long successful courtship had been a happy part of Barnfield's life; but even then we must fear that many a young lady of twenty in 1595 was called Elizabeth.

A final item of interest in the address to the readers is Barnfield's announcement that *Cynthia* "is the first imitation of the verse of that excellent Poet, Maister *Spencer,* in his *Fayrie Queene.*" The statement is accurate as far as anyone has been able yet to ascertain. Drayton preceded Barnfield in imitating Spenser, but Drayton's model was *The Shepheardes Calender;* except for *The Shepheards Garland,* "Cynthia" is the earliest extended imitation of Spenser in any form.

T. T.'s[8] commendatory verses are panegyric and pedestrian. In rime royal, they are frequently awkward and sometimes ungrammatical. Providing little more than a table of contents, the four stanzas refer to all poems in the volume except "Nights were short." They concur with the poet as to his youthful years ("the noneage of his skill") and claim for him "more thē cōmon praise," which seems modest enough and just. But to turn the page from the lines of T. T. to those of Barnfield in address "To his Mistresse," also in rime royal, is to be aware immediately of the easy grace of Barnfield's pen. The poet's verses are conventional also, praising highly, promising devotion and labor, and denying self-worth; but the syntax is unstrained, the images attractive, the measure even, and the rimes unforced. The first stanza offers the

---

[8]Grosart thought the initials might be Thomas Tuke's, but they may stand as well for Thomas Thorpe.

book to his mistress, "Rare president of peerelesse chastity," the
usual terms of eulogy to the Queen. The second stanza refers
briefly to those detractors mentioned in the preface, whom he is
incapable of pleasing because they are "maliciously enuious," and
then invokes his mistress as his only muse. The third stanza makes
it unquestionable, I think, that his mistress is the Queen:

> But ah (alas) how can myne infant Muse
> (That neuer heard of Helicon before)
> Performe my promise past: when they refuse
> Poore Shepheards Playnts? yet will I still adore
> Thy sacred Name, although I write no more:
>   Yet hope I shall, if this accepted bee;
>   If not, in silence sleepe eternally.
>   (A₆^r)

The poems are offered and a plea is made for acceptance. It is
difficult to believe that Barnfield could offer "Cynthia" and the
sonnets to any lady whom he hoped to make his love-sovereign.
Instead "Cynthia" and "Nights were short" are poems in adoration of the same lady addressed in this invocation, his legal sovereign. Her name is sacred, and he will have hope—the same hope,
I take it, that Spenser held—if the verses are accepted. The promise
to remain silent if his "Poore Shepheards Playnts" are refused was
very nearly kept. Barnfield published only one more volume, although it went through two separate editions, seven years apart,
before he retired permanently from the public pursuit of poetry.

Barnfield presents his elaborate panegyric to Queen Elizabeth
—the title poem "Cynthia"—in the old form of the dream-vision.
In so much is he original. His is the only piece taking this form
in the rather large body of literature comparing Elizabeth to im-
mortal goddesses.[9] In all other matters, his treatment is derivative,

---

[9]The convention of praising the queen in terms of the judgment of
Paris is well reviewed by T. S. Graves, "*The Arraignment of Paris* and
Sixteenth Century Flattery," *MLN*, XXVIII (1913), 48-49. Still Graves'
article has some notable omissions. In an unpublished dissertation, W. P.
James (*The Life and Work of Richard Barnfield* [Northwestern, 1952],
p. 98) cites Gascoigne's *Griefe of Joye* as another instance of the Paris-
Elizabeth theme. An interesting parallel can be found also in Francis
Sabie's *Pans Pipe*, entered in the Stationers' Register January 3, 1595. In
Thestilis' ode, in the third Eclogue, there is a Paris-judgment episode in
which Juno, Pallas, and Venus all want Citheria (Queen Elizabeth) as
their own. The judgment is given to Zeus, who praises the Queen out-
rageously and says "Sweet Eliza, Ladies,/ Shall be mine onlie" (D₄^r).

emulative, and plagiaristic.[10] The verse form follows the stanza of
The Faerie Queene; the content derives from *The Arraignment of
Paris*. Although one scholar has expressed disbelief in Barnfield's
indebtedness to Peele,[11] there can be little doubt that the younger
poet leaned heavily upon *The Arraignment*. Lines 90-110 of I.iii.[12]
in Peele's pageant are the unmistakable source for the fourth stanza
of "Cynthia":

> There might one see, & yet not see (indeede)
> Fresh *Flora* flourishing in chiefest Pryme,
> Arrayed all in gay & gorgeous weede,
> The Primrose & sweet-smelling Eglantyne,
> As fitted best beguiling so the Tyme:
> And euer as she went she strew'd the place,
> Red-roses mixt with Daffadillyes fine.
>
> (B^v)

In stanza ten Barnfield uses a word so unexpected as *trindled*,
which appears in no eulogy to the Queen that I have seen other
than *The Arraignment*: "Ate hauing trūdled the ball into place
. . . " (Stage direction following line 381). Barnfield calls the
inscription on the ball a "Poesie" as does Peele and records it as
Pvlcherimae, while Peele writes *Detur Pulcherimmae*. Barnfield
diverges from Peele in having Mercury present the golden apple to
Elizabeth, whereas in *The Arraignment* it is Diana who perhaps
more fittingly, as the chaste huntress, approaches the virgin
Queen.[13] Undoubtedly Barnfield saw much of the poetry so dedicated to the Queen. His possible friend and assured poetic master,

---

Sabie's work is the more significant for eight lines on signature As^r, first
pointed out by Sidney Lee, *Poems and Pericles* (Oxford, 1905), pp. 31-32,
in relation to Barnfield's ode beginning, "As it fell vpon a Day." But
more important still are three works which I treat below, two of them
by men to whom Barnfield was close in spirit if not in actuality: Watson
and Sidney. The third was by the anonymous T. H., probably Thomas
Heywood, who wrote *Oenone and Paris* (1594).

   [10]See Waldo F. McNeir, "Barnfield's Borrowings From Spenser,"
N & Q, CC (Dec., 1955), 510-511.

   [11]See W. P. James' dissertation, p. 98.

   [12]Malone Society reprint, ed. H. H. Child (Oxford, 1910), pp.
As^r-As^v.

   [13]T. H. in *Oenone and Paris*, ed. J. Q. Adams (Washington, 1943),
entered in the Stationers' Register May 17, 1594, has Mercury present
the ball also. T. H.'s Flora is a clear echo of Peele's and may have been
intermediary between *The Arraignment of Paris* and "Cynthia":

Thomas Watson, had written two poems suggestive of the theme of "Cynthia": Passion XXXIII of *Hecatompathia* (1582) and song VIII in *The first Sett, of Italian Madrigalls Englished* (1590).[14] In Passion XXXIII, Watson praises his lady, someone other than the Queen however:

> When *Priams* sonne in midst of *Ida* Plaine
> Gaue one the price, and other two the foile,
> If she for whome I still abide in paine
> Had liued then within the *Troyan* soile,
>> No doubt but hers had bene the golden ball,
>> *Helen* had scaped rape, and *Troy* his fall.
>> (E^r)

> There had the Silvanes planted many a thing,
> Flora bedecked it with eche smelling flower,
> The Primrose, Cow-slippe, and the Daffadillie,
> The Pinke, the Daysie, Violet, and Lillie.
>> (p. 6)

Compare also line 115 of *Oenone and Paris* with lines 1-2, stanza nine of "Cynthia":

T. H.:
> Then did thy eies with pearled teares reueale

Barnfield:
> By this the formost melting all in teares,
> And rayning downe resolued Pearls in showers.

However, the line more likely comes from Marlowe's *Tamburlaine*: "Rainst on the earth resolved pearls in showers" (I.v.i) as Charles Crawford pointed out, *N & Q*, 9th Series, Vol. VIII (1901), 219. Line 234 of *Oenone and Paris* seems also midway between Peele and Barnfield:

> I read the posie: *Detur Pulchriori.*

[14]Song VIII is less important, I think, than the piece in *Hecatompathia*, yet significant for the same reasons as *Pans Pipes*: a marked similarity to "As it fell vpon a Day":

> This sweet & merry month of May,
> While nature wantons in her Pryme,
> & Byrds do sing & Beasts do play:
> for pleasure of the ioyfull time,
> I choose the first for holly daie,
> & greet Elyza with a Ryme,
> O Beauteous Queene of second Troy,
> Take well in worth, a simple toy.
>> (B₄^v)

It is not absolutely clear that the words to this madrigal are by Watson. They may belong to William Byrd, who wrote the music.

Usually giving the sources for those of his Passions which are based on other writers, Watson gives none for this. But the thirteenth sonnet in *Astrophel and Stella,* with some considerable variation admittedly, is of a type with Watson's poem, with Peele's *Arraignment,* and with Barnfield's "Cynthia": Jove, Mars, and Love appoint Phoebus to be judge of their heraldic devices; Love's shield displays Stella's face; his crest her hair; and Phoebus, because of Stella's beauty, judges Love the winner. Mona Wilson, on the basis of other evidence, believes that Sidney knew Watson's *Hecatompathia,*[15] and possibly there is some interplay between these poems. Perhaps finding these themes in his early masters suggested to Barnfield a panegyric to the Queen; but it is to Peele that he goes for his basic theme and to Spenser for his verse.[16]

The sonnets that follow "Cynthia" are more the poet's own work than anything he had done up to the time of their inception. Not only had no writer published a sequence addressed to a young man but also it is unlikely that Barnfield had seen any of Shakespeare's sonnets before publication, for they are not mentioned in the "Remembrance of some English Poets" (1598), wherein *Venus and Adonis* and *Lucrece* are praised, nor are there any clear echoes of the poems to Shakespeare's young man in any of those to Ganimede. Surely if this poet, often charged with imitativeness, had read Shakespeare's sonnets, images, phrases, and ideas would have made their way into the *Cynthia* sequence. Janet Scott, who has an amazing eye for correspondences, sees similarities to other sonnets in only four of Barnfield's. She believes the sestet of Sonnet X follows the sestet of Constable's *Diana* II.v. Vague ideas come in one case from Daniel and in two from Sidney; but, in general, "Barnfield ne paraît pas avoir imité aussi directement. Il est hanté par la poésie de ses prédécesseurs et nous trouvons parfois un demi-

---

[15]*Sir Philip Sidney* (New York, 1932), pp. 164, 174. The passage Miss Wilson cites would indicate unfriendliness between Sidney and Watson but establishes nevertheless Sir Philip's familiarity with the *Hecatompathia.*

[16]It is all the more probable that Barnfield came to Peele through Watson or Sidney since *The Arraignment* had been published in 1584, when Barnfield was 10, and undoubtedly was never produced after its appearance in print. The evidence that Barnfield knew the works of Watson and Sidney is overwhelming, and the similarity between Barnfield's second sonnet and Sidney's fifty-second is proof that *Astrophel and Stella* was included in the younger poet's reading.

vers utilisé dans un contexte différent." Even when he does use an idea from a forerunner, he does so "de telle façon qu'il garde son indépendance de langage."[17] The sequence is very short, twenty sonnets, and throughout Barnfield confines himself to a single form, a modification of the English sonnet: abba cddc effe gg. In general the couplet is epigrammatic and summary, but the first twelve lines are not always divided into quatrains, Barnfield's practice in this matter showing some lack of discipline. The last sonnet in the cycle refers to Spenser and Drayton under their pastoral guises of Colin and Rowland and leads us to look in vain in *Amoretti* and *Idea* for suggestive similarities; but the tribute is general, praising the poets for their pastoral verse rather than for their sonnets. As I have stated previously in this chapter, it is highly doubtful that Barnfield had seen Spenser's *Amoretti* before he wrote Sonnet XX, and he could have seen only eighteen from Drayton's *Idea* in 1595, unless he had access to manuscript poems of his "professed friend." Still, no echoes are to be found.

"Nights were short," the ode which follows the sonnets, should be looked upon as the strongest argument there is in favor of Barnfield's authorship of "As it fell vpon a Day," the poem claimed for Shakespeare by several nineteenth-century editors. "Nights were short" is superior to "As it fell," and there is some reason to believe that it was composed later than the more famous piece, although it was published four years earlier.[18] Both "Nights were short" and "As it fell" employ the same verse form: a tetrameter line, beginning and ending on a stressed syllable. Barnfield allows himself considerable freedom in slipping away, in both poems, from rigid regularity—a characteristic much less prevalent in his longer poems. But the metrical variations in "Nights were short" are more adept than those in "As it fell." The images are fresher throughout the 1595 ode, as can be shown in the imitative nature of the opening in that of 1598.[19] "Nights were short" is a

---

[17]*Les Sonnets Élisabéthains* (Paris, 1929), p. 187.

[18]See especially the lines of dedication to Nicholas Blackleech prefacing *Poems: In diuers humors*, wherein the verses in the volume are called "fruits of vnriper yeares." "Nights were short" was reprinted in *Englands Helicon* (1600) as "The Sheepheards Ode" (K4r-Lr) and was taken directly from *Cynthia* as its fidelity to the 1595 text indicates.

[19]Although the matter of sources for "As it fell vpon a Day" is treated thoroughly in Chapter 4, attention has been called already to the poems of Sabie and Watson, both of which suggest that Barnfield

more extensive work, numbering ninety-six lines; "As it fell" comprises only fifty-six. "Nights were short" is a totally unified poem, having for its subject the single theme of love-transference from the shepherd boy Ganimede to the poet's mistress Eliza, whereas much controversy has resulted over a marked change of tone that appears at line twenty-seven of "As it fell vpon a Day." So great is the difference that several critics have theorized that the first twenty-six lines are the work of some poet greater than Barnfield,[20] the final thirty being the lesser poet's. Yet the mastery of "Nights were short," greater even than the first twenty-six lines of "As it fell," indicates beyond any doubt that Barnfield could have written the best there is in the 1598 ode.

If Barnfield, when naming Elizabeth in this ode, is indeed referring to some lady other than the Queen, "Nights were short" is then his only love poem to a woman. Even the two short pieces already discussed—the epigram and the address to his mistress— provided they can be proved to invoke some lesser lady, can hardly be called love poems. But in "Nights were short" Barnfield assumes a puzzling mask. An unnamed observer, wandering through the woods, comes upon a shepherd weeping. The shepherd is Daphnis, the same pastoral figure we find in *The Affectionate Shepheard* and the sonnets. As the ode opens, Daphnis still loves Ganimede; the narrator-observer himself holds for Daphnis affection of an ambiguous nature:

> (For who is not payn'd to heare
> Him in griefe whom heart holdes deare?)
>   (D^r)

While it is dangerous always to identify a poet with any of his creations, Barnfield has presented Daphnis so convincingly in earlier works that we have come to think of the shepherd as the poet's mouthpiece. Also Daphnis is the name undersigned to the dedication to Penelope Rich and the name by which H. C. refers to Barnfield in *Piers Plainnes*. We are faced then with the amusing confidence that narrator-Barnfield holds shepherd-Daphnis-Barnfield dear, or with the fiction—supplied for parallel structure— that there is another who loves the shepherd unnaturally just as Daphnis loves Ganimede.

---

was at least using a conventional opening if not borrowing outright from an earlier composition. See footnotes 9 and 14 of this chapter.

[20]See for instance, J. B. Henneman, "Barnfield's Ode: 'As It Fell Upon A Day,'" *An English Miscellany* (Oxford, 1901), pp. 158-164.

But more important is the transference of Daphnis' love from Ganimede to a

> (Lasse) that did in beauty passe,
> (Passe) fayre *Ganimede* as farre
> As *Phoebus* doth the smallest starre.
>
> (D^v)

The lady to whom Daphnis has shifted his love is Eliza, an Eliza whom I identify with the lady of the epigram, a lady not his love-mistress, but a Queen his sovereign mistress. The matter descriptive of her beauty is brief and conventional, not at all unlike the usual tributes to the Queen: in addition to surpassing all other mortals in loveliness, Eliza has "fair eies" through which she wounds the shepherd with love. The effect of this love is more lengthily treated, but the terms are recognizable still as the courtly gallantry now grown old with the Queen:

> Her it is, for whom I mourne;
> Her, for whom my life I scorne;
> Her, for whom I weepe all day;
> Her, for whom I sigh, and say,
> Either shee, or els no creature,
> Shall inioy my loue: whose feature
> Though I neuer can obtayne,
> Yet shall my true loue remayne:
> Till (my body turn'd to clay)
> My poore soule must passe away,
> To the heauens; where (I hope)
> Hit shall finde a resting scope:
> Then since I loued thee (alone)
> Remember mee when I am gone.
>
> (D₂^r)

At this point the laments of Daphnis cease and the narration is put back into the hands of Daphnis' eavesdropper:

> Scarce had hee these last words spoken,
> But me thought his hart was broken;
>
> . . . .
>
> In whose hart (thus riu'd in three)
> ELIZA written I might see:
> In Caracters of crimson blood,
> (Whose meaning well I vnderstood.)
>
> (D₂^r-D₂^v)

As in the lines introductory to the epigram ("I vse the name of *Eliza* pastorally: wherein, least any one should misconster my meaning [as I hope none will] I haue heere breifly discouered my harmeles cōceipt"), Barnfield again inserts a parenthetical explanation and apology, insisting, even at the expense of artistry, that we are dealing here with a conceit. He seems more afraid that someone will construe that he is in love with a flesh and blood lady than that the queen will take offense. But, surely, the very fact that Barnfield tells us a conceit is involved implies that the Elizabeth is not an Elizabeth like Spenser's beloved; instead she must be the Queen represented pastorally, and the poet does not want any reader to misconstrue his tone. It is to be seen as respectful, reverential, and innocent. But, we might ask, what is meant by the heart rived in three? Are we to understand that one part belongs to Ganimede, one part to Eliza, and that one remains with Daphnis? Or is one part Ganimede's, another Eliza the Queen's, and the third Eliza the lady friend's, about whom Grosart wished to know more in vain?

Perhaps help is to be found elsewhere in the ode. When Daphnis tells of his love for a woman who replaces Ganimede, there is no ambiguity. She is a single woman. His affections are not split: "Either shee, or els no creature,/ Shall inioy my loue." It would seem there is only one Eliza, and she is a woman whom Daphnis "neuer can obtayne," not because she scorns his love, as Ganimede has, but because she is out of his sphere. In the only remaining place that the name *Eliza* appears, stanzas 36-37 of "Cassandra," the lady's identity is established beyond a reasonable doubt:

> Yet famous *Sabrine* on thy bank's [*sic*] dost rest
> The fayrest Mayde that euer world admired:
> Whose constant mynde, with heauenly gifts possest,
> Makes her rare selfe of all the world desired:
>   In whose chast thoughts no vanity doth enter;
>   So pure a mynde *Endymions* Loue hath lent her.

> Queene of my thoughts, but subiect of my verse,
> (Diuine *Eliza*) pardon my defect:
> Whose artlesse pen so rudely doth rehearse
> Thy beauties worth; (for want of due respect)
>   Oh pardon thou the follies of my youth;
>   Pardon my fayth, my loue, my zeale, my truth.
>   (D8ᵛ-Eʳ)

The terms of affection and address are no less extreme as love verse than in the epigram, than in the address "To his Mistresse," or than in the ode, but the apology for presumption is clearer here.

In the second stanza, Barnfield cries pardon three times, and in the last cry, pardon for four offenses. That two of these request pardon for his love and for his truth ought to raise some eyebrows. His love is not sufficient, either because Eliza shares it with Ganimede or because no subject can love his sovereign adequately, and his truth is imperfect because the literal statement of pastoral allegory is not to be taken seriously. The first of the two stanzas above helps to explain the seemingly two distinct Elizabeths of the epigram. "The fayrest Mayde that euer world admired" and one "In whose chast thoughts no vanity doth enter" is one woman whom Barnfield wants to associate with two virtues: beauty and chastity. That is exactly what he does in "Cynthia"; it is exactly what many poets had done who wanted to flatter the Queen. In "Cynthia" Elizabeth contains all the virtues of Venus, Juno, and Minerva; in "Cassandra" and in the epigram she contains the virtues of Venus and Vesta. In effect the entire *Cynthia* volume, with the exception of the sonnets and the narrative sections of "Cassandra," is a eulogy to Queen Elizabeth, and *Cynthia,* as a title, applies as much to the complete work as it does to the first poem in it. The ode, then, is in the Petrarchan convention, which demands that at some point in the lover's life he give over the follies of his wilder days. "Leave off these toys in time!" is the way Thomas, Lord Vaux, puts it:

> I loathe that I did love;
> In youth that I thought sweet,
> As time requires for my behove,
> Me thinks they are not meet.

This convention employs usually an aging poet, but Barnfield liked to play the old man; and Vaux, dying at forty-six, could hardly be called doddering no matter when he wrote his poem. Sidney, whose "Leave me O love" is perhaps a better model to cite, although it does not associate repentance with age, illustrates that reform of this kind can take place even in the very young, since Sidney died in his thirty-second year. But strongest of all in the argument I am trying to establish is the difference between the ode as a love poem and one of the sonnets to Ganimede:

> Long haue I long'd to see my Loue againe,
>> Still haue I wisht, but neuer could obtayne it;
>> Rather then all the world (if I might gaine it)
> Would I desire my loues sweete precious gayne.

Yet in my soule I see him euery day,
    See him, and see his still sterne countenaunce,
    But (ah) what is of long continuance,
Where Maiestie and Beautie beares the sway?
Sometimes, when I imagine that I see him,
    (As loue is full of foolish fantasies)
    Weening to kisse his lips, as my loues fee's,
I feele bvt Ayre: nothing but Ayre to bee him.
    Thus with *Ixion*, kisse I cloudes in vayne:
    Thus with *Ixion*, feele I endles payne.
                  (C₅ᵛ)

Certainly the pretence of love in the ode does not approach the emotion of this sonnet[21] nor the conviction we feel in many lines of *The Affectionate Shepheard*.

Barnfield returns in "Cassandra," second longest of his works, shorter only than the combined two days' lamentations of *The Affectionate Shepheard*, to the six-line stanza that he seems to handle more easily than other verse forms. Almost no commentary on this poem exists. C. S. Lewis is amused at "a good many delights unintended by the poet."[22] C. K. Pooler and Douglas Bush, perhaps both indebted to Sidney Lee for the observation, claim that "Cassandra" owes something to Shakespeare's *Rape of Lucrece*.[23] Bush adds that "much of the Trojan matter seems to be taken from the *Recuyell* (ed. Sommer, pp. 509, 526 ff., 658 ff., 667, 673)"; and that the death of Agamemnon apparently comes from the *Agamemnon* of Seneca.[24] Hallett Smith's assertion that "Cassandra" is a sample of the "Ovidian-erotic poem" and that "the heroine reflects the current fashion . . . both victim of Fortune and a warning to girls,"[25] just about concludes all that has been written on this poem. It deserves better treatment, for it is not as derivative as these commentators imply. Pooler, who looked carefully,

---

[21]For a contrary opinion, see L. E. Pearson, *Elizabethan Love Conventions* (Berkeley, 1933), p. 141.

[22]"Apollo, wooing Cassandra, 'briefly t'her relates his pedigree', refers to her as 'my Cass', and no one 'seemed more fair' than this god on an occasion when he 'invisibly did glide'." *English Literature in the Sixteenth Century* (Oxford, 1954), p. 497.

[23]*Shakespeare's Poems*, The Arden Shakespeare, ed. C. K. Pooler (London, 1911), pp. xi-xiii; Douglas Bush, *Mythology and the Renaissance Tradition in English Poetry* (Mpls., 1932), p. 310; *Poems and Pericles*, ed. Sidney Lee (Oxford, 1905), pp. 31-32.

[24]*Mythology and the Renaissance Trad.*, p. 310.

[25]*Elizabethan Poetry* (Cambridge, Mass., 1952), pp. 94, 119.

apparently found only three encroachments upon Shakespeare: two from *Venus and Adonis* and one from *Lucrece*. "Cassandra" is no more nor less dependent on other works than many another poem of the period. Scholars should stop pointing out verbal similarities between one Elizabethan work and another for the sole purpose of establishing indebtedness. The task is too exhausting, the fruits rarely worth the effort. The scholar finds always the thing he is looking for: interdependence, borrowing, paraphrase, or plagiarism; but in the long run, little that is exposed contributes in any real way to an understanding or an appreciation of the poem or the poet. Neither has any Elizabethan borrower ever been "rased" from the canon of English Renaissance literature as a plagiarist.

More than its verbal echoes or specific situations, "Cassandra" owes to *Lucrece* the fusion of the eroticism that is found best in *Venus and Adonis* and the lament that originates perhaps in the *Mirror for Magistrates*. Hallett Smith is correct to call the poem Ovidian-erotic in one part of his book and a complaint in another. But, in one respect, "Cassandra" goes counter to a movement which *Lucrece* helped to support in the last decade of the sixteenth century. In 1592, Daniel revived the complaint genre and used the old *Mirror* rime royal stanza; but Lodge, Chute, and Drayton, imitating Daniel's themes and continuing the *Mirror* tradition, rejected the seven-line stanza for the much more widely used six-line ababcc.[26] Then, when *Lucrece* appeared in 1594 in the old rime royal stanza, the subsequent complaint poems such as Drayton's *Matilda* and even Barnfield's own Matilda poem, "The Complaint of Chastitie," returned with Shakespeare to the seven-line stanza. But Barnfield, who is charged with following always the lead of any older poet, chose to write "Cassandra" in the by then unfashionable six-line stanza. Clearly, *Venus and Adonis* exerted more influence upon Barnfield than *Lucrece*. The central idea of an importunate lover trying to break down the resistance of a sexually virtuous maiden plus a few verbal echoes are all that *Lucrece* lends to "Cassandra"; but Charles Crawford lists five borrowings from *Venus and Adonis*.[27] The plot, which includes a

---

[26]Hallett Smith, *Elizabethan Poetry*, p. 113, attributes the vogue of the six-line stanza to *Venus and Adonis*.

[27]"Richard Barnfield, Marlowe, and Shakespeare," *N & Q*, 9th Series, Vol. VIII (1901), 278.

deity enamored of a scornful mortal, a Greek rather than a Roman setting, a lover moved by softness rather than foul lust, plus the six-line stanza all show Barnfield to rely more heavily upon *Venus and Adonis* than upon *Lucrece.*

The materials claimed by Douglas Bush to be the sources for the Trojan matter and the death of Agamemnon seem to have only the slightest relationship to "Cassandra." Though it is true that Barnfield uses the tradition found in the *Recuyell* in which Aeneas, along with Antenor, is a traitor to Troy,

> What, ten-yeeres siedge by force could not subuert,
> That, two false traytors in one night destroy'd:
> Who richly guerdond for their bad desert,
> Was of *Aeneas* but small time inioy'd:
>   Who, for concealement of *Achilles* loue [Polyxena],
>   Was banished; from *Ilion* to remoue,
>   (E₂ʳ)

there is hardly any medieval version of the Troy legend which does not concur with the *Recuyell* on this point. Bush cites p. 509 of Sommer's edition, which provides, and tenuously only, the location where Priam determines for war:

> (Old princely *Pryamus Troy's* aged King)
> Was gon into *Ioues* Temple, to conspire
> Against the Greekes.
>   (Eᵛ)

Pages 526-527 (Sommer) also cited by Bush supply only Cassandra's prophecy of the city's destruction:

>   truely she fore-tolde
> The fall of *Troy.*
>   (E₂ʳ)

But the *Recuyell* does not state or imply that her words were ignored, as the story goes in "Cassandra":

> They count her hare-braynd, mad, and ouer-bolde,
> To presse in pressence in so graue a place.
>   (E₂ʳ)

The further references of Bush to pp. 658 ff., 667, and 673 all treat of the treason of Aeneas and Antenor. Taken all together these pages enumerated by Bush supply materials for only three of the seventy-eight stanzas of the poem; some connections are so remote as to constitute nothing more than the adherence of both the *Recuyell* and "Cassandra" to the widely accepted versions of the Troy story peculiar to post-classical treatments. One wonders why, for instance, Barnfield, for the death of Agamemnon, did not use the *Recuyell,* which has it simply "that the fyrst nyght that agamemnon shold lye with her/ he [Aegisthus] shold renne vpon hym & slee hym. This thinge was doon in like wise as she had purposid./ And Agamemnon was slayn and put in the erth" (p. 680). Bush suggests that Seneca's *Agamemnon* provides the method of the murder, but the Roman play contributes no more than the cloak which has no outlet for the victim's head. The murder itself is altered. Although Seneca has Aegisthus stab Agamemnon—the assassin is so inept and fearful that he botches the job and Clytemnestra has to finish it—John Studley's translation (1581)[28] misconstrues the passage and makes Clytemnestra the weapon-wielder for both blows. But "Cassandra" follows neither the original Latin nor Studley's erroneous version; Aegisthus accomplishes the murder quite efficiently all by himself. Barnfield was probably calling upon a vague remembrance of several versions of the Agamemnon story when he composed the passage concerning the murder.

The only imitativeness of "Cassandra" then is its following the vogue of *Venus and Adonis* and *The Rape of Lucrece* (a failing common to several poets of the age) and its making some slight verbal levies from these same poems. In general, the poems of *Cynthia* do not fit the charge made by some critics that Barnfield borrowed from his contemporaries more than did other Elizabethans. The title poem is highly indebted to Spenser and Peele, but the intention to imitate the *Faerie Queene* is announced in the preface. The sonnets owe very little to other sonneteers, English or continental. The ode not only is original but also of a high order of poetry, a peak not often arrived at by imitation. "Cassandra" owes no more to *Venus and Adonis,* its chief inspiration, than *Venus and Adonis* owes to *Hero and Leander.*[29] Barnfield's tendency to become independent of his friends and fellow poets is a sign of increasing maturity. At the publication of *The Affectionate Shepheard,* Barnfield had just passed his twentieth birthday, and some of the verse in that volume had been written as early

---

[28]*Seneca, His Tenne Tragedies* (1581).

[29]The point I am here trying to make is valid equally if *Hero and Leander* is the debtor.

as 1592, his eighteenth year. At the publication of *Cynthia*, he was young still, but the success of the first volume gave him apparently confidence and courage to cut the ties binding him too closely to older or more widely-known poets. The mark of a firmer mind, an approach of dignity to his craft, this tendency to be independent, to attempt new and different things, missing from a writer like Nicholas Breton, for all that poet's occasional charm, continued to grow in Barnfield as his third volume, *The Encomion of Lady Pecunia* (1598), shows:

> Being determined to write of somthing, & yet not resolued of any thing, I considered with my selfe, if one should write of Loue (they will say) why, euery one writes of Loue: if of Vertue, why, who regards Vertue? To be short, I could thinke of nothing, but either it was common, or not at all in request. At length I bethought my selfe of a Subiect, both new (as hauing neuer beene written vpon before) and pleasing.
>
> (A₃ʳ) (A$_8$ᵣ)

What is to be lamented is that the growth promised by such resolution was cut short. *Lady Pecunia* was Barnfield's last poetic venture, and all growth stopped together.

II

Apart from the soaring eulogies of the nineteenth century,[30] scholars and critics have been too hasty to urge the imitativeness of Barnfield. As a result little has been written truly analytical of the works of this interesting poet. He has sometimes considerable originality. "Cynthia," though highly derivative, is the only panegyric of Queen Elizabeth that uses the dream-vision framework, a device that gives Barnfield the advantage of a measure of sanity in otherwise outrageous flattery of the Queen. He is not forced

---

[30]High praise begins with T. Warton's *History of English Poetry*, ed. W. C. Hazlitt (London, 1871), IV, 436-437; "[Barnfield] of all the minor poets of Elizabeth's reign may perhaps be fairly regarded as occupying the first place." Grosart's edition of the complete poems for the Roxburghe Club in 1876 is sprinkled with moderate but solid praise, and it remains for the irrepressible Swinburne to deliver the accolade in his own inimitable prose: "Barnfield, our elder Shelley and our first-born Keats; the singer of Cynthia in verse well worthy of Endymion, who would seem to have died as a poet in the same fatal year of his age that Keats dies as a man; the first adequate English laureate of the nightingale, to be supplanted or equalled by none until the advent of his mightier brother." *A Study of Shakespeare* (London, 1880), p. 65.

to produce gods and goddesses walking the earth like natural men.
He reminds his reader several times that these are the images of a
dream. In both the first and second stanzas Barnfield retains
carefully this visionary quality:

> (I) Then loe (me thought) I saw or seem'd to see,
>
> (II) But straight (me thought) I saw a rout of heauenlie
> Race.
>
> (B^r)

In the fourth stanza we are warned pointedly: "There might one
see, & yet not see (indeede) / Fresh *Flora* flourishing in chiefest
Pryme" (B^v). The poem ends as do all dream-visions, with the
poet's waking. Even the flattery is saved some unctuousness by its
removal from the real.

"Cynthia" is dramatic, with nine of its nineteen stanzas in
dialogue, the speakers being Juno and Jupiter. The words of Venus
and Minerva are reported by Juno. The diction is unstrained but
compact; it has conversational ease yet avails itself, as in this speech
of Jove's, of poetic devices which add no little charm:

> Thou *Venus,* art my darling, thou my deare,
> (*Minerua,*) shee, my sister & my wyfe:
> So that of all a due respect I beare,
> Assign'd as one to end this doubtfull stryfe,
> (Touching your forme, your fame, your loue, your lyfe,)
> Beauty is vayne much lyke a gloomy light,
> And wanting wit, is counted but a tryfe,
> Especially when Honour's put to flight:
> Thus of a louely, soone becomes a loathly sight.
>
> (B$_4^r$)

The varied syntax of the first two lines is lively yet natural; the
series of the fifth line follows the poetic convention of referring
to several different things or persons without adequate pronominal
relationships, the antecedents being clear only through respective
order; Jove refers to Venus' form, Minerva's fame, Juno's love
and Paris' life. The rhetoric is effective, still not obscure, and the
stanza ends strongly with a noun which is removed from the first
of its double adjectives by half a line.

Adding to the fluidity of the poem is metrical control of
considerable skill. Barnfield has progressed from the somewhat
too-regular iambs of *The Affectionate Shepheard* to a happy mixture of appropriate substitutions such as in the opening line of the
third stanza: "Downe in a Dale, hard by a Forrest side" (B^v), or

the opening line of the fifteenth stanza: "Wit without wealth is bad, yet counted good" (B₄ᵛ). Seven of the stanzas begin with a stressed syllable, adding strength and variety; only one stanza uses feminine rime. The hexameters are handled extremely well, most of them breaking strongly at the center and providing pleasant balance through various rhetorical constructions:

A fayrer nere was seene, if any seene so fayre.
(Bᵛ)
With euery one a Lampe, & euery one a light.
(B₂ʳ)
Thus was his Blisse to Bale, his Honey turn'd to gall.
(B₂ᵛ)
And on our beautyes look't, & of our beauties stole.
(B₃ᵛ)

But Barnfield does not need the mid-caesura to produce some very competent lines:

Was neuer mortall eye beheld so fayre a Shee.
(Bʳ)
Both Wisdom, Beauty, Wealth, & all in her shall find.
(B₄ᵛ)
Fame borrowing al mens mouthes to royalize ẙ same.
(B₅ʳ)

I do not mean to suggest that "Cynthia" is a superlative poem; it is far from that. Certainly it is as far below the Spenserian stanzas of their originator as one might expect them to be. But it is not significantly poorer than other panegyrics to the Queen. The lyric grace and fresh imagery of Barnfield's pentameters, especially in the description of Flora's arrayal of the cave in Ida, are only slightly less impressive than Peele's.

Diehard critics, who produce many ingenious ways of circumventing the charge of pederasty brought against Barnfield by less friendly writers, apply to the sonnets in *Cynthia* the critical commonplace quoted often about Shakespeare's sonnets: that many of them could be addressed to a woman and others would require no alteration other than in their pronouns to make conventional tributes to a lady. Through this reasoning Shakespeare's defenders as well as Barnfield's claim that there is no real emotion or historical accuracy in the sonnets; they are exercises merely.[31] Still it seems strange to me that the argument used to convince us of

---

[31]See, for instance, the Yale Shakespeare *Sonnets,* p. 94 and L. E. Pearson, *Elizabethan Love Conventions,* p. 141.

Barnfield's orthodoxy is the very one which establishes his hetero-doxy. If these poems satisfy us as love poems to a woman when we alter the pronouns, why do they not stand as love poems to a man as they are? I am convinced, despite the evidence of marriage after his retirement from London, that Barnfield held a decided preference for young boys. Not only are his three volumes devoid of love poetry addressed to women, but also the existing poems to Ganimede are too personal, too charged with feeling to be ac-counted for in any other way. Still it is true that much of the diction, imagery, and thought is convention- and device-ridden, having not a jot of emotion. Sonnet I opens in a way reminiscent of the first five sonnets of Thomas Watson's *Teares of Fancie* (1593); the poet's aloofness in love is proof against Cupid; but Cupid, through the beloved, quickly triumphs. This opening is not uncommon in love poems other than Watson's. Sidney's Sonnet II in *Astrophel and Stella* follows the tradition. Barnfield devotes only two lines to the same pose:

> Sporting at fancie, setting light by loue,
> There came a theefe, and stole away my hart.
> (B₆ʳ)

With only twenty sonnets to go, he cannot spend more time in the company of Watson and Sidney's scornful foes of the winged boy. But the rest of the sonnet is heavy-handed, with no spark of fresh-ness or originality, and ends, as Janet Scott has shown, imitating the conclusion of Constable's *Diana*, II.v.

Sonnet II owes undoubtedly something to Sidney's Sonnet LII. In Barnfield's poem, Beauty, Majesty, and Virtue strive with one another to possess Ganimede. Beauty is called *Loue* in lines six and nine. Virtue and Love contend for Stella in Sidney's poem, with Virtue winning out nominally there too, though Sidney says wittily that Virtue must leave Stella's body to Love and to him.

Barnfield's third sonnet is a clever discourse of the various schools of philosophy and what they hold to be the chiefest good, with the poet concluding,

> Let Stoicks haue their Vertue if they will,
>   And all the rest their chiefe-supposed good,
>   Let cruell Martialists delight in blood,
> And Mysers ioy their bags with gold to fill:
>   My chiefest good, my chiefe felicity,
>   Is to be gazing on my loues fayre eye.
> (B₇ʳ)

The poem is competently handled—the verse and conceptual matter well-blended—but we do not find yet the moving poem for which we are looking.

Sonnet IIII is a thoroughly conventional effort, comparing Ganimede's eyes with a variety of bright, clear objects. The only line of interest is the comparison of the Italian river with the English: "As much as *Po* in clearness passeth *Trent*," raising the question, which cannot be answered with the biographical evidence now available, of whether Barnfield traveled on the continent. Sonnet V may be an elaboration merely of lines 13-14 of Barnabe Barnes' "Elegy XXI" in *Parthenophil and Parthenophe* (1593)[32] but I do not much think so. Although the Achilles metaphor is used in both, there is little other similarity.

With Sonnet VI we feel at once a difference. Although the conventions appear, there is a new note, an immediacy, a conviction that the poet is a part of the lines:

> Sweet Corrall lips, where Natures treasure lyes,
> The balme of blisse, ẙ soueraigne salue of sorrow,
> The secret touch of Loues hart-burning arrow,
> Come quench my thirst or els poor *Daphnis* dyes.
> (B₈ᵛ)

The rest of the sonnet lapses into an elaborate conceit, stating that a dream of the kiss for which he asks makes Daphnis young and strong. He wonders what the kiss itself would do. Sonnet VII might be added to Douglas Bush's list of poems indebted to Marlowe's *Hero and Leander,* though appearing before the earliest printed edition (1598).[33] Barnfield honors the Thames: "For on thy waues, (thy Christal-billow'd waues,)/ My fairest fayre, my siluer Swan is swimming" (Cʳ). The poet, his beloved in the water, thinks of the ocean god, and we think of lines 155-201 of the second sestiad of *Hero and Leander.* Ganimede may suffer the fate of the swimmer to Abydos:

> . . . *Neptune* his fayre feete with water laues,
> *Neptune,* I feare not thee, nor yet thine eye,
> And yet (alas) Apollo lou'd a boy,
> And *Cyparissus* was *Siluanus* joy.
> (Cʳ)

---

[32]Grosart calls attention to their likeness. *The Complete Poems,* p. 234.

[33]*Mythology and the Renaissance Trad.*, pp. 125-126.

But Daphnis fears Thetis more. The fear of the shepherd that his boy will be seen by some female and won by her was prevalent in *The Affectionate Shepheard* and has a ring of reality about it, lending credence to the theory that these sonnets as well as Barnfield's other love poems to a boy have some basis in fact. Sonnet VIII contains this personal note also. Daphnis alters the commonplace wish to be Ganimede's pillow to the rather spontaneous conceit of wondering why the bees do not suck his lips for honey. The lover's warning to the bees not to sting Ganimede for fear of his angry words leads to the living part of the poem:

> Kisse him, but sting him not, for if you doe,
> His angry voyce your flying will pursue:
> But when they heare his tongue, what can controule,
> Their back-returne? for then they plaine may see,
> How honey-combs from his lips dropping bee.
>
> (C^v)

Fluctuation from the highly artificial and conventional to accents of warm originality and seeming truth remain one of the strangest aspects of the sequence. Just when the reader is convinced he is being allowed a glimpse of a deep, sensual, illicit passion, the tone changes and he is brought up sharply with the old familiar terms and cadences of well-worn Petrarchism. In such a sequence Sonnet IX follows VIII. Diana pricks her foot and Venus retrieves some of the blood, which she puts into a human shape, fashioned from snow. The creature thus brought into being is Ganimede, who obviously is made for love, but who carries Diana's frosty blood in his snow-formed body. Sonnet X, the first of Barnfield's sequence to be the continuation of a preceding poem, elaborates the snow-blood image, concluding in a couplet which Janet Scott has observed is similar to lines 9-12 of *Astrophel and Stella* XXXI:[34]

> And thus it is: as far as I can proue,
> He loues to be belou'd, but not to loue.
>
> (C₂^v)

Sonnets XI and XII are both hackneyed. In the first Ganimede asks why Daphnis is so sad; Daphnis answers he is in love:

> And what is she (quoth he) whō thou do'st loue?
> Looke in this glasse (quoth I) there shalt thou see
> The perfect forme of my faelicitie.
> When, thinking ẏ it would strange Magique proue,

---

[34]*Les Sonnets Élisabéthains*, p. 187.

He open'd it: and taking off the couer,
He straight perceau'd himselfe to be my Louer.
                                                 (C₃ʳ)

In the second Barnfield writes that many have praised Ganimede's
namesake, Jove's beloved; others have praised Adonis, Castor, or
Narcissus. These were, perhaps, not quite so fair as Daphnis' love,
only better praised: "But he is fayrer then I can indite" (C₃ᵛ).

Sonnet XIII is what Janet Scott calls "L'inévitable sonnet
avec Echo."[35] Barnfield's version is quite pedestrian. He does not
let Echo reiterate the end of every line as Barnes and Watson do
in similar poems. Only four words are repeated. The first is exact
duplication, but in the remaining three, Barnfield somewhat clev-
erly uses sound equivalents of the given word for Echo's responses:
"christaline—Eyne, aire—Haire, grows—Rose." But Barnes had
done the same thing in 1593 and Sidney occasionally in the fifty
lines of his echo poem in 1590.

Sonnet XIIII plays most pedestrianly upon the word *gloue*,
the entire fourteen lines existing solely for the epigrammatic close:

If thou from gloue do'st take away the g,
Then gloue is loue: and so I send it thee.[36]
                                                 (C₄ᵛ)

Sonnets XV through XX, the final six of the sequence, all, to a
greater or lesser degree, have both charm and originality. In XV,
the poet pleads that Ganimede not disdain him because he is a
shepherd only: "*Apollo, Ioue*, and many Gods beside,/ S'daind not
ẏ name of coūtry sheepheards swaines" (C₅ʳ), and recalls his own

---

[35]*Les Sonnets Élisabéthains*, p. 185. I have found echo poems in
Watson, Barnes, Sidney, Shakespeare (in *Venus and Adonis*), and Peele,
among the poets with whose work we know Barnfield to have been
familiar.

[36]As bad as the concept is, William Strode (1600-1645) thought
well enough of the final couplet to copy it almost verbatim:

If that from glove you take the letter g,
Then glove is love, and that I send to thee.

See *The Poetical Works of William Strode*, ed. Bertram Dobell (London,
1907), p. 46. Strode, at least, found the whole idea worth no more than
two lines. An interesting alternative explanation is that the lines in Strode
are only some variant of Barnfield's couplet that he copied into his commonplace book, a frequent source for Dobell's edition of Strode's work.
Thus a charming lesser poet of the early seventeenth century was familiar
with the work of a charming lesser poet of the late sixteenth century.

"Country Content" with perhaps a new note of personal bitterness over the Court:

> Nor want we pleasure, though we take some paines,
> We liue contentedly: a thing call'd pryde,
> Which so corrupts the Court and euery place,
> (Each place I meane where learning is neglected,
> And yet of late, euen learnings selfe's infected)
> I know not what it meanes, in any case.[37]
>   (C₅ʳ)

Any association Barnfield may have had with the Court must have been very slight, if indeed he had any; just what brings on this attack is difficult to determine. But far-fetched and highly speculative as it may be, the explanation for these lines might possibly be found in irritation generated by Barnfield over some friend or idol's mistreatment at Court. It is even possible that he was angered over the fate of Spenser (whom he apostrophizes in Sonnet XX), remembering the fable of *Mother Hubberds Tale* (1591) and Spenser's lines therein: "For men of learning little he [the Ape] esteemed;/ His wisedome he above their learning deemed."

Sonnet XVI, quoted in its entirety above,[38] is the finest poem in the sequence, containing in almost every line a note of convincing desire and disappointment. It appears not to owe any of its parts to other writers, suffering only from too much reliance upon penultimate rime and feminine endings. The best effects come from the successful variation of anaphora in the first two lines: "Long haue I long'd . . ./ Still haue I wisht," and the standard anaphora of the last two:

> Thus with *Ixion*, kisse I cloudes in vayne:
> Thus with *Ixion*, feele I endles payne.
>   (C₅ᵛ)

Sonnet XVII gives Barnfield a chance again to work with the images of nature, which he employs so effectively in *The Affectionate Shepheard*:

---

[37]Sonnet XV was reprinted in *Englands Helicon* as "The Sheepheards Sonnet" (P₂ʳ) and attributed there to "Rich. Barnefielde." It was taken directly from *Cynthia*, altering only A[h] to *my* and *pleasure* to *pleasures*.

[38]See pp. 63-64.

[Ganimede's] rosiate red excels the crimson grape,
. . . .
His cheekes, the Lillie and Carnation dyes
With louely tincture which *Apolloes* dims.
His lips rype strawberries in Nectar wet,
His mouth a Hyue, his tongue a honey-combe,
Where Muses (like Bees) make their mansion.
His teeth pure Pearle in blushing Corrall set.
(C₆ʳ)

Although this poem does not have the affective quality of XVI,
it is in every way as successful formally, if not happier in its rimes
and images. The three-syllable pronunciation of *mansion* saves the
measure of the eleventh line, but even as *man-si-on,* riming, as it
does, with *honey-combe,* it mars slightly an otherwise fully
satisfying structure. The closing couplet is a human cry—not
completely articulate—unlike anything else that I have seen in
contemporary sonnet literature:

Oh how can such a body sinne-procuring,
Be slow to loue, and quicke to hate, enduring?
(C₆ʳ)

Sonnets XVIII and XIX are linked. In the first the poet compares
Ganimede with beautiful boys out of Plutarch, giving the palm
to his own. All persons love Ganimede so greatly that they shower
him with gifts, a list of which gives Barnfield again the opportunity to catalogue nature, something he performs well:

Some weaning Lambs, and some a suckling Kyd,
Some Nutts, and fil-beards, others Peares & Plums,
Another with a milk-white Heyfar comes;
As lately *AEgons* man (*Damaetas*) did.
(C₆ᵛ)

Although the reference to a rival causes wonder (in vain) as to
whom Damaetas might represent pastorally, the names and the
relationship of Damaetas to AEgon come from Virgil's third eclogue, as does the bisexual contest for the shepherd's favors:

But neither he, nor all the Nymphs besyde,
Can win my *Ganymede*; with them t'abyde.
(C₆ᵛ)

The failure of others provides the link to the next sonnet:

Ah no; nor I my selfe: though my pure loue
   (Sweete *Ganymede*) to thee hath still beene pure,
   And euen till my last gaspe shall ay endure,
Could euer thy obdurate beautie moue.
                (C$_7$^{r})

Of particular interest in XIX is the closing couplet, not for its
childish game with the alphabet,

Euen so of all the vowells, I and V,
Are dearest vnto mee: as doth ensue,
                (C$_7$^{r})

but for the apparent promise of verses to follow. However, Sonnet
XX cuts off abruptly any continuation, almost as though Barnfield
had composed it prematurely, planning, when appropriate, to use
it as a graceful conclusion to the sequence; for the poet seems to
have wearied early and, with great callousness as to continuity,
plucked up his finale and tacked it on:

But now my Muse toyld with continuall care,
   Beginns to faynt, and slack her former pace,
   Expecting fauour from that heauenly grace,
That may (in time) her feeble strength repayre.
Till when (sweet youth) th'essence of my soule,
   (Thou that dost sit and sing at my harts griefe. [*sic*]
   Thou that dost send thy shepheard no reliefe)
Beholde, these lines; the sonnes of Teares and Dole.
                (C$_7$^{v})

The poem and the cycle end with a tribute to Spenser and Drayton and with a modest appraisal of the poet's own powers:

Ah had great *Colin* chiefe of Sheepheards all,
   Or gentle *Rowland*, my professed friend,
   Had they thy beautie, or my pennance pend,
Greater had beene thy fame, and lesse my fall:
   But since that euery one cannot be witty,
   Pardon I craue of them, and of thee, pitty.
                (C$_7$^{v})

The total sequence is above mere competence because it de-
parts from the conventional and fixed figures, images, and themes,
which it eschews because it is touched with unmistakable personal
involvement; in their single-mindedness of purpose, their concen-
tration on obtaining the physical love of a young boy, these poems
are unlike any other extant sonnet cycles of the age.

The beauty of "Nights were short, and dayes were long" has been stressed already:

> Nights were short, and dayes were long;
> Blossoms on the Hauthorn's hung:
> *Philomaele* (Night-Musiques King)
> Tolde the comming of the spring.
> Whose sweete siluer-sounding voyce
> Made the little birds reioyce:
> Skipping light from spray to spray,
> Till *Aurora* shew'd the Day.
>   (C_8^r)

This perfect control of materials is felt throughout the poem. Many of the poetic devices, the lessons in rhetoric learned from his master Fraunce, that are either inept or badly chosen in *The Affectionate Shepheard* and also in other poems of *Cynthia*, are used again, but here with no amateurishness. The poem represents the highest reaches of Barnfield's poetic achievement. Mid-line rime is here woven with success into a moment of revelation:

> Scarce might one see, when I might see
> (For such chaunces sudden bee).
>   (C_8^r)

The poet's favorite device of anaphora was never more organic to the emotional responses of the speakers:

> Weepe she did for companie:
> Weepe she did for her sweete sonne,
>   (C_8^r-C_8^v)

> Loue I did, (alas the while)
> Loue I did, but did beguile
> My deare loue with louing so,
>   (D^r)

> Him I thought the fayrest creature;
> Him the quintessence of Nature:
>   (D^r)

> Loue at last (though loath) preuaild;
> (Loue) that so my hart assayld;
>   (D^v)

> Her it is, for whom I mourne;
> Her, for whom my life I scorne;
> Her, for whom I weepe all day;
> Her, for whom I sigh.
>   (D_2^r)

Considerable unity is gained through tear or weeping imagery, a
pervasive element throughout Barnfield's works. First the narrator
comes upon Daphnis weeping; then the image is reproduced in
Aurora, who weeps in sympathy for the shepherd. The dew, which
is Aurora's tears, covers the entire scene, and as the tears which
Daphnis shed "Made the fading flowers spring," so also the silver
tears of Aurora "Giue moysture to each liuing thing,/ That on
earth increase and grow." Flora cannot resist these tears, and so
she blossoms, but then the image is again picked up to show that
no amount of tears can make the unresponsive beloved unfold.
Yet, as we have seen in the anaphora above, the shepherd weeps
the day through. It cannot be denied that the poem is slight and
artificial, as it must be when the emotion recorded is the fluff of
flattery; but airy scrollwork can be exquisitely wrought, and so it
is in this ode. We can be content that Barnfield recognized his
limitations and tried nothing more demanding. We can claim for
him only that he is occasionally a fine artificer, but "Nights were
short" makes that much of a claim safe.

  While "Cassandra" is not any more imitative than many
poems by other Elizabethans, still it is less original than several of
its companion pieces in *Cynthia*. Its closeness to *Venus and Adonis*
and *Lucrece* in form and content as well as its borrowings from
them has been illustrated. Its place in the genres of Ovidian-erotic
and lament poetry has been cited, but its success or failure as a
poem has not yet been demonstrated. Other writers have either
overlooked the poem completely or denied that it is worth much
consideration. C. S. Lewis alone has been attracted and then to one
quatrain only:[39]

> Looke how a brightsome Planet in the skye,
> (Spangling the Welkin with a golden spot)
> Shootes suddenly from the beholders eye,
> And leaues him looking there where she is not.
>   (D₇ʳ)

But there are other bright lines which are neither imitations of
contemporaries nor variations of overworked conventions. The
poem opens with lines descriptive of Cassandra, lounging upon her
couch, lines which bring to mind Enobarbus' reminiscence of
Cleopatra:

---

[39]*English Literature in the Sixteenth Century*, p. 497. Lewis notes,
of course, that the image is taken from Shakespeare, but admits that
Barnfield has contributed "something worth adding."

Vpon a gorgious gold-embossed bed,
With Tissue curtaynes drawne against the sunne,
(Which gazers eyes into amazement led,
So curiously the workmanship was doone,
    Lay fayre *Cassandra*, in her snowie smocke,
    Whose lips the Rubies and the pearles did locke.

And from her Iuory front hung dangling downe,
A bush of long, and louely curled hayre;
Whose head impalled with a precious Crowne
Of orient Pearle, made her to seeme more fayre.
                                    (D₃ʳ)

The anger of Apollo shows strength and originality, with a tonal
echo of Spenser:

Then angry *Phoebus* mounts into the skye:
Threatning the world with his hot-burning eye.
Now nimbly to his glyst'ring Coach he skyps,
And churlishlie ascend's [*sic*] his loftie chayre,
Yerking his head-strong Iades with yron whyps,
Whose fearefull neighing ecchoes through the ayre,
    Snorting out fierie Sulphure from their nosethrils:
    Whose deadly damp the worlds poore people kils.
                                    (D₇ʳ)

Cassandra's unheeded prophetic warnings are rejected with colloquial forcefulness and prose-like syntax, but holding still firm
measure and moving pity:

They count her hare-braynd, mad, and ouer-bolde,
To presse in pressence in so graue a place:
But in meane season *Paris* he is gone,
To bring destruction on fayre *Ilion*.
                                    (E₂ʳ)

Still it cannot be denied that the poem is an artistic failure.
Hallett Smith shows us that Cassandra "is both the victim of fortune and a warning to girls,"[40] a dual role which causes the poem
to become diffuse, and to lose whatever artistic unity and firmness
it might otherwise have had. Barnfield presents us a picture of a
girl whose sorrows begin not because she was unchaste but because
she refuses to give herself to Apollo. By the end of the poem sight
is lost of her crime, the cause of her downfall, which is her treachery in promising love to Apollo for the gift of prophecy and then

---

[40]Smith, *Elizabethan Poetry*, p. 119.

reneging. She becomes instead a girl whose life should be a warning
to others to retain their virtue:

> I liu'd (quoth she) to see *Troy* set on fire;
> I liu'd to see, renowmed [*sic*] *Hector* slayne;
> I liu'd to see, the shame of my desire;
> And yet I liue, to feel my greeuous payne:
> > Let all young maydes example take by mee,
> > To keepe their oathes, and spotlesse chastitie.
> > > (E₆ᵛ)

It is true that after Troy falls and Cassandra becomes the spoil
of Agamemnon, she becomes his lover, but the relationship is
forced upon her:

> *Cassandra* then to *Agamemnon* fell,
> With whom a Lemman she disdaynd to dwell.
>
> She, weepes; he, wooes; he, would; but she would not;
> Hee, tells his birth; shee, pleades virginity;
> He sayth, selfe-pryde doth rarest beauty blot;
> (And with that worde he kist her louingly:)
> > Shee, yeeldingly resists; hee faynes to dye:
> > Shee, falls for feare; hee, on her feareleslye.
> > > (E₂ʳ-E₂ᵛ)

More clearly, Cassandra is the victim of circumstance or Fortune;
no matter how Cassandra had behaved with Apollo, the Trojan
War would have occurred, the Greeks have won, and Cassandra
have fallen to the lot of Agamemnon. Despite Apollo, still might
Cassandra cry, in recognizable Greek sentiment,[41] and also in one
of the best stanzas in the poem,

> Happy are they, that neuer liu'd to know
> What tis to liue in this world happilye:
> Happy are they, which neuer yet felt woe;
> Happy are they, that dye in infancye:
> > Whose sins are cancell'd in their mothers wombe;
> > Whose cradle is their graue, whose lap their tombe.
> > > (E₇ʳ)

It is difficult to understand how the theme of chastity got into
the poem. Possibly Barnfield, who tried a *Mirror* lament in the
story of Matilda and found he could not do the poem—no doubt

---

[41]Compare Barnfield's stanza with the choral lines that terminate
Oedipus Rex: "Count no mortal happy till/he has passed the final limit
of his life secure from pain" [Trans. David Greene].

because Drayton had so completely handled the legend before him
—felt compelled to attempt the theme again; but once again it
did not work. Matilda triumphs by her virtue, but Barnfield
would have us accept Cassandra triumphing by her fall:

> Euen so by death her purest soule was eased,
> From bodyes pryson, and from endlesse mone:
> Where now shee walkes in sweete *Elysium*,
> (The place for wrongfull death and Martyrdum.)
>
> (E_7^v)

If Barnfield had shown the heroine solely as a tragic victim of the
vagaries of Fortune, as she is most often presented, if he had left
out the chastity theme entirely, "Cassandra" might have been successful as an Ovidian-erotic *de casibus* poem.

Barnfield's second volume, then, is a mixture of imitative,
derivative work and some originality. The title poem is heavily
indebted to other writers in almost all its aspects, but the sonnets,
the ode, and even "Cassandra" show the tendency that was to
carry Barnfield in his third volume to seek new subjects to write
about in new ways. Following *Cynthia* Barnfield was silent for
three years, publishing no more until 1598, a considerable gap
when we remember how closely *Cynthia* followed upon *The Affectionate Shepheard. The Encomion of Lady Pecunia* (1598) is Barnfield's final work and possibly marks the date of his departure
from London, although a second edition of *Lady Pecunia*, with
considerable changes, was issued in 1605. It is not inconsonant,
however, with the nature of the new edition and with publishing
and authorial practices of the end of the sixteenth century, for
Barnfield to have done the revisions at his home in Staffordshire,
sending or taking the new copy to London after several years of
quiet country living. *Cynthia* is the final volume of the poet's
apprenticeship, although Barnfield was hardly anything more than
an apprentice ever, ceasing to write at the age of twenty-four; and
The Encomion of Lady Pecunia is the first and last book of his
journeyman days, with the 1605 revision as a mere epilogue. His
poetry, in the ode, reached rare heights, and nothing he did later
was quite so good, but *Lady Pecunia* has a certain ease, a certain
professionalism, that shows a wiser head, a more craftsmanlike
hand.

CHAPTER IV

LADY PECUNIA

In effect Barnfield published only one additional volume after *Cynthia, The Encomion of Lady Pecunia: OR The Praise of Money* in 1598. It was printed by G. S. [haw?] for John Jaggard and carried for the first time Barnfield's name upon a title page.[1] A revised and altered edition of this work appeared in 1605 with the title changed to read *Lady Pecunia, OR The Praise of Money.* The new printing was performed by W. [illiam] I. [aggard] and the publisher was John Hodgets.[2] Neither volume was entered in the Stationers' Register. The 1598 edition comprises four major divisions, the first three being each devoted to a single poem and the fourth to a collection of shorter pieces. Each of the four sections has its own title page identical with those of the other three insofar as the publisher's imprint and place and date colophon are concerned.[3] The only differences are the omission of Barnfield's name from all but the first, the Latin inscription gracing each, and of course, the titles themselves. An address "To the Gentlemen Readers" follows the first title page, but no dedication prefaces the volume as a whole; the second, third, and fourth sections, however, have verse dedications to Edward Leigh, John Steventon, and Nicholas Blackleech respectively. Section one contains only the title poem which is renamed on Sig. A^{3r} *The Prayse of Lady Pecunia.* Section two contains *The Complaint of Poetrie, for the Death of Liberalitie,* and the signatures begin again from A^r. Section three contains *The Combat, betweene Conscience and Coue-*

---

[1] The copy that I consulted for this chapter is in the Folger Shakespeare Library. There are at this time only two other copies known to exist, one in the Bodleian, the other in the Huntington.

[2] Again I used the copy in the Folger. Another, but imperfect copy, is in the Bodleian; and a third is in the Huntington. MS. Ahsmolean 1152, xii has been identified as a phonetic transcription of the 1605 *Lady Pecunia.* It has been reprinted in *The Phonetic Writings of Robert Robinson,* ed. E. J. Dobson, EETS (London, 1957).

[3] It was common for a publisher to have a book printed with several separate title pages so that if a poor sale ensued, the edition could be divided into smaller pamphlets and sold under different titles. See E. E. Willoughby, *A Printer of Shakespeare* (London, 1934), p. 56.

tousnesse, in the minde of Man but continues the signatures begun in Section Two. Section four contains eight short pieces and is entitled *Poems: In diuers humors*. These eight poems are as follows: "Sonnet I. To his friend Maister R. L. In praise of Musique and Poetrie," "Sonnet II. Against the Dispraysers of Poetrie," "A Remembrance of some English Poets," "An Ode" (As it fell vpon a Day), "Written, at the request of a Gentleman, vnder a Gentlewomans Picture," "An Epitaph vpon the Death, of Sir Philip Sidney, Knight: Lord-gouernour of Vlissing," "An Epitaph vpon the Death of his Aunt, Mistresse Elizabeth Skrymsher," and "A Comparison of the Life of Man."

The 1605 edition was reset completely, with many variations of spelling and typography throughout. Only a single title page was used in place of the four distinct and separate title pages of 1598. Full titles of the *Complaint* and the *Combat* appeared on A^r directly under the title poem, which had been altered from the previous edition to read simply *Lady Pecunia, OR The praise of Money*. The original address "To the Gentlemen Readers" was retained with only three minor alterations, which appear to be more the result of careless compositing than anything else; but the verse dedications of 1598 that followed each of the second, third, and fourth title pages were dropped. A single new dedication was inserted at the beginning of the volume, intended apparently to cover the entire book. Signatures were numbered consecutively throughout, and the order of *The Complaint* and *The Combat* was reversed. Of the eight shorter poems concluding the 1598 edition only two were kept: "A Comparison of the Life of Man" and "A Remembrance of some English Poets" respectively. The stanzas of *Lady Pecunia* and *The Complaint* were numbered in the 1605 edition for the first time. *Lady Pecunia* itself was swelled by the addition of eight entirely new stanzas, growing out of the succession of the new king in 1603. There were other minor changes throughout the title poem alone. All other pieces included were virtually the same as their 1598 predecessors.

The address "To the Gentlemen Readers" is modelled upon that in *Cynthia*. Encouragement Barnfield has received through the reception of his previous book has stirred him to publish again. But he has gotten the desire to publish before having enough in hand to make up a volume. The decision over what to write is influenced by his desire to be different:

> Being determined to write something, & yet not resolued
> of any thing, I considered with my selfe, if one should
> write of Loue (they will say) why, euery one writes of
> Loue; if of Vertue, why, who regards Vertue? To be short,
> I could thinke of nothing, but either it was common, or
> not at all in request. At length I bethought my selfe of a
> Subiect, both new (as hauing neuer beene written vpon
> before) and pleasing (as I thought) because Mans Nature
> (commonly) loues to heare that praised, with whose pres-
> sence, hee is most pleased.
>
> (A8^r)

The jocular nature of this paragraph is in keeping with the title
poem to which alone the address alludes. The subject, of course,
is money, and Barnfield's claim to be here writing about something
new appears justified. No sources for this poem have been found,
nor has any work been turned up in which money is personified
under the title of Lady Pecunia.[4] The use of *Encomion* in the title,
however, shows that while the subject was new the genre was not;
by the time Barnfield was writing, the body of such literature had
grown to sizable proportions. Its tradition is represented best by
Erasmus' *Praise of Folly*, to which Barnfield links his *Encomion*
specifically:

> *Erasmus* (the glory of *Netherland*, and the refiner of the
> Latin Tongue) wrote a whole Booke, in *the prayse of Folly*.
> Then if so excellent a Scholler, writ in praise of Vanity,
> why may not I write in praise of that which is profitable?
>
> (A8^r)

Much of the humor of Barnfield's poem comes from a tongue-in-
cheek praise of that which ordinarily deserves censure. Even in
the address to the readers Barnfield uses this type of irony:

> There are no two Countreys, where Gold is esteemed, lesse
> than in *India*, and more then in *England*: the reason is,
> because the Indians are barbarous, and our Nation ciuill.
> (A8^r)

Further similarity between the address to the readers of
Cynthia and that of *Lady Pecunia* is Barnfield's inclusion of epigrammatic verses. In *Cynthia* there was the six-line enigmatic

---

[4]A fifteenth-century ballad in praise of money would seem to have
been unknown to Barnfield. See *Nugae Poeticae*, ed. J. O. Halliwell
(1844), pp. 46-49.

tribute to the Queen; in *Lady Pecunia* Barnfield prints a pair of couplets in honor of two great sea rovers, loosely connecting their mention with the search for riches:

> The brauest Voyages in the World, haue beene made for Gold: for it, men haue venterd (by Sea) to the furthest parts of the Earth: In the Pursute whereof, *Englands Nestor* and *Neptune* (*Haukins* and *Drake*) lost their liues. Vpon the Deathes of the which two, of the first I writ this:

> > *The Waters were his Winding sheete, the Sea was made his Toome;*
> > *Yet for his fame the Ocean Sea, was not sufficient roome.*

> Of the latter this:

> > England *his hart; his Corps the Waters haue:*
> > *And that which raysed his fame, became his graue.*
> > (A8^r-A8^v)

One wonders over Barnfield's statement about these epigrams. Were they ever published elsewhere and are there other pieces of the poet's which, published or not, are in anonymous existence or in undiscovered repositories? Hawkins died in 1595, Drake in 1596. The nature of the couplets is such that most probably they were written at the height of public interest in these famous men's deaths. Either the verses saw publication elsewhere or they were kept in a commonplace book to be extracted, when the poet had need, for inclusion in a volume like *Lady Pecunia*. It is not improbable that in like ways other pieces might survive.[5]

The epitaph on Drake is only a variation on the commonest kind of funereal verse. Ralegh's epitaph on Sidney, which appeared as late as 1593 in *The Phoenix Nest*, supplies most of the matter for Barnfield's couplet and some of the language:

---

[5]The Isham MS. found at Lamport Hall, first mentioned by Charles Edmonds in 1870 and reprinted by Grosart in his edition of Barnfield in 1876, raises the question of Barnfield's authorship of various pieces in this commonplace book. Certainly a poet who had published two volumes within six months and then nothing for three years would be collecting his work in some manner. The Isham MS. presents complex issues, however, that must be treated at length in their proper place. See Chapter V.

England doth hold thy lims that bred the same,

. . . .

Thy friends, thy want; the world, thy vertues fame.[6]

An epitaph on Ralegh himself almost thirty years later shows how widespread the formula had become:

> Heaven hath his Soul, the World his Fame,
> The Grave his Corps, Stukley his shame.[7]

Why the 1598 edition carries no dedication for the *Lady Pecunia* section is difficult to understand. Two of the verse dedications prefacing the three following sections have the same jocular quality of the dedication to *Lady Pecunia* when it appears finally in the 1605 edition. It cannot be that Barnfield was any more or any less desirous of patrons in 1598 (he never seemed urgently concerned in the dedications of any of his volumes). Nor is it likely that William Jaggard prodded him to obtain a benefactor any more earnestly than John Jaggard. Nevertheless, whatever the facts, no dedication accompanied *Lady Pecunia* until 1605. At its appearance, however, it is so much in the tone of the poem itself that it must have been written at the composition of *Lady Pecunia*:

> Led by the swift report of winged Fame,
>   with siluer trumpet, sounding forth your name
>   To you I dedicate this merry Muse,
> And for my Patron, I your fauour chuse:
> She is a Lady, she must be respected:
> She is a Queene, she may not be neglected.
>   This is the shadow, you the substance haue,
>   Which substance now this shadow seems to craue.
>   (A₃ʳ)

The dedication has no addressee, but in the Isham MS., where it is reproduced with several minor variations, it is headed with the following inscription:

> To the right Worˡˡ Sir John Spenser Knighte
>   Alderman of the honourable Citty of
> London and lorde treasurer of Lady pecunia.

Because of the somewhat merry if not flippant nature of the ad-

---

[6]*The Poems of Sir Walter Ralegh*, ed. Agnes Latham (London, 1951), p. 7.

[7]Anthony Wood, *Athenae Oxonienses* (London, 1721), I, 440.

dress, one does not expect that it moved any patron to magnanimity, but with the addressee identified as Sir John Spencer, the joke apparently increased in sarcasm. The worthy alderman was a known miser.[8] However, it is to be doubted that Barnfield was ever seriously in need of money. The fact that he was able to retire to the country at some time between 1598 and 1606 suggests that he led a comfortable life in the city, secure in the knowledge of his future ease. Freedom from want may account as well for the rather relaxed quality of all his dedications.

The eight lines, as they appear in the 1605 *Lady Pecunia*, are introduced as "The Authors First Epistle Dedicatory." "First" is somewhat puzzling since it is the only dedication in the 1605 volume, since it does not appear in the 1598 volume where there are second, third, and fourth dedications, and since it is appended to the edition (1605) which was issued second, not first. I can conceive of two explanations only. Either the dedication was written for the 1598 edition, in which case the modifier *First* would have some meaning, and was omitted by accident; or the 1605 edition, in its planning stages, was intended to include the other three dedications of the earlier volume, but these were left out at the last moment. Sir John Spencer, not to be confused with Sir John Spencer of Althorp,[9] would be as appropriate a dedicatee in 1598 as in 1605. He had terminated his Lord Mayoralty of London only a few years before in 1595. He had been knighted also in 1595 and had been enormously wealthy for a long time before his aldermanship, to which he had been elected in 1587.

Lady Pecunia, the title poem, as already noted, is the only poem that undergoes change in the 1605 edition. In 1598 the poem runs for 49 stanzas, in 1605 for 56, five of the additional eight

---

[8]For information about Sir John Spencer, I am indebted to the *DNB* (1898), pp. 357-358.

[9]A student of Barnfield might be led into such an error, remembering Barnfield's dedication to William Stanley in *Cynthia*, and remembering also William Stanley's elder brother's marriage to Alice Spencer, daughter of the Althorp Sir John. Another trap leading to such error might be found in Barnfield's expressed admiration for Edmund Spenser and that poet's claim to kinship with the Spencers of Althorp. But these very facts should lead the student away from identifying the London alderman with the other, for Barnfield would hardly address the impolitic dedication of *Lady Pecunia* to a relative of either the Stanleys or Edmund Spenser. Furthermore Sir John Spencer of Althorp died in 1586.

being taken up in tribute to the new ruler who ascended the
throne between the first and second versions. For *Lady Pecunia*
Barnfield reverts to his favorite form, the six-line pentameter
stanza, riming ababcc. He developed it in the two-days' lament of
The Affectionate Shepheard as the vehicle in which he performed
most successfully, and he used it again, in an extended poem, in
"Cassandra," which comes to mind as we read *Lady Pecunia*. When
Barnfield wrote "Cassandra," he went counter to the established
convention of writing a *Mirror for Magistrates*-complaint poem
in rime royal. Instead he employed the six-line stanza of *Venus
and Adonis*, fusing the components of the Ovidian-erotic poem
with the complaint narrative. He has the complaint genre in mind
as he starts *Lady Pecunia*, if only to use the lament as a point of
departure and an origin for his verse form. He mentions one of
the great protagonists of complaint literature and another whose
story would make a fine addition to the type as he introduces his
own heroine:

> I Sing not of *Angellica* the faire,
> (For whom the Palladine of *Fraunce* fell mad)
> Nor of sweet *Rosamond*, olde *Cliffords* heire,
> (Whose death did make the second *Henry* sad)
> But of the fairest Faire *Pecunia*,
> The famous Queene of rich *America*
>   (A₄ʳ)

The reader familiar with the addresses in the 1598 edition,
and especially that of 1605, recognizes immediately the comic
note that enters at line five. Prepared as he may have been for a
Mirror-complaint at the mention of Rosamond, or prepared only
for a tragic narrative at the mention of these two heroines of
unhappy tales, he is reoriented the moment he reads of "fairest
Faire *Pecunia*." Despite the growing importance of the rising middle class and their money, despite the late sixteenth-century break
from the severe control of the medieval church, there was enough
carry-over of the *contemptu mundi* teachings of the theologians
to prevent anything but the denigration of money. Barnfield's
association of Pecunia with America may be attributed either to
the voyages of Drake, mentioned in the address to the reader, or
to the voyages of Ralegh to Guiana in 1595, accounts of which
were published in the 1598 edition of Hakluyt. Ralegh's account
of the Guiana voyage had been published separately as early as

1596 and is the likelier work to have influenced Barnfield. Some
association between Barnfield and Ralegh might be sought on the
basis of Barnfield's admiration for and imitation of Marlowe and
Spenser, two of Ralegh's closest acquaintances among the poets.

A further tone of *Lady Pecunia* derives from Barnfield's reversal of the usual epic opening: "I sing not of *Angellica*," suggests
the mock-heroic. The lady is, of course, Orlando's beloved in
Ariosto's *Orlando Furioso*. Then, since an announcement of exalted
purpose must be accompanied by an invocation to the muse, Barnfield, somewhat anticipating Milton, calls not upon Calliope, but
upon a Christianized substitute:

> Of thee Ile sing, and in thy Prayse Ile write;
> You *golden Angels* helpe me to indite.
>   (A₄ʳ)

Barnfield requires angelic muses for the pun he intends upon the
Elizabethan coin. We can hardly miss any of the puns in *Lady
Pecunia,* for Barnfield italicizes all words of double meaning.

At this point the reader is sure that he has entered the domain
of pseudo-encomiastic literature. The tradition went back in classical works at least as far as Isocrates but had also by Barnfield's
time an English heritage in Abraham Fleming's translation of
Synesius' praise of baldness (1579), Gabriel Harvey's "Encomium
lauri" (1580), Sir John Harington's *Metamorphosis of Ajax*
(1596), and most important, Edmund Spenser's translation of
Culex as *Virgil's Gnat* (1591).[10] It is impossible to determine
whether it was Barnfield's admiration for and study of Spenser
or his knowledge of the works of Virgil that turned him to the
pseudo-encomium. In the Prayer at the end of *Lady Pecunia,*
Barnfield refers to "*Ovids* vaine" and "*Virgils* spirit," clearly
linking the poem to *Culex* and *Nux.* But many poems of mock
praise allude to these works,[11] and Barnfield's invocation of the
two Latin writers may have been nothing more than his own way
of identifying with a long-established genre. Actually, *Lady
Pecunia* was not Barnfield's first venture into the pseudo-
encomium. The long section in the second day's lamentation of

---

[10]For a detailed history of the pseudo-encomium, see Henry K.
Miller, "The Paradoxical Encomium with Special Reference to Its Vogue
in England, 1600-1800," *MP*, LIII (1956), 145-178.

[11]See for instance the preface to *Metamorphosis of Ajax* or Nashe's
list in *Nashes Lenten Stuffe, Works,* III, 176-178.

The Affectionate Shepheard, in which black is praised at the expense of white, fits squarely into the tradition.

After the invocation the poem moves immediately into its
satire, working primarily through irony and sarcasm. The poet
affirms paradoxically that in the golden age of Saturn, money
was not admired, only truth and honesty; but as the world grew
wiser and charity waned, money began receiving the respect of
all. As the world grew older, Pecunia's followers increased, but
the first to worship her were the aged. Opposed to these are the
youth, few of whom "could euer gaine her:/ Of if they did, she
soone was gone againe" (B^r). Barnfield then digresses for eight
stanzas, commenting upon the varying attitudes toward money
of youth and old age, winding up in an attack upon misers and
usurers whom he associates with old men. In stanza sixteen, Barnfield returns to his primary purpose of praise and initiates a list
of all those who devote themselves to the pursuit of wealth, a
list that covers nearly all the professions of Man:

> For her the Lawyer pleades; the Souldier fights.

> For her, the Merchant venters on the Seas:
> For her, the Scholler studdies at his Booke:
> For her, the Vsurer (with greater ease)
> For sillie fishes, layes a siluer hooke:
> > For her, the Townsman leaues the Countrey Village:
> > For her, the Plowman giues himselfe to Tillage.

> For her, the Gentleman doeth raise his rents:
> For her, the Seruingman attends his maister:
> For her, the curious head new toyes inuents:
> For her, to Sores, the Surgeon layes his plaister.
> > In fine for her, each man in his Vocation,
> > Applies himselfe, in euerie sev'rall Nation.
>
> > > (B₂^v-B₃^r)

In these three stanzas we see again Barnfield's dependence upon
his favorite rhetorical device of anaphora.

Following the list of the corrupted, Barnfield, in stanzas 19
through 25, shows more specifically the nature of the corruption.
Stanzas 20-21 provide a homely little sketch of the power of
money on the small scale. We are reminded of the adventures of
Joseph Andrews and Parson Adams:

> Admit thou come, into a place vnknowne;
> And no man knowes, of whence, or what thou art:
> If once thy faire *Pecunia,* shee be showne,
> Thou art esteem'd a man of great Desart:
>   And placed at the Tables vpper ende;
>   Not for thine owne sake, but thy faithfull frende.
>
> But if you want your Ladies [Pecunia] louely grace,
> And haue not wherewithall to pay your shot,
> Your Hostis pressently will step in Place,
> You are a Stranger (Sir) I know you not:
>   By trusting Diuers, I am run in Det;
>   Therefore of mee, nor meate nor Bed you get.
>   (B₃ʳ-B₃ᵛ)

Contrasted to the common village inn is the great empire of Troy and its destruction, no less easily accomplished than the undoing of the innkeeper or his customer:

> When nothing could subdue the *Phrygian Troy,*
> (That City through the World so much renowned)
> *Pecunia* did her vtterly destroy:
> And left her fame, in darke Obliuion drowned.
>   (B₄ʳ)

The reference is to the treason of Antenor and Aeneas, who sold out Troy to the Greeks in most of the medieval versions of the Troy story. Barnfield had alluded to the villainy in "Cassandra."

Stanzas 26-31 describe how Pecunia has usurped Honesty and how Pecunia is found in many forms: lead, brass, silver, gold. Three of these stanzas expose counterfeiting practices and provide instructions for recognizing fraudulent coin. But since Pecunia has replaced Honesty and rules as queen, Barnfield takes the opportunity to compare this regent with his own English queen and devotes stanzas 32-36 to Elizabeth's reformation and refinement of coinage and her reformation of religion:

> And as the Coyne she hath repurifyde,
> From baser substance, to the purest Mettels:
> Religion so, hath she refinde beside,
> From Papistrie, to Truth; which daily settles
>   Within her Peoples harts; though some there bee,
>   That cleaue vnto their wonted Papistrie.
>   (Cᵛ)

He shifts into a pastoral metaphor to continue the attack on

Romanism and produces a fine stanza in the best tradition of his *Affectionate Shepheard*:

> No flocke of sheepe, but some are still infected:
> No peece of Lawne so pure, but hath some fret:
> All buildings are not strong, that are erected:
> All plants proue not, that in good ground are set:
>> Some tares are sowne, amongst the choicest seed:
>> No garden can be cleansd of euery Weede.
>>> (C₂ʳ)

These stanzas establish Barnfield as a staunch Protestant and vehement anti-Papist. They lend some credence to the possibility that the answer to Chidiock Tichbourne's elegy, found in the Isham MS. may have been written by Barnfield, although I do not believe so.[12] There is even some similarity of imagery between Tichbourne's poem, the answer in the Isham MS., and the stanza above in the employment of the tares-seed-garden-weed metaphor. All these stanzas to the Queen were altered for the 1605 edition by the simple expedient of changing verb tenses. However, either Barnfield or his publisher felt that more than these slight modifications were necessary. If a tribute had been given to the old Queen, it might be best not to slight the new King. Consequently, immediately following stanza 36, five new stanzas praise King James in terms of outrageous flattery. After these the poet returns to his praise of Pecunia, avowing that much of her beauty comes from the annual coinage of new mint in the Tower of London. Stanza 39 in the 1958 edition merely announces the routine mintage under Elizabeth. This stanza is completely recast in 1605 and expanded into two:[13]

---

[12]See pp. 139-141.

[13]The commentators and editors write consistently of "seven" additional stanzas in the 1605 edition. This is, in fact, an error. Stanza 39 of the 1598 text is no less new than its counterpart, stanza 44, of 1605. Actually stanza 44 retains only one line of the 1598 stanza, whereas stanza 45 of 1605 utilizes two lines of the old 39th. I print the 1598 stanza here for easy comparison:

> New Coyne is coynd each yeare, within the Tower;
> So that her Beauty neuer can decay:
> Which to resist, no mortall man hath Power,
> When as she doeth her glorious Beames display.
>> Nor doeth *Pecunia*, onely please the eie,
>> But charms the eare, with heauenly Harmonie.
>>> (C₂ᵛ)

New Coine is yearlie stamped in the Tower,
But these faire daies of ioy, addes alteration:
In faire Elizaes raign, none had that power;
But kingly glorie, clothes her new in fashion,
    Ads beautie to her beames, by adding more
    Then grayest haires in life, ere saw before.

Stand forth who can and tell, and trulie saie
When England, Scotland, Ireland, and France,
He euer saw Pecunia to displaie
Before these daies; O wondrous happie chance.
    Nor doth Pecunia onelie please the eie,
    But charmes the eare, with heauenlie harmony.

                         (C$_3^r$-C$_3^v$)

These somewhat confusing stanzas refer merely to the addition of
Scotland to the Crown through the accession of James I. Not the
oldest living Englishmen (those with greyest hairs) can tell of a
time when the nation included the Northern kingdom or when
coins displayed the word *Scotland*. Two additional stanzas on the
coins of the period immediately follow in the 1605 edition; in
1598 only the first of these appeared, the second being the eighth
and final of those stanzas added later:

Like to an other Orpheus, can she plaie
Vpon her treble Harpe, whose siluer sound
Inchants the eare, and steales the hart awaie,
That hardlie the deceit thereof is found.
    Although such Musicke, some a shilling cost,
    Yet is it worth but Nine-pence, at the most.

But Ireland alone, this Musicks sound
Being clad in Siluer, challenge for their coine,
What though amongst vs much thereof be found,
Authoritie, no subiect dooth inioyne
    Aboue his worth to countenance the same,
    Then men, not coin, are worthy of that blame.

                              (C$_3^v$)

Unless the new stanza was included only to clear up some of the
obscurity of the first, it is difficult to understand why Barnfield
added the second of these only in 1605 since it has no particular
pertinence to James' reign. During her reign Elizabeth coined
shillings to be used especially in Ireland. These were called

Harpers, from the Arms of that Kingdom, *viz.* three Harps crown'd on the Reverse. It was a fair Coin, tho' of a baser kind than the *English,* and pass'd only for Ninepence in *England;* and towards the latter end of her Reign she paid her Army there with much baser Coin, three parts Copper, and a fourth part Silver, valued at but Twopence Halfpenny, but pass'd by Proclamation for a Shilling in Ireland.[14]

The *treble Harpe* is thus explained. The Irish shilling was a silver coin and the three harps on its reverse supply "Musicks sound." The music, like Orpheus's lulls the senses, and the receiver of the debased Irish shilling in exchange for a good English coin is unaware of the loss in real value. Apparently many Irish coins were finding their way across the Irish Sea into England because of payment to the English Army in 1601 with these "Harpers." Barnfield's second stanza says simply that no one has the courage to complain about the debased coinage, and therefore men are to blame for the situation, not Lady Pecunia (the coin). One must understand from the fact that the second of these two stanzas did not appear until 1605 that inhabitants of London were still upset about "Harpers" though James did not perpetuate the coinage.[15]

Stanzas 41 through 49 of the 1598 edition are essentially the same as stanzas 48 through 56 of 1605. Barnfield returns for the third time to the praise of Pecunia. Money itself is held not to blame for the evils it fosters. No man is proof against the beauty of Lady Pecunia. A second attack on Rome is indulged by ridiculing the practice of buying pardons; but, says Barnfield, since no man can contend against the beauty of Pecunia, it is small wonder that so great a sinner as the Pope is tempted to pursue her. The entire section leads to the commonplace observation that

---

[14]Stephen Martin Leake, *Nummi Britannici Historia* (London, 1726), pp. 71-72.

[15]James not only added the name of the Scottish kingdom to his coins but also he changed the coat of arms on the reverse. Elizabeth quartered the fleur de lis of France with the English triple lion, the first and fourth quarters bearing the French arms, the second and third bearing the English. James reduced Elizabeth's entire four quarters and stamped them in the first and fourth quarters of his own arms. The second quarter then contained a single lion rampant within a double tressure fleury for Scotland, and the third quarter contained a single harp for Ireland.

> *Pecunia,* is, as shee is vsed;
> Good of her selfe, but bad if once abused.
> (C$_3$^{v})

The poem concludes with a single stanza, separated from the others, and headed with the legend, "His Prayer to Pecunia":

> Great Lady, sith I haue compylde thy Prayse,
> (According to my skill) and not thy merit:
> And sought thy Fame aboue the starrs to rayse;
> (Had I sweete *Ovids* vaine, or *Virgils* spirit)
> I craue no more but this, for my good-will,
> That in my Want, thou wilt supplye me still.
> (C$_4$^{r})

The prayer, then, like the rest of the poem, is in the comic mode, and as always, Barnfield modestly depreciates his own talents.

Lady Pecunia is a good poem. It is novel and it is sprightly. Apparently it was very popular. Not only did it achieve a second edition in 1605 but also it was imitated on a considerable scale.[16]

Without doubt the title poem and nothing else in the volume called forth the second edition. As a comic poem, it is very successful.[17] Barnfield, already shown to be very fond of punning, utilizes the pun as a comic instrument very heavily in *Lady Pecunia.* The subject lends itself nicely, and the poet helps the

---

[16]Grosart has pointed out that Samuel Nicholson borrows from all of Barnfield, including *Lady Pecunia* in *Acolastus His After-Witte* (1600). See *Occasional Issues of Unique or Very Rare Books* (Manchester, 1876), II, xx. A ballad called "The Silver Age" uses the term *Lady Pecunia* three times and is a humorous poem, but along lines different from Barnfield's. See *The Pepys Ballads,* ed. Hyder Rollins (Cambridge, Mass., 1929), I, 200 ff. "The World's Sweet heart" (1630) employs *Lady Pecunia* in its second stanza. See *Roxburghe Ballads,* ed. John Payne Collier (London, 1847), p. 7. Collier believes the poem "made its original appearance before 1600," but he gives no support for his contention. Ben Jonson, in *The Staple of Newes* (1631) creates "Pecunia doe-all," a great lady, who owes nothing more than her name to Barnfield. And as late as 1654 Humphrey Crouch wrote "Lady Pecunia's Journey unto Hell." See *Cavalier and Puritan,* ed. Hyder Rollins (Cambridge, Mass., 1923), pp. 354-360. Collier, *Biblio. Acct.,* I, 9, observes that *The Massacre of Money* (1602) by T. A. resembles *Lady Pecunia.*

[17]Collier believes that "The World's Sweet-heart" "touches humorously upon topics Barnfield had treated more seriously," *Roxburghe Ballads,* p. 7. It might be suspected that Collier lacked a sense of humor. Actually Barnfield's is both a better and a more humorous poem than "The World's Sweet-heart."

reader by italicizing all word-play. Various coins are punned upon
such as angels and crosses; and counterfeiting practices along with
the slang used to identify them, terms such as *slip* and *Clypt*, provide matter for further wit. Sometimes the inscriptions or devices
upon the coins themselves are used for a kind of punning. But the
humor of *Lady Pecunia* is not confined to this, the often-called
lowest form. Comic elements are obtained also from the methods
of satire: ridicule, paradox, irony, scourging, and understatement.
Barnfield's use of rime and diction also lend humor. C. S. Lewis
finds "comic stanzas that almost anticipate Byron."[18] Several of
the devices employed for humorous effect can be demonstrated
with the following lines:

> You, [Pecunia] you alone, can make my Muse to speake;
> And tell a golden Tale, with siluer Tongue:
> You onely can my pleasing silence breake;
> And adde some Musique, to a merry Songue:
>   But amongst all the fiue, in Musicks Art,
>   I would not sing the *Counter*-tenor part.

> The Meane is best, and that I meane to keepe;
> So shall I keepe my selfe from That I meane:
> Lest with some Others, I be forc'd to weepe,
> And cry *Peccaui*, in dolefull Scaene.
>   (A₄ᵛ)

Barnfield pretends he will write only when paid to do so. Money,
made of gold and silver, has a silver tongue and tells a golden tale.
The poet's silence is a pleasing thing. Readers are happier when
Barnfield is not writing. The italicized *Counter* warns us of a pun,
and unless we work it out, the following stanza does not make
much sense. *Counter* is a cant term for prison, a place the poet
does not want to be. Thus the threefold play on the word *mean*
in the next stanza may be paraphrased as "The middle road is
safest, and I intend to follow it; in that way I shall keep myself
out of that place I am talking about above, prison. If I wind up
in prison, I, along with other inmates, will drop tears and cry I
have sinned in the general doleful scene of Newgate." Feminine
rime always lends itself well to humorous verse, and Barnfield
uses it liberally throughout the poem: *respect her, reiect her; despyse*

---

[18]*English Literature in the Sixteenth Century* (Oxford, 1954),
p. 497.

her, Myser; infect her, respect her; tearme it, confirme it; Albion, Apparell on; etc.

Technically, *Lady Pecunia* exhibits Barnfield's easy mastery of metrics. Scarcely a line in the entire poem, or even in all three volumes, does not scan or is not smooth. Diction is always precise, but varied. It is never Latinate, even though *pecunia* is used for the title. Instead, as Warton had remarked, "surely no author, whom we could name, has fairer pretensions to be regarded as a writer of genuine, untainted vernacular English."[19]

Since I have been quoting primarily from the 1598 text and since the first edition, except for *Lady Pecunia*, is fuller than that of 1605, I shall follow the order of the earlier and consider next *The Complaint of Poetrie, for the Death of Liberalitie.* It will be remembered that each of the last three sections of the 1598 volume has its own verse dedication. The six lines prefacing *The Complaint of Poetrie* contain the ring of personal friendship:

> To his Worshipfull wel-willer, Maister
> *Edward Leigh,* of Grayes Inne.
>
> Image of that, whose losse is here lamented;
> (In whom, so many vertues are contained)
> Daine to accept, what I haue now presented.
> Though Bounties death, herein be only fained,
>   If in your mind, she not reuiue (with speed)
>   Then will I sweare, that shee is dead indeed.
>
>   (A2^r)

The Edward Leigh of the dedication, despite Grosart's identification,[20] is, as far as I have been able to determine, unknown. These lines and the dedication to Nicholas Blackleech, whom Barnfield also associates with Gray's Inn, have raised the question of Barnfield's possible enrollment in that institution. But nothing has been turned up to place the poet there. Arber assuredly goes too far to refer to Barnfield as "this young barrister (as we should now call him)"[21] merely because of these friends. A young London

---

[19]*History of English Poetry,* ed. W. Carew Hazlitt (London, 1871), IV, 440.

[20]Grosart, *The Complete Poems,* p. xiii, seems to confuse Barnfield's dedicatee with Edward Leigh (1602-1671) who wrote *Critica Sacra* (1639) and who was enrolled at the Middle Temple. He was, however, M. P. for Stafford, Barnfield's county, and possibly came from the same family as the dedicatee.

[21]*Poems,* xxii.

poet may have two acquaintances at the same law institute without having been a student there himself. Although these lines to Leigh are friendly and not particularly mercenary, still they ask for pecuniary patronage. Furthermore, the request is made in the somewhat joking terms of *Lady Pecunia*. The poem itself complains of the death of liberality, which Barnfield equates with bounty, both being the benevolence showed to poets by rich patrons. Bounty is personified in the dedication; and Barnfield implies that if Leigh does not prove that she is alive, by presenting the author with some monetary gift, why then the poem is not a fantasy at all but painful reality. The jest is very deftly handled, and it is not difficult to believe that Barnfield wrote the dedication more for the humor than out of any real expectation of success. Mainly the dedication tends to link *The Complaint of Poetry* to *Lady Pecunia*. If they can be tied together, the composition of both can be dated by the address "To the Gentlemen readers" as works thought up especially for a new volume. The dating of many of the pieces in the third volume is not always so easily arrived at, since Barnfield elsewhere implies that some were written at an earlier time.[22]

----

[22]The appearance the same year (1598) of a poem signed J. M. and entitled *A Health to the Gentlemanly Profession of Seruing-men* perhaps throws some light on the date of publication of *Lady Pecunia*. As Collier has noted (*Biblio. Acct.*, IV, 30), the poem by J. M. "reminds" us of *The Complaint*. It was entered in the Stationers' Register for May 15, 1598. Since J. M. seems to be satirizing *The Complaint* and since his penultimate stanza carries suggestions of stanza five of *Lady Pecunia*, it would seem that Barnfield's volume was in print before May 15:

> The golden world is past and gone,
>   The Iron age hath runne his race:
> The lumpe of Lead is left alone
>   To presse the poore in every place:
> Nought els is left but miserie,
>   Since death of Liberalitie.
>   (*A Health*)

> When *Saturne* liu'd, and wore the Kingly Crowne,
> (And *Ioue* was yet vnborne, but not vnbred)
> This Ladies fame was then of no renowne;
> (For Golde was then, no more esteem'd then Lead)
>   Then Truth and Honesty were onely vs'd,
>   Siluer and Golde were vtterly refus'd.
>   (*Lady Pecunia*, A₄ᵛ)

J. M. turned the bantering tone of *Lady Pecunia* against the poet himself

In one sense *The Complaint of Poetrie, for the Death of Liberalitie* is a work which excerpts one small item out of *Lady Pecunia* and elaborates upon it: "You, you alone, can make my Muse to speake" (A₄ᵛ). Of course, the new poem is a complaint of very special kind and obviously not in the comic mode of *Lady Pecunia*. In fact, it is somewhat strange to find Barnfield devoting himself to a poem of some length on this particular subject at all. He seems to have been a man who had no money troubles, much less a poet who feared he may have to find a new profession if no patron stepped forward. Perhaps his very detachment from his material in this case explains the unique quality of the poem, for unique it is. Despite its title, which misleads the reader to expect a poem in the lament tradition of *The Affectionate Shepheard* or perhaps in the complaint genre of the *Mirror* poems, *The Complaint of poetrie, for the Death of Liberalitie* is a pastoral elegy from the precise mold that fashioned *Lycidas* and *Adonais*. But the difference between Barnfield's elegy and all others in the great sweep from Theocritus to Arnold is that the Elizabethan is not commemorating a human being. Employing personification, Barnfield puts the pastoral elegy to unusual lamentation, and perhaps debases the form in the process. Given great dignity and pathos by the grief of the bereaved and the tragedy of the dead, the elegy loses something when invoked for a fantasy in which the dead creature is only an abstraction. Nevertheless Barnfield proceeds exactly as though Bounty were some shepherd recently deceased and adheres to the conventions of the form as closely as if the victim's name were Adonis or Daphnis or Thyrsis. It appears that the initiating inspiration for The *Complaint* was again Spenser. The poem is a combination of the materials from the October and November eclogues. *October* develops Cuddie's complaints over the sparse rewards of his poetry. *November* is Spenser's famous pastoral elegy lamenting the death of the anonymous Dido. But quite clearly, Barnfield has not confined his use of elegiac models to Spenser. Typical of the Greek elegy as it is employed by Bion and Moschus is the opening dirge. All elegists provide a scene of weeping shepherds and mourning nature, but only Bion and

when satirizing his more serious *Complaint*. Note that J. M. uses a tetrameter line although his stanza follows the ababcc of both *Lady Pecunia* and *The Complaint*.

Moschus begin their poems with tears. Barnfield seems closest to the *Lament for Bion* in his first stanza:

> Weepe Heauens now, for you haue lost your light;
> Ye Sunne and Moone, beare witnesse of my mone:
> The cleere is turnd to clouds; the day to night;
> And all my hope, and all my ioy is gone:
>   Bounty is dead, the cause of my annoy;
>   Bounty is dead, and with her dide my ioy.
>
>   (A8ʳ)

But since Barnfield's lamentation is not for a dead human, the poem launches immediately into the satire that is part of this elegy. In combining an attack upon vice with the traditional materials of the pastoral elegy, Barnfield is among the freest. Surely political allegory was a part of Virgil's fifth eclogue, but the matter was well masked. Barnfield, though employing allegory, is easily understood. Personification, in which the vice or virtue carries its own name, clearly presents the poet's complaints. When patronage was generous, "I neuer then, did write one verse in vaine" (A8ᵛ); but now all that the poet can expect is "Good wordes." The debt to Spenser's October eclogue is most evident. Stanza 4 concludes,

> Tis not *Good wordes*, that can a man maintaine;
> Wordes are but winde; and winde is all but vaine.
>
>   (A8ᵛ)

Spenser's Pierce suggests to Cuddie that praise is better than monetary reward, but Cuddie answers,

> Sike prayse is smoke, that sheddeth in the skye,
> Sike words bene wynd, and wasten soone in vayne.
>
>   (35-36)

Barnfield's fifth stanza then goes into an *ubi sunt* query over various famous patrons of poetry:

> Where is *Mecoenas*, Learnings noble Patron?
> (That *Maroes* [Virgil's] Muse, with Bountie so did cherish?)
>   (A8ᵛ)

Following a reference to Zenobia, the sixth stanza alludes to Augustus. These twelve lines seem to be Barnfield's rendering of Spenser's two six-line stanzas beginning,

> Indeede the Romish *Tityrus* [Virgil], I heare,
> Through his *Mecoenas* left his Oaten reede,
>   (55-56)

and developing into an image that we associate with Barnfield
both in this poem and in the ode "As it fell vpon a Day":

> But ah *Mecoenas* is yclad in claye,
> And great *Augustus* long ygoe is dead:
> And all the worthies liggen wrapt in leade.
>
> (61-63)

Barnfield, in the ode, alters his borrowing to "King Pandion hee
is dead:/ And all thy friends are lapt in Lead." Spenser liked the
image so well he used it in the June eclogue to bemoan the death
of Tityrus: "Nowe dead he is, and lyeth wrapt in lead"; and repeated it again in the November eclogue, in which Dido is described
as "Dead and lyeth wrapt in lead." Barnfield's answer to the
ubi sunt question is not the same as Spenser's. The patrons are
not all dead; rather Avarice has perverted the otherwise noble
minds of once generous benefactors, and it is Avarice who has
killed Bounty, at least killed her so far as the poet is concerned.
With Bounty lost, Barnfield seizes the opportunity to cram two full
stanzas with his favorite rhetorical device of anaphora:

> Neuer againe, shall I thy presence see:
> Neuer againe, shal I thy bountie tast:
> Neuer againe, shall I accepted bee:
> Neuer againe, shal I be so embrac't:
>   Neuer againe, shall I the bad recall:
>   Neuer againe, shall I be lou'd of all.
>
> Thou wast the Nurse, whose Bountie gaue me sucke:
> Thou wast the Sunne, whose beames did lend me light:
> Thou wast the Tree, whose fruit I still did plucke:
> Thou wast the Patron, to maintaine my right:
>   Through thee I liu'd; on thee I did relie;
>   In thee I ioy'd; and now for thee I die.
>
> (A₄ᵛ)

In the last two lines of the second stanza, the recurrent use of
thee provides an additional internal repetition.

According to George Norlin,[23] the second element in the

---

[23]At the end of the first decade of this century, a revival of interest
in English pastoral poetry, spurred perhaps by W. W. Greg's seminal
study, *Pastoral Poetry and Pastoral Drama* (London, 1906), produced a
series of monumental essays on the pastoral elegy and other bucolic
eclogues: W. P. Mustard, "Later Echoes of the Greek Bucolic Poets,"
AJP, XXX (1909), 245-283; Herbert E. Cory, "The Golden Age of the
Spenserian Pastoral," *PMLA*, XXV (1910), 241-267; James Holly Han-

pastoral elegy, an element to be found as early as Theocritus and present in almost all elegies, including Spenser's November eclogue, is the mourning of all nature. Jackals, wolves, and lions in Theocritus; mountains, rivers, and trees in Bion; nightingales and nymphs in Moschus; all these and more in Virgil accompany the shepherd in his weeping. Spenser invokes the muse of tragedy to aid him:

> Vp then *Melpomene* thou mournefulst Muse of nyne,
> Such cause of mourning neuer hadst afore.
> (*November*, 53-54)

Barnfield would seem to have made a survey of all these elegies and culled selectively from each:

> Faire *Philomela*, cease thy sad complaint;
> And lend thine eares vnto my dolefull Ditty:
> (Whose soule with sorrowe, now begins to faint,
> And yet I cannot moue mens hearts to pitty:)
>   Thy woes are light, compared vnto mine:
>   You waterie Nymphes, to mee your plaints resigne.
>
> And thou *Melpomene*, (the Muse of Death)
> That neuer sing'st, but in a dolefull straine;
> Sith cruell Destinie hath stopt her breath,
> (Who whilst she liu'd, was Vertues Soueraigne)
>   Leaue *Hellicon*, (whose bankes so pleasant bee)
>   And beare a part of sorrowe now with mee.
>
> The Trees (for sorrowe) shead their fading Leaues,
> And weepe out gum, in stead of other teares;
> Comfort nor ioy, no Creature now conceiues,
> To chirpe and sing, each little bird forbeares.
>   The sillie Sheepe, hangs downe his drooping head,
>   And all because, that *Bounty* she is dead.
>   (B^r-B^v)

---

ford, "The Pastoral Elegy and Milton's *Lycidas*," PMLA, XXV (1910), 403-447; and George Norlin, "Conventions of the Pastoral Elegy," *AJP*, XXXII (1911), 294-312. Despite their close searching, none of these men discovered that Barnfield's *Complaint* was cast in the form of the classical pastoral elegy; neither has any researcher since. Norlin's essay is most helpful, however, in illustrating just how closely Barnfield conforms to the classical structure. The first of the conventions—the framework of a shepherds' gathering of two or more who decide after an opening scene of dramatic quality to sing the praises of the dead—Barnfield omits. But he has classical authority even in this matter: Bion and Moschus as well as Virgil in his Tenth Eclogue omit the dramatic setting.

Here is the nightingale of Moschus, used in such a manner that we cannot help but recall Barnfield's ode "As it fell vpon a Day." In the ode the poet lends his tears to the bird, whereas in *The Complaint* he asks the bird to cease its own and mourn with him. Here too are the nymphs of Moschus and the others. Here is Spenser's Melpomene, and here are the mourning trees, birds, and sheep of Bion, Virgil, and other elegists.

At the conclusion of the "weeping-nature" section, the vices responsible for the death of Bounty are again attacked. Avarice before, now it is Adulation or "smooth-Tongd Flatterie" who is the culprit. Bounty is dead only to the poet; she lives still for those who find the sugary words to awake her largess. In one compact stanza, the fable of the fox and the magpie is retold, but the denunciation of *Flatterie* in more abstract terms is drawn out for eight stanzas (18-25). Then, as a substitute for the third element common to all classical elegies—decking of the grave with flowers[24] —Barnfield deposits first "ten thousand Teares" and after inscribes upon the tomb an epitaph. Though this practice may not follow very closely the convention of strewing blossoms, the fourth convention of the pastoral elegy is observed minutely. Norlin calls it seeking "the riddle of this painful earth."[25] It begins usually with the bereaved asking the inevitable question: "Why was this person beloved of me taken away?" Stanza 29 opens the lament, and the elegiac strain continues to stanza 44, the next to last of the poem. Greed is found to be the villain: "Vile *Auarice*, why hast thou kildd my Deare?" The poet is struck with the realization that all who suffer tragedy renew at some time their lives with hope; he only despairs hopelessly:

> The Merchants wife; the Tender-harted Mother:
> That leaues her Loue; whose Sonne is prest for warre;
> (Resting, the one; as woefull as the other;)
> Hopes yet at length? when ended is the iarre;
>   To see her Husband; see her Sonne againe:
>   "Were it not then for Hope, the hart were slaine.   [*sic*]
>
> But I, whose hope is turned to despaire,
> Nere looke to see my dearest Deare againe.
>   (B₄ʳ)

The first seven lines above form one of those rhetorical stanzas in

---

[24]Norlin, "Conventions of the Pastoral Elegy," pp. 304-305.
[25]"Conventions of the Pastoral Elegy," p. 306.

which a double narrative is carried on contrapuntally, the caesura being the alternating point. This device, so widespread in Elizabethan verse, is used frequently by Barnfield, although not on so elaborate a scale. More often he devotes to it only two lines.[26] Of some interest also is stanza 32, in which Barnfield lists others who have lamented the loss of someone dear. Selected as illustrations are four sets of lovers: Pythias and Damon, Pylades and Orestes, Hercules and Hylas, and Theseus and Pirithous. This rather distressing choice raises again the old charge of pederasty. Barnfield seems to have at hand many of the classical references to this unnatural love. However, the remaining stanzas of lament become general, and the effect of Bounty's death upon persons and professions other than poets and poetry is explored. The section concludes in stanzas 42, 43, and 44 with a close and somewhat surprising imitation of Bion's *Lament for Adonis*. Whereas the Greek Cytherea wails that she must live on wretchedly, since she is a goddess and has eternal life, Barnfield says of himself,

> Then come (sweet Death) O why doest thou forbeare me?
> Aye mee! thy Dart is blunt, it will not enter.
> Oh now I knowe the cause, and reason why;
> I am immortall, and I cannot dye.
> ($C_2{}^r$)

While these words are appropriate for a deity, they are patently absurd for an Elizabethan. That they owe their origin to an unthinking imitation of Bion is clear from an unmistakable allusion which Barnfield brings in as inappropriately as the misapplied immortality itself:

> So *Cytheraea* would haue dide, but could not;
> When faire *Adonis* by her side lay slaine.
> ($C_2{}^r$)

As ridiculous as these sentiments are, they do not go so far as the final couplet of stanza 44, in which the poet intends to punish death for not taking away his miserable life at the height of his grief:

> Sith, when I would, thou doost my sute denie,
> Vile Tyrant, when thou wilt, I will not die.
> ($C_2{}^r$)

---

[26]See, for instance, "Shepheards Content," stanzas 4, 10, 18; "Cassandra," stanza 46; *Greenes Funeralls*, Sonnet I.

How Barnfield will flout death when it comes to take him is not explained. So absurd is his pose that one can suspect only that the poet's comic and satiric muse has supplanted Melpomene.

Only one stanza is left in *The Complaint* and only one stanza therefore to carry the fifth and final convention of the pastoral elegy, in Norlin's terms the "peace, peace, he is not dead" conclusion.[27] Although this sentiment is hinted at by Bion and Moschus, their employment of it is only vague and ambiguous. The convention begins unmistakably with Virgil's fifth eclogue, in which there is an elaborate song of apotheosis. Barnfield incorporates this part of the elegy in a way unique to the genre. All death's victims in other elegies are literally revitalized in accord with the theological concepts of the writer. Barnfield's Bounty receives continuing life in the memory of mortals only:

> And *Bounty*, though her body thou [Death] hast slaine,
> Yet shall her memorie remaine for euer:
> . . . .
> Then Sorrowe cease, and wipe thy weeping eye;
> For Fame shall liue, when all the World shall dye.
>   (C₂ᵛ)

In another instance of his frequent illogic, Barnfield fails to explain in this concluding line how fame can continue when there are no mortals left to perpetuate it. *The Complaint of Poetrie, for the Death of Liberalitie* then is a surprising variation of the pastoral elegy, although the sentiments become somewhat mocking when dedicated to the abstraction of Bounty.

The third poem of the 1598 volume, *The Combat, betweene Conscience and Couetousnesse, in the minde of Man,* is prefaced by the briefest of the verse dedications in any of Barnfield's books. Addressed "To his Worshipfull good friend, Maister *Iohn Steuenton,* of *Dothill,* in the County of *Salop,*" it runs but four lines:

> Sith Conscience (long since) is exilde the Citty,
>   O let her in the Countrey, finde some Pitty:
> But if she be exilde, the Countrey too,
>   O let her finde, some fauour yet of you.
>   (C₄ʳ)

We recognize again the formula used in the dedications to Spencer and Leigh. The subject matter of his poem is in the keeping of the dedicatee; therefore it is only appropriate that such a patron show

---

[27]"Conventions of the Pastoral Elegy," pp. 309-310.

favor to a poem celebrating the patron's unique virtue. Grosart was not able to identify Steventon,[28] and I have not unearthed any information of significance. The Harleian Society transcripts of the visitation of Shropshire record the Steventon family of Dothill as going back at least as far as Edward III. A John Steventon, whose wife was Margery Bridgman, named his first son Richard, noted as living in 1564. Richard had no male heirs, and the second son, John, possibly became *pater familias* upon the death of his elder brother. This John may be Barnfield's dedicatee, although he too had a son named John. The last named, however, was a fourth son and unlikely to have merited consideration as a patron.[29] Like the others prefacing the poems of the 1598 volume, this dedication was dropped in 1605 and, also like the others, apparently produced no results since the whole volume was rededicated to Spencer in 1605. Thus the identities of Steventon, Leigh, and Blackleech have little importance other than as a list of the poet's non-literary associates.

The Combat, betweene Conscience and Couetousnesse, in the minde of Man is a curious throwback to medievalism, although in some respects Barnfield's inclinations are often reactionary. "The Complaint of Chastitie" is close to the original *Mirror* poems in its excessive moralizing, a quality found throughout even the most modern of Barnfield's pieces; and the poet's love of allegory has a distinctly aging effect on much of his otherwise fresh, young pastoralism. The Guendolena episode of *The Affectionate Shepheard* does nothing so much as to take some of the bloom off the vernal loveliness of the bucolic landscape. *Lady Pecunia* escapes the heaviness of a morality piece only when it is furthest from allegory. *The Complaint of Poetrie, for the Death of Liberalitie* almost sinks completely under the weight of its allegory. And finally, *The Combat* founders utterly. What there was in the young poet that turned him toward the Middle Ages must have been the same quality that took him to Spenser as a master; again, the closest analogue for *The Combat* can be found in the author of the *Faerie Queene*, just as suggestions for *Lady Pecunia* and *The Complaint of Poetrie* had their germination in *Virgils Gnat* and the November Eclogue. Although *The Combat* is a *débat*,

---

[28]*The Complete Poems*, p. xiii.
[29]See *The Visitation of Shropshire*, II, Publications of the Harleian Society, XXIX (London, 1889), pp. 444-445.

belonging to the genre of such poems as the *Disputation between the Body and the Soul,* the *Owl and the Nightingale,* and other *estrif,* it is also allegory similar to Spenser's House of Alma in Book II, Canto IX, of the *Faerie Queene.* But in addition to the poem's relationships with *débats* and "castle of the body" allegory, *The Combat* fits also the general motif of the *Lady Pecunia* volume. The title poem as well as *The Complaint of Poetrie, for the Death of Liberalitie* are poems in the larger category of the contests between the vices and the virtues. If we were to call the roll in these first three poems, on the side of virtue we should find Charity, Wisdom, (well-used) Wealth, Liberality, Bounty, Generousness, Conscientiousness, Truth, Honor, and Good Deeds; on the side of vice we should find Miserliness, Avarice, Covetousness, Flattery, Adulation, Hardness of Heart, Falsehood, and Deceit. For some reason, Barnfield's outlook is bitter, and in these poems the vices triumph. Lady Pecunia is in the hands of flatterers, Bounty is dead, and Covetousness sends Conscience packing. In so much he differs from Spenser, whose Alma, although heavily besieged inside her castle of the body by numerous forces of vices, wins victory through aid given by Guyon and the Prince.

Instead of the entire body, Barnfield confines his psychomachia to the mind of man, as stated in the title to the poem. The conflict is simplified tremendously, with only two combatants: Conscience and Covetousness. All is a dream vision, with the poet first succumbing to sleep before the debate begins and, at its end, awaking from the sorrow "which my Soule did take/ At sight hereof" (D⁴ᵣ). Conscience appears first, almost naked, but clad in Good Deeds, Truth, and Honesty. "Nor any other Ornament shee had." The echo is of Spenser's Alma, who is dressed only in a robe of "lilly white," whose hair is "trimly wouen, and in tresses wrought" and who "Ne other tyre . . . on her head did weare" (II. ix. xix. 1-8). Barnfield's Covetousness follows Conscience to the field, dressed in a cassock like a usurer. Covetousness is called (lines 21 and 140) a *Carle,* a word so popular with Spenser that in Canto XI, Book II, the canto that concludes the Alma story, he uses it six times in 31 stanzas. Barnfield does not use the word in any other place. The debate, beginning at line 25, takes up most of this relatively short poem. Covetousness reprimands Conscience for appearing on the plain called the mind of man, for by right it belongs to the forces of evil. Covetousness lists his followers, and again we get a list similar to that in stanzas 16-18

of *Lady Pecunia*: princes, kings, captains, courtiers, country-men,
lawyers, politicians, surgeons, and physicians. Covetousness hopes
to clinch his claim to man's mind by the treachery of Judas, who,
driven by avariciousness, sold Christ for thirty pieces of silver.
Conscience counters with the argument that, since the Lord placed
a conscience in man in Paradise, Conscience is the elder of them
both and by right of seniority should hold the mind of man. Then
in a bit of antifeminism, another strong hold-over from the Middle
Ages, Barnfield allows Covetousness to claim that Eve's transgression was greed:

> What was it else, but *Auarice* in *Eue*,
> (Thinking thereby, in greater Blisse to liue)
> That made her taste, of the forbidden fruite?
>
> (D₂ᵛ)

Man never used the conscience he was given; covetousness was
employed first; therefore says the Vice, covetousness is the older.
Conscience accepts the argument, placing all the blame upon Eve:

> Man had a *Conscience*, to obey his will,
> And neuer would be tempted thereunto,
> Vntill the Woeman, shee, did worke *man woe*.
>
> (D₃ʳ)

Again Barnfield italicizes his pun, making certain the reader does
not miss his spelling of *woeman*, an arrangement hardly necessary
since the pun had been used since the Middle Ages. Covetousness,
in the final argument, destroys Conscience's reasoning by stating
it was not goodness that kept Adam from sinning prior to Eve's
transgression: it was fear. Conscience gives up the battle with a
long lament, in which Barnfield again employs his favorite device
of anaphora, this time fourteen lines beginning with the same two
words. The poem concludes with a return to the "castle of the
body" device. Covetousness becomes the king and lord of the
plain, which has but one gate, "Repentance cald":

> he causd that to be kept,
> Lest *Conscience* should returne, whilst as he slept:
> Wherefore he causd it, to be wacht and warded
> Both night and Day, and to be strongly guarded:
> To keepe it safe, these three he did intreat,
> *Hardnesse of hart*, with *Falshood* and *Deceat*.
>
> (D₄ʳ)

Although almost all allegories of this sort employ a porter at the
gate, usually some Virtue keeping watch against the entrance of

some Vice, Barnfield's language may be traced to the porter passage
in Spenser's House of Alma:

> Within the Barbican a Porter sate,
> *Day and night* duely keeping *watch and ward.* [my italics]
> (II. ix. xxv. 1-2)

The influence from Spenser in the first two poems of *Lady
Pecunia* is felt also in the third, although much abounds that is
completely alien to the author of the *Faerie Queene.*

The Combat employs pentameter couplets, a form not often
used by Barnfield, but one managed with the same fluid ease he
gets in all his verse. Many run-on lines keep the form from be-
coming heroic couplets, and the strong caesura, marked almost
always by some otherwise unneeded punctuation keeps the lines
from monotonous regularity. Nevertheless, there is very little
poetry of merit in *The Combat.* The allegory is flat and uninterest-
ing. The duel of wit itself between Conscience and Covetousness
is unimaginative and somewhat illogical. Conscience gives up too
easily, though actually making a point not refuted by Covetousness, the point being that man could not sell his soul since it did
not belong to him. Christ's sacrifice upon the cross was an act
through which Christ bought man's soul dearly, an argument
never answered whether or not it had any validity to begin with.
Because of the shortness of the poem,—it is only 164 lines—the
allegory never really gets started, and the debate is terminated
abruptly. While it has greater unity and completeness than many
of Barnfield's poems from earlier volumes and while it shows
greater control and surer touch, *The Combat* is the least disting-
uished of all Barnfield's verse. Even the shorter pieces, produced
on occasion and collected in the last section of *Lady Pecunia* as
"fruits of vnriper yeares," give more pleasure and exhibit a happier
vigor, a more charming grace.

The final division of *Lady Pecunia* is *Poems: In diuers
humors.* A six-line stanza addressed to Nicholas Blackleech of
Gray's Inn dedicates this section in the 1598 edition:

> To you, that know the tuch of true Conceat;
> (Whose many gifts I neede not to repeat)
> I write these Lines: fruits of vnriper yeares;
> Wherein my Muse no harder Censure feares:
> Hoping in gentle Worth, you will them take;
> Not for the gift, but for the giuers sake.
> (E^v)

Although less information can be gleaned about Nicholas Black-leech, either in a negative or a positive way, than about any of the other dedicatees, this prefatory stanza is more interesting than those to Spencer, Leigh, and Steventon for its oft-quoted half-line, "fruits of vnriper yeares." The dates of composition of the eight poems included in 1598 become matters of dismay for the bibliographer. If Barnfield was only twenty-four when this statement was published, to what years is he referring as unripe? At least four of the eight poems have clearly datable references, and in "A Remembrance of some English Poets" it can be seen that Barnfield's remark is just a trifle disingenuous. An allusion to Drayton's plays and epistles indicates that these lines at least could not have been written before 1597, the date of the earliest of those productions unless Barnfield, who calls "gentle *Rowland,* my professed friend," had seen them in manuscript. I do not think it likely that Barnfield read many of Drayton's works before they went to the printers, since if such were the case one would expect to find a more pervasive influence coming from the older man. Instead, the greatest influence on Barnfield's poems comes from Spenser and from works that had been long in print before they found their way into works like *Cynthia, Lady Pecunia,* and *The Complaint of Poetrie, for the Death of Liberalitie.*

The initial poem of the group is one of the two that have given to Barnfield most of what little attention he has received in the past. Along with "As it fell vpon a Day," Sonnet I of *Poems: In diuers humors,* "If Musique and sweet Poetrie agree," has been attributed to Shakespeare, primarily because of the subsequent appearance of both poems in *The Passionate Pilgrim* (1599). The various editors of Shakespeare who at one time or another (some of them reversing their opinions) attributed the poem to the playwright are Malone, Dyce, White, Hudson, Drake, Boswell (tentatively), and Knight. Drake's words of praise for the poem have stuck with it. He reproduces it in its entirety "not only for its beauty as a sonnet, though this be considerable, but as it makes mention of his great poetical contemporary, Edmund Spenser, for whose genius, as might naturally be expected, he appears to have entertained the most deep-felt admiration."[30] The first admission that the poem might have been by Barnfield was perhaps Malone's silent removal of the poem in the 1790 edition of Shakespeare's

---

[30]*Shakespeare and His Times* (London, 1817), II, 49.

works. In 1832 Dyce had given it to Barnfield, but reversed this opinion in his editions of 1857-1876, possibly influenced by Collier, who is the real culprit in the story. Other editors giving the poem to Barnfield are Knight (a reversal of opinion), Bell, Halliwell-Phillipps, Edmonds, Furnivall, Dowden, Craig, Hudson, Gollancz, and Herford. In his 1843 edition of Shakespeare, Collier had assigned the poem to Barnfield: "There can be little doubt that he was the author of it."[31] But in various other writings, beginning in 1856,[32] Collier altered his opinion, claiming that Shakespeare was the author since Barnfield omitted the poem in the 1605 edition.[33] But authorship is not the only problem in this sonnet. It is addressed "To his friend Maister R. L.," whose identity has by some been arrived at without great difficulty. In the Variorum edition of Shakespeare's poems, Hyder Rollins first gives credit to Grosart for the original detection and then proceeds, in a note to line three, "Then must the Loue be great twixt thee and me," to gloss accordingly: "I. e., between the author, Barnfield, and R (ichard) L (inche), to whom this sonnet was addressed."[34] Grosart was not the originator of the Richard Linche identification, and furthermore, he was not as certain in his opinion as Rollins. Grosart had written only that R. L. "was perhaps Richard Lynch (or Linch), the poet of 'Diella' (1596)." But the speculation carried a footnote: "It is not known for certain. It is to be noted that while Barnfield says 'and Both in thee remaine,' in the rest he very distinctly and twice puts in apposition R. L.'s love for music and his own love for poetry. 'Diella,' however, is so slight a verse-attempt that it might be as nothing to his musical gifts and tastes."[35] Grosart does not give the source for his identification of R. L., but his frequent references to the work of Charles Edmonds assures us that he got it from the Isham reprint of *Venus and Adonis*, which includes *The Passionate Pilgrim*. Ed-

---

[31]*Works* (1843), VII, 577.

[32]In *The Athenaeum*, May 17, 1856, pp. 616 ff.; in *N & Q*, July 5, 1856, pp. 8 ff.; in his editions of Shakespeare of 1858 and 1878; in his *Bibliographical Account* (1865), I, 47-50; and in the introduction to his edition of *Lady Pecunia* (1866).

[33]Since Collier's arguments include also "As it fell vpon a Day" and pertain more directly to that poem than to the sonnet, his pronouncements are taken up more fully in the treatment of the ode.

[34]*A New Variorum of Shakespeare* (Phila., 1938), XXII, 282.

[35]*The Complete Poems*, p. xiii.

monds writes that Sonnet I "is openly addressed to a friend, R. L., presumed to be Richard Linch, author of 'Diella,' 1596."[36] No writer that I have come upon gives any reason for such an identification. Apparently finding it necessary to give some name to the anonymous R. L., scholars could find no Elizabethan of record whom the initials would fit other than Richard Linche. Absolutely nothing is known about Linche, and a close study of his sonnet sequence, a collection of thirty-nine poems, discloses only two metaphors related to music or to musical instruments:

Sonnet XV

. . . .
Where, under umbrage of some aged tree
   with lute in hand I sit and, sighing, say,

Sonnet XVI

But thou, my dear sweet-sounding lute, be still!
   repose thy troubled strings upon this mosse!
Thou hast full often eased me 'gainst my will:
   lie down in peace, thy spoil were my great loss!

I'll speak enough of her too cruel heart,
   enough to move the stony rocks to ruth!
And cause these trees weep tears to hear my smart,
   though cruel She will not once weigh my truth.[37]

Although these references state clearly that the poet has relied upon the lute often to ease his troubled passions, the passage is only a fiction invented for the moment; otherwise, in a sequence of thirty-nine poems, there would be more imagery of music and instruments than this. R. L., elsewhere in *Diella,* is given to extended metaphors on various objects: sun-moon, love as army-enemy, war-truce-parley, falcon, renewing and burgeoning nature, book, seamen in danger on the sea, uprooted tree, winter raging upon nature, conqueror-prisoner, elaborate ship metaphor, etc. Several of these images overlap and recur, but the lute never recurs and seems only to be a natural extension of the Orpheus myth which the poet implies in the moving rocks-weeping trees image. Are these lines then enough to establish the R. L. of Barnfield's poem as the author of *Diella?* No other evidence can be brought to bear.

---

[36]*Shakespeare's Venus and Adonis,* (London, 1870). The individual works are paginated separately. See p. xi of *The Passionate Pilgrim.*

[37]*Elizabethan Sonnets,* ed. Sidney Lee (Westminster, 1904), II, 309.

The sonnet itself, as well as the one following it, "Against the Dispraysers of Poetrie," varies in its rime scheme from the form Barnfield had used in *Cynthia*. All twenty of the earlier sequence had employed an abba cddc effe gg pattern, whereas the two sonnets of *Poems: In diuers humors* rime abab cdcd efef gg. The poem plays upon the harmony to be found between music and poetry and pays elaborate tributes to Dowland, as the idol of R. L., and Spenser as the inspiration of the poet:

> *Dowland* to thee is deare; whose heauenly tuch
> Vpon the Lute, doeth rauish humaine sense:
> *Spenser* to mee; whose deepe Conceit is such,
> As passing all Conceit, needs no defence.
>
> (E_2^r)

The evocation of Spenser is only appropriate since almost every piece in *Lady Pecunia* shows Barnfield's reliance upon his great contemporary. The idea that Shakespeare should pay tribute to Spenser enticed Drake and others[38] uncritically to ascribe the poem to Shakespeare, but Dowden felt "that it would be wholly exceptional to find Shakespeare mentioning by name, in his verse, any of his contemporaries."[39] Barnfield, on the other hand, takes great delight in praising and complimenting his contemporaries and does so more often, in a relatively small body of work, than almost any other writer of his time. The sonnet concludes with an enigmatic claim that "One Knight loues Both, and Both in thee re-maine." All commentators have taken "Both" to refer to Dowland and Spenser; and Sidney Lee, adding to a footnote by an unidentified "L,"[40] glossed "Knight" as Sir George Carey, to whom Dowland dedicated his *First Book of Ayres* (1597) and to whose wife Spenser dedicated *Muiopotmos* (1591).[41] However, the entire sestet of the sonnet tends to cast doubt upon such an interpretation:

---

[38]Boswell, in his edition of the works of Shakespeare in 1821, wrote "I should be glad if I could claim them with more confidence for our great poet, not on account of their merit, which is small, but as showing his admiration of Spenser, and the warm terms in which he expressed it."

[39]*The Passionate Pilgrim*, Facsimile reproduction (London, n.d.), p. xi. Dowden's introduction is dated 1883.

[40]*The Modern Readers' Shakespeare*, ed. H. N. Hudson, I. Gollancz, and C. H. Herford (New York, 1909), X, 86.

[41]*The Passionate Pilgrim*, facsimile reproduction (Oxford, 1905), p. 31.

Thou lou'st to heare the sweete melodious sound,
That *Phoebus* Lute (the Queene of Musique) makes:
And I in deepe Delight am chiefly drownd,
When as himselfe to singing he betakes.
     One God is God of Both (as Poets faigne)
     One Knight loues Both, and Both in thee remaine.
                                             (E₂ʳ)

Dowland and Spenser have been dropped in the sestet. R. L. enjoys Apollo's lute (music); Barnfield delights in Apollo's voice (poetry). Apollo is the god of both music and poetry (here *Both* cannot refer to Dowland and Spenser since "Poets faigne" Apollo's godhead not the musician's and the poet's adoration of him). One knight loves both music and poetry, and both music and poetry reside in R. L. Since two of the three *both*'s in the final couplet cannot refer to anything other than music and poetry, it is unreasonable to assume that the poet expected the reader to identify the remaining *both* with Dowland and Spenser. The identity of the knight becomes folly to speculate upon since the only clue left is his love for two of the arts. The poem is not so good as several critics have found it. Perhaps they were led to their opinions either by belief that Shakespeare authored it or that it was good enough for people to mistake as his. But the first quatrain is based on a false syllogism, and the rest of the poem is given over to rather conventional diction and sentiments. Three lines are padded by parenthetical statements (an identifying mark of Barnfield's) and the entire poem, to use a phrase of Barnfield's, is "Bath'd in a melting Sugar-Candie stream" (*Affec. Shep.,* Cᵛ).

The second sonnet is a companion piece to its predecessor. Linked together by numbering, they have also common themes. The first is, in part, in praise of poetry; the second is, as its descriptive title tells us, "Against the Dispraysers of Poetrie." It has a haunting opening quatrain:

> *Chaucer* is dead; and *Gower* lyes in grave;
> The Earle of *Surrey,* long agoe is gone;
> Sir *Philip Sidneis* soule, the Heauens haue;
> *George Gascoigne* him beforne, was tomb'd in stone,
>   (E₂ʳ)

but it quickly deteriorates into undistinguished verse. The second quatrain depends upon the conventions, Barnfield borrowing from himself in the seventh line, "Their liuing fame, no Fortune can confound." The sestet, though somewhat original, descends into bathos, especially in the final couplet made famous by Meres' allusion in *Palladis Tamia* (1598):

> The King of *Scots* (now liuing) is a Poet,
> As his *Lepanto*, and his *Furies* shoe it.
>   (E₂ʳ)

C. S. Lewis, who felt that comic stanzas in *Lady Pecunia* "almost anticipate Byron"[42] might better have quoted the rime above as a forerunner of some of those in *Don Juan*. The only difference is that Barnfield did not intend to be comical.

The third poem of the 1598 edition, "A Remembrance of some English Poets," is one of the two pieces retained in 1605, the final selection of the book. The other poem reprinted is the relatively insignificant seven-line "Comparison of the Life of Man." The length of each of these poems becomes important when the makeup of the 1605 quarto is examined. Barnfield's best poems were not retained. If two were to be kept, why were they not "If Musique and sweet Poetrie agree," and "As it fell vpon a Day"? The 1605 edition shows that *The Complaint of Poetrie, for the Death of Liberalitie* carried over into gathering G, employing all of Gʳ and Gᵛ. A short poem was required to fill up Gᵛ. The only possibilities were the six-line epigraph to the "Gentlewoman's Picture" and the seven-line "Comparison of the Life of Man." The better poem was chosen. However a blank recto still remained. Of the seven poems left to choose from in the 1598 quarto, none filled up exactly one page so well as "A Remembrance of some English Poets." The whole solution was a publisher's arrangement and suggests strongly that Barnfield was not around to supervise or even have voice in the printing, despite the fact that he wrote special stanzas for *Lady Pecunia*. While it may be impossible to determine which poems any poet may think his best, it is hard to see how Barnfield himself could have picked the completely conventional and very slight "Comparison" over either of the sonnets or "As it fell vpon a Day." One might even expect that Barnfield would have urged that the gathering be filled out simply to keep more of his work before the public; but he probably was up against a publisher who, resetting the whole volume anyhow, refused to waste type, ink, and a compositor's wages when he

---

[42]*English Literature in the Sixteenth Century*, p. 497.

didn't have to; and Barnfield, probably up in Staffordshire, was not present to press his point.

"A Remembrance of some English Poets" is neither a very good nor a very bad poem. Its chief interest lies in the mention of Barnfield's contemporaries whom the poet thought worthy of praise and of the works which merited that praise. No surprise attends the discovery that the first stanza, and therefore first place, is given to Spenser:

> Liue *Spenser* euer, in thy *Fairy Queene*:
> Whose like (for deepe Conceit) was neuer seene.
> Crownd mayst thou bee, vnto thy more renowne,
> (As King of Poets) with a Lawrell Crowne.
>
> ($E_2{}^v$)

The second line is a variation of the tribute paid Spenser in the sonnet to R. L. and, if necessary, might be brought in as further evidence of Barnfield's authorship of the sonnet. The citation of the *Faerie Queene* alone cannot startle anyone either, although Barnfield knew all Spenser's work and was heavily indebted to many pieces other than the longer work. The *Faerie Queene* was Spenser's most widely admired poem as well as his best intrinsically. In 1598, the first appearance of Barnfield's accolade, Books IV-VI of the *Faerie Queene* had been out only two years and, except for the *Foure Hymnes* (Fall, 1596), was Spenser's most recently published work of any magnitude, although the reissue of an edition of *The Shepheardes Calender* in 1597 may well have accounted for the influence of the October and November eclogues on the *Lady Pecunia* volume. Finally, Barnfield's greatest debt, covering all his works, is to the *Faerie Queene*. The use of the distinctive stanza in *Cynthia* and the reliance upon Spenser's allegorical methods, especially in the imitation of the psychomachia of the House of Alma, make it imperative that Barnfield acknowledge the *Faerie Queene*. If a second work could have been mentioned, it should have been *The Shepheardes Calender*, which may possibly have launched Barnfield upon his charming pastorals and which certainly supplied him throughout his poetic career.

The inclusion of Daniel, in the second stanza, is somewhat of a surprise since no influence by this poet has been found in Barnfield. Why not some other poet, someone whom Barnfield, through the testimony of his other writings, was known to have held in high esteem, someone like Sidney, Watson, Greene, Marlowe, or Fraunce? In three of the poem's four stanzas, the pivotal word is "live" and in the fourth stanza it is implied. Apparently Barnfield chose to write only about living poets. With the possible exception of Abraham Fraunce all his early masters were dead by 1597, the earliest he could have written the "Remembrance." The exclusion of Fraunce may be one more bit of evidence that he was dead long before Hunter's date of 1633, or it may mean only that Barnfield did not consider Fraunce praiseworthy enough for company with Spenser, Drayton, and Shakespeare. Casting about for a poet to lodge in his pantheon of the great, Barnfield well may have hit upon Daniel, who was perhaps at the peak of his fame immediately following the appearance of the *Civil Wars* (1595), who had published in Sidney's *Astrophel and Stella,* who was a member of the Countess of Pembroke's circle, and whose *Complaint of Rosamond* (1592) was in a genre that Barnfield admired and imitated. Significantly enough the works of 1592 and 1595 are those selected by Barnfield for mention. The younger man's predilection for *Mirror* tragedies appears in the fine verse on Rosamond, whereas the line on the *Civil Wars* reads as though the poet had never read the poem:

> And *Daniell,* praised for thy sweet-chast Verse:
> Whose Fame is grav'd on *Rosamonds* blacke Herse.
> Still mayst thou liue: and still be honored,
> For that rare Worke, *The White Rose and the Red.*
> (E₂ᵛ)

Drayton's appearance in the third stanza is easily understood, although the choice of works for which he is elevated—"Trage-dies,/ And sweete Epistles"—should be explained on the grounds that they were recent and would perhaps be recognized more readily by a reader than such pieces as *The Shepheardes Garland, Endymion and Phoebe,*[43] or *Matilda* to which Barnfield had been indebted in *The Affectionate Shepheard.* Throughout the works of Barnfield, Drayton is alluded to four times, more than any poet still living at the composition of the "Remembrance" with the exception of Spenser. If we bring in the dead also, only Sidney and the enigmatic Amyntas receive more attention than Drayton, and for sheer number of times their names appear, they outdo Spenser as well. The fourth stanza of the poem, which increases

---

[43]Perhaps more than any other poem by Drayton, *Endymion and Phoebe* should be cited by Barnfield in the "Remembrance." There is no

the aa bb quatrain of the first three to a six-line conclusion, is
Barnfield's only mention of Shakespeare:

> And *Shakespeare* thou, whose hony-flowing Vaine,
> (Pleasing the World) thy Praises doth containe.
> Whose *Venus,* and whose *Lucrece* (sweete, and chaste)
> Thy Name in fames immortall Booke haue plac't.
> Liue euer you, at least in Fame liue euer:
> Well may the Bodye dye, but Fame die neuer.
>   (E₂ᵛ)

Many scholars, some overenthusiastically, have taken great pains
to show Barnfield's indebtedness to Shakespeare, and certainly
there is a significant amount. Furthermore, all that has been
gathered comes from the poems that Barnfield acknowledges above,
although Sir Sidney Lee has claimed that Barnfield borrowed from
the sonnets as well;[44] but Lee does not give any evidence, and I
have not been able to find any. They had not been published by
1598; and I doubt that Barnfield saw them in manuscript, although that is precisely what Lee argues. Mention of Shakespeare
at all is somewhat incongruous when we remember that Barnfield

---

doubt in my mind that Barnfield imitated lines 993-1010:

> Deare *Collin,* let my Muse excused be,
> Which rudely thus presumes to sing by thee,
> Although her straines be harsh untun'd & ill,
> Nor can attayne to thy divinest skill.
> And thou the sweet *Museus* of these times,
> Pardon my rugged and unfiled rymes,
> Whose scarce invention is too meane and base,
> When *Delias* glorious Muse dooth come in place.
> And thou my *Goldey* which in Sommer dayes,
> Hast feasted us with merry roundelayes,
> And when my Muse scarce able was to flye,
> Didst imp her wings with thy sweete Poesie.
> And you the heyres of ever-living fame,
> The worthy titles of a Poets name,
> Whose skill and rarest excellence is such,
> As spitefull Envy never yet durst tuch,
> To your protection I this Poem send,
> Which from proud *Momus* may my lines defend.
>   (*The Works of Michael Drayton,* ed. J. W. Hebel, I, 155)

Not only is an identical structure, rime scheme, and meter employed but
also a catalogue of poets (in both poems begun by Spenser and Daniel),
each introduced with the verbal formula *and thou* or some variation of it.
    [44]*The Passionate Pilgrim,* p. 32.

was identified with what might be called a rival camp. As a defender of Greene, he may even have disliked Shakespeare. As an imitator-student of Marlowe, he may have been further estranged. Actually, Barnfield's work is curiously free of any real influence from the drama, although Greene and Marlowe were importantly associated with the stage. The younger poet uses, almost exclusively, the pastoral and lyrical expressions of these men, and where he turns to Shakespeare, it is to the lyrical and narrative. With every reason to ignore Shakespeare, Barnfield was of such integrity that he felt impelled apparently to cite a poet whose fame was mounting and whose works he had utilized. Noticeably, Shakespeare comes last in the procession. This is not a place of honor as the concluding couplet might imply. Although these two lines were not separated from the final quatrain, I believe that they were intended as an envoi to the entire poem, and the "you" of line five is plural, encompassing all four men. Shakespeare then is the least of these, and although we might rank them differently, we must not impress our sensibilities upon a poet, writing possibly in 1597 and uninterested in the drama.

"As it fell vpon a Day" has elicited perhaps more commentary than all the other works of Barnfield combined. Called by most critics the poet's best endeavor,[45] it was, along with "If Musique and sweet Poetrie agree," claimed for Shakespeare on the basis of its appearance in *The Passionate Pilgrim*. In 1600, the poem was printed in *England's Helicon* in a truncated version. It is Barnfield's most celebrated poem, whether or not it is his best. The publishing history of "As it fell vpon a Day" is somewhat complicated. Appearing first in the 1598 edition of *Lady Pecunia*, it was printed as by Shakespeare the following year in *The Passionate Pilgrim*. The first twenty-six lines, with no author given, were included in *England's Helicon* as poem number 36. A con-

---

[45]Among those who rank it without equal in Barnfield's other work are G. Saintsbury, W. W. Greg, and C. S. Lewis. Swinburne, in a characteristic effusion, singles out "As it fell vpon a Day" in the course of a general encomion on Barnfield: " . . . our elder Shelley and our first-born Keats; the singer of Cynthia in verse well worthy of Endymion, who would seem to have died as a poet in the same fatal year of his age that Keats died as a man; the first adequate English Laureate of the nightingale, to be supplanted or equalled by none until the advent of his mightier brother," *A Study of Shakespeare* (London, 1880), p. 65.

cluding couplet, unique to the 1600 version, replaced the last
thirty lines of the two other versions:

> Euen so poore bird like thee,
> None a-liue will pitty mee.[46]

"As it fell vpon a Day" was reprinted in all early editions of
Shakespeare's poems, including Malone's first (1780). In his second
edition (1790), Malone omitted the poem, possibly having noticed
it in Barnfield's *Lady Pecunia.* Most subsequent editors of Shake-

---

(ed. Hyder Rollins [Cambridge, Mass., 1929], I, 186-189)
in *Pepys Ballads*, printed about 1620, in which the poem was expanded
into ten six-line stanzas and called "A Louers newest Curranto, or the
Lamentation of a young mans folly." Lines 55 and 56 were omitted and
the following eighteen added:

> First entised by many wiles,
>   and by fortunes fickle smiles:
> Griefe it is my cheefest song,
>   sorrow to me doth belong,
> Still I waite and moane to see,
>   my hard hap and misery.

> When all my money it was spent,
>   no credit vnto me he lent:
> But straight they turnd me out of doore,
>   to beg my bread among the poore.
> Thus fortune first on me did smile,
>   and afterwards did me beguile.

> Wherefore I wish all youthes that see,
>   to take warning heere by mee.
> How that they follow *Venus* trace.
>   feare least they come to great disgrace,
> For she like Syrens will them intice,
>   and afterwards will them despise.

(ed. Hyder Rollins [Cambridge, Mass., 1929], I, 186-189)

Whoever pilfered the song from *Lady Pecunia* apparently read the title
poem as well and fashioned the second stanza above chiefly from stanza
21:

> But if you want your Ladies [Pecunia] louely grace,
> And haue not wherewithall to pay your shot,
> Your Hostis pressently will step in Place,
> You are a Stranger (Sir) I know you not:
>   By trusting Diuers, I am run in Det;
>   Therefore of mee, nor meate nor Bed you get.

(B3^v)

speare give the poem to Barnfield, as did Collier in 1843. However, on May 17, 1856, writing in the *Athenaeum*, Collier reversed his position, muddying the waters for years to come. He reaffirmed his 1856 position in two subsequent editions of Shakespeare (1858, 1878), in an item in *Notes and Queries* (July 5, 1856), in *A Bibliographical and Critical Account of the Rarest Books in the English Language* (1865), and in his reprint of *Lady Pecunia* (1866). Collier's chief argument was that Barnfield did not reprint the poem in question in 1605 because he would not willingly claim what was not his. Several writers took Collier to task—Edmonds (1870), Grosart (1876), Arber (1882) and Dowden (1883)— but Edmonds, the earliest, did all the work that was necessary.[47] First he demolished completely Collier's suggestion that the ode, as it appears in *The Passionate Pilgrim*, was two poems, the first comprising the version found in *England's Helicon*, the second beginning, "Whilst as fickle Fortune smilde." Collier was misled because at this line the *Passionate Pilgrim* poem begins a new page. His argument ignores totally the arrangement in *Lady Pecunia*, which in itself shows Collier's theory to be absurd. Edmonds proceeds with an explanation for the unique couplet which appears in *England's Helicon*:

> "We are driven to the conclusion that the editor of 'England's Helicon,' instead of following Barnfield's publication, where he would have found the ode complete, made use of that in 'The Passionate Pilgrim,' imagining that it terminated, as there printed, at the bottom of the page. But feeling, like most readers, probably, that this ending was too abrupt for the subject, and falling into the same error as Mr. Collier, that the lines on the next page began a new ode, he added the couplet in question as a more appropriate termination.

Edmonds' subsequent points are that Barnfield was too upright to steal the works of others since he repudiated two volumes in the preface to *Cynthia*, since he specifically claimed the works

---

[47]Rollins, in his review of the controversy in the Variorum Shakespeare, attributes several of the chief points of attack against Collier to various critics, to wit: Grosart is responsible for the explanation of the concluding couplet to the *England's Helicon* version and Dowden responsible for the argument that Barnfield also excluded in 1605 the epitaph to his aunt. But both these points, and virtually all others put forward by Grosart, Arber, Dowden, Lee and others were presented first by Edmonds.

in the dedication to Blackleech, and since he eulogized his supposed victim in "A Remembrance of some English Poets." His final point, in two parts, is that the omission in 1605 of the two poems in question cannot be attributed to Barnfield's refusal to keep what was not his, as Collier asserts, since the "Epitaph upon the Death of his Aunt" is excluded also; and the selection of those poems retained was based upon the needs of the publisher to fill up exactly one page and a half.[48]

The suggestion that "As it fell vpon a Day" was two poems remained a dead issue until J. B. Henneman took it up again in 1901. Writing only in terms of wishfulness, Henneman was somewhat mistreated when attacked by H. C. Beeching[49] and summarized by Hyder Rollins.[50] Both these men charged that Henneman categorically claimed the first twenty-six lines, plus the *Helicon* couplet, as Shakespeare's, when all that Henneman wrote was "One is almost tempted to wish that the evidence in point could render unto Shakespeare what is good enough to be Shakespeare's and unto Barnfield what there is neither question nor disposition to doubt is Barnfield's."[51] Henneman sees two different poems in the ode, not because of the typography in *The Passionate Pilgrim* (Collier's argument) but because "even if the question of authorship be not involved, the composite character and changed conception of the poem are readily seen."[52] Using the faulty Cambridge text, which, upon no authority whatever, prints the ode from *The Passionate Pilgrim* as including the *Helicon* couplet, Henneman believed that the poem had reached a third stage of development by the time it appeared there: the first version would have been a now lost twenty-eight line poem, exactly as it appears in *England's Helicon*; the second version would be Barnfield's, as it appears in *Lady Pecunia*; and the third version would be the imaginary fifty-eight line poem of the Cambridge Shakespeare. All Henneman's theories, however, were exploded by Beeching

---

[48]All the materials taken from Edmonds can be found in pp. xi-xxiv of his edition of *The Passionate Pilgrim*.

[49]"English Literature and American Professors," *The Athenaeum* (May 25, 1901), p. 661.

[50]Variorum Shakespeare, *The Poems*, pp. 557-558.

[51]"Barnfield's Ode: 'As It Fell Upon A Day,' " *An English Miscellany* (Oxford, 1901), p. 163.

[52]Henneman, p. 163.

in a rather nasty attack upon "American Professors," and we may
now hope that the matter is laid once and for all.

"As it fell vpon a Day" is second to "Nights were short" as
a successful lyric. The disparateness between the first twenty-six
lines and the last thirty, as they appear in *Lady Pecunia*, cannot
be overlooked. While there may be no break in sentiment, meaning, or intention, there is assuredly a diminution in skill. The first
part of the poem is dramatic, made up of a single concrete image,
and unified. The second part is didactic, broken up into a series
of weak images, and dispersed. But to explain these facts with a
theory of dual authorship or even to find Shakespeare the sole
author of the whole poem is to ignore all the other work of Barnfield. He had shown himself capable in *The Affectionate Shepheard*
of juxtaposing arresting lyric poetry with the most earthbound
didacticism. He had shown the ability to write verse of the level
of "As it fell vpon a Day" in such lines as "Nights were short"
and in isolated stretches in all three volumes. He had toyed with the
Philomela legend in at least three other poems (*The Aff. Shep.*,
"Nights were short," and *The Complaint of Poetrie, for the Death
of Liberalitie*). Few critics remember these facts. Two writers,
especially, seem to think that, though Barnfield wrote the first
part, he was not capable of arriving at such fine lines, haunting
meter, and charming images by himself. Charles Edmonds, with
no asperity whatsoever, brings back the ghost of Amyntas: "One
of Watson's odes bears so great a resemblance in its commencement
to that of Barnfield's poem, 'As it fell upon a day,' published eight
years afterwards, that I cannot resist the temptation of calling
attention to it. It is a Birthday Ode to Queen Elizabeth, written
probably in the May of 1590:—

> 'This sweet and merry month of May,
> While nature wantons in her pryme,
> And byrds do sing, and beasts do play,
> For pleasure of the joyfull time,' &c."[53]

Sidney Lee, with greater heat, suggests a different source: "There
was a crude sort of justice in the attribution of Barnfield's verse
to another. Thoroughly well read in contemporary poetry, Barnfield had already shown himself an unblushing plagiarist. His
popular ode beginning 'As it fell upon a day' secretly levies heavy

---

[53]*The Passionate Pilgrim*, p. xxx. As I pointed out, p. 57, footnote
14, the poem may be by William Byrd.

loans on a poem by a little-known versifier, Francis Sabie. In his
'Pan his Pipe: conteyning three pastorall Eglogues in Englyshe
hexameter; with other delightfull verses' (London. Imprinted by
Richard Jones, 1595, 4to) Sabie opens his volume thus:

> It was the moneth of May,
> All the fields now looked gay,
> Little Robin finely sang,
> With sweet notes each green wood rang;
> Philomene, forgetfull then
> Of her rape by Tereus done,
> In most rare and joyfull wise
> Sent her notes unto the skies:
> . . . .
> Fish from chrystall waves did rise
> After gnats and little flies:
> Little lambs did leape and play
> By their dams in medowes gay."[54]

Henneman, incidentally, thinks that Shakespeare was the inspirer
and molder in his song from *Love's Labour's Lost*:[55]

> On a day (alacke the day)
> Loue whose month was euer May
> Spied a blossome passing fair,
> Playing in the wanton ayre.
>   (IV. iii. 106-109)

With all these suggested sources for "As it fell vpon a Day,"
one or more of these writers must be wrong. Lee jumps several
lines in order to quote "Little lambs did leape and play," hoping
to show that Barnfield's "Beastes did leape, and Birds did sing"
originated with Sabie. But by that very token did not Sabie's line
come first from Watson's "And byrds do sing, and beasts do play"?
Beeching, who cites the poem for other reasons, inadvertently
brings in another possibility when he invokes Breton's

> In the merry month of May,
> In a morn by break of day
> Forth I walked by the wood-side,
> Whenas May was in his pride.

This poem was sung as early as 1591 to Queen Elizabeth during

---

[54]*The Passionate Pilgrim*, pp. 31-32.
[55]Henneman, p. 163.

her entertainment at Elvetham.[56] Does it owe anything to Watson's poem, printed in *The first sett, of Italian Madrigalls Englished* (1590)? Is Sabie indebted to Breton, to whose poem his opening line is closer? or does *Pan his Pipe* go directly back to Watson? What is the relation of all these poems to "On a day (alacke the day)," which may have been written earlier than even Watson's poem, although probably not? These questions are really unimportant, for, clearly, the "May-time" opening in a large number of poems, especially poems written in this distinctive four-beat line, was just as conventional to the Elizabethans as the "April" opening was to Chaucer and the fifteenth century. In this very poem, Barnfield shows he is capable of better lines than the opening eight; he is capable of anything in the lyrical vein that Watson, Breton, or Sabie could write. In fact what he has done in the first eight lines is to take the convention and do it better than anyone else before or since:

> As it fell vpon a Day,
> In the merrie Month of May,
> Sitting in a pleasant shade,
> Which a groue of Myrtles made,
> Beastes did leape, and Birds did sing,
> Trees did grow, and Plants did spring:
> Euery thing did banish mone,
> Saue the Nightingale alone.
>   (E₃ᵛ-E₃ʳ)

Unlike the poems of Watson, Breton, and Sabie, "As it fell vpon a Day" presents a sorrowing shepherd as well as a sorrowful nightingale. It is the bird, remembering her tragedy, that gives the poem its pathos and its best lines:

> *Fie, fie, fie;* now would she cry
> *Teru Teru,* by and by:
>
> . . . .
> Senslesse Trees, they cannot heere thee;
> Ruthlesse Beares, they will not cheer thee.
> King *Pandion,* hee is dead:
> All thy friends are lapt in Lead.
> All thy fellow Birds doe singe,
> Carelesse of thy sorrowing.
>   (E₃ʳ)

[56]Beeching, p. 661; *Tudor Poetry and Prose*, eds. Hebel, Hudson, Johnson, Green, and Hoopes (New York, 1953), pp. 165, 1219.

The Philomela myth evokes the king of Troy dead, evokes the nightingale as a kind of ineffectual Orpheus who cannot move the trees and the beasts, and evokes an indifferent nature which continues its happy songs though the mutilated-raped-transfigured girl sings her dirge. At this point the dramatic section of the poem ends and the didactic begins. The remaining thirty lines fit closely the general scheme of the *Lady Pecunia* volume, an attack on the vices that include flattery, avarice, and niggardliness.

The shepherd who comes upon the lamenting nightingale grieves over false friendship. A catalogue on flattery follows: seeming friendship for the wealthy man but abandonment for the unfortunate; service, fawning, pandering, insincere praise if a man's purse-strings are open, disdain if his purse is empty. The conclusion awakes echoes of the male friendship presented in *The Affectionate Shepheard* and the sonnets:

> If thou sorrowe, hee will weepe;
> If thou wake, hee cannot sleepe:
> Thus of euerie griefe, in hart
> Hee, with thee, doeth beare a Part.
> These are certaine Signes, to knowe
> Faithfull friend, from flatt'ring foe.
> (Eₐᵛ)

Barnfield, at the end of the second day's lamentation of *The Affectionate Shepheard,* appended a didactic lesson completely out of keeping with the attempt at seduction of a young boy. In the ode, didacticism forms the bulk, and male attachment a brief digression. It is perfectly possible that the ode was written several years before the publication of *Poems: In diuers humors* and is one of the "fruits of vnriper yeares." As such it would place one of Barnfield's best productions contemporary perhaps with *The Affectionate Shepheard* and would be a poem of considerable merit for a youth of twenty or less.

The four remaining poems, the final four of Barnfield's career as a poet, are relatively undistinguished. Three are in fourteeners, the best of these being the epitaph to Sidney, and one is a single rime royal stanza, the "Comparison of the Life of Man" that was retained in 1605. The first of the poems in fourteeners contains all the faults of that rambling meter. The line, too long usually under the best of conditions, should be broken up with more than a single strong caesura in each line, and the iambics should be varied to avoid the pitfall of sing-song; but Barnfield's poem "Written, at the Request of a Gentleman, vnder a Gentle-womans Picture" not only fails in five of its six lines to get a caesura of any strength at all, it also employs in one couplet triple feminine rime to add to the too-regular cadence:

> Even as *Apelles* could not paint *Campaspes* face aright,
> Because *Campaspes* Sun-bright eyes did dimme *Apelles* sight:
> Euen so, amazed at her sight, her sight all sights excelling,
> Like *Nyobe* the Painter stoode, her sight his sight expelling,
> Thus Art and Nature did contend, who should the Victor bee,
> Till Art by Nature was supprest, as all the worlde may see.
>   (E₃ᵛ)

Excessive repetition in so short a poem suggests that this piece was a very early attempt. It is very much like the fourteeners in "Sonnet I" and, in its word play, like the hexameters in "Sonnet VII," both of *Greenes Funeralls*. If it were not probable that the poem is a piece of juvenilia, one might suspect that Barnfield didn't like the gentleman for whom he wrote the piece, nor the gentlewoman, nor the painter. The poem is so bad its author would hardly offer it to a friend or present it as a tribute to a lady he admired. As for the painter, the ambiguity (unconscious, I suspect) of the final line is not very flattering.

The lines to Sidney are more successful, although they were written probably at about the same time as the previous poem. They carry also echoes of "Sonnet VII" in *Greenes Funeralls,* which was written before 1594 and possibly as early as 1592. Similarities in cadence and in matter to the elegy written for Sidney, beginning "Silence augmenteth grief, writing encreaseth rage" are apparent as well. Given by some to Fulke Greville, by others to Sir Edward Dyer, the poem was appended to Spenser's *Astrophel* (1595), but had appeared earlier in *The Phoenix Nest* (1593). Whether Barnfield could have seen it any earlier than 1593 must depend on the date of his arrival in London and the speed with which he became associated with the remains of the Sidney circle, then gathered about the Countess of Pembroke. Judging on the basis of his relationship with Watson or Fraunce or both, I believe it is highly possible that Barnfield might have seen the poem in manuscript. The older epitaph's second line seems echoed in Barnfield's first:

Stald are my thoughts, which lou'd, and lost, the wonder
of our age.
* * * *
That *England* lost, that Learning lov'd, that euery mouth
commended.
(E₄ʳ)
and the older's fourth line in Barnfield's seventh:

Enrag'd I write, I know not what: dead, quick, I know
not how.
* * * *
Belov'd, bewaild; aliue, now dead; of all, with Teares
for euer.
(E₄ʳ)
These correspondences are very slight it must be admitted; the
real nature of the former's influence is on the cadences throughout.

The last of these three poems in fourteeners can be dated
with some certainty. A funeral elegy upon the death of his aunt,
Elizabeth Skrymsher, it was, I assume, composed reasonably close
in time to her death, which came on October 14, 1594.[57] The manner throughout is very close to that in the epitaph on Sidney,
although veneered with greater sentimentality. One couplet,
though little more than cliché or folk-wisdom, carries some slight
strength and grace:

He [Death] spareth none: both rich and poore, both young
and olde must die;
So fraile is flesh, so short is Life, so sure Mortalitie.
(E₄ʳ)
The poet liked one of the lines so well that he used it again with
little variation in the lines "To his Mistresse" prefacing *Cynthia*:
"A President of modest Life, and peerlesse Chastitie" (E₄ʳ).

Barnfield concludes the book with a single stanza in rime
royal, the best of the final four poems. Based on a life-feast metaphor, it raises an interesting question:

Mans life is well compared to a feast,
Furnisht with choice of all Varietie:
To it comes Tyme; and as a bidden guest
Hee sets him downe, in Pompe and Maiestie;
The three-folde Age of Man, the Waiters bee:
Then with an earthen voyder (made of clay)
Comes Death, & takes the table clean away.
(E₄ᵛ)

---

[57]Grosart, *The Complete Poems*, p. xlv.

In 1595 were published the posthumous works of the Jesuit priest Robert Southwell. In *St. Peter's Complaint*, Southwell included "I Dye Alive," a poem not using the life-feast metaphor in any extended sense, yet nevertheless employing this couplet:

> My feast is done, my soule would be at ease,
> My grace is saide, O death! come take awaye.[58]

Barnfield, who shows familiarity with Tichbourne's elegy, could possibly have gotten interested in the verse of other Catholics, thereby reading the poems of Southwell. Southwell is thought to have known about the Babington plot, although opposed to it. He may even have known Tichbourne since it is clear he was acquainted with some of the other conspirators.[59] Barnfield, caught up in vigorously assailing the Catholics (witness his attack on the Pope in *Lady Pecunia*), may well have read the opposition.

The most notable feature about Barnfield's third volume is its Spenserian orientation. For many years now the history of the followers of Spenser has been written, omitting Barnfield from its pages, but perhaps no figure among them all was any more indebted (perhaps no one quite so much) to that master poet of the age than Barnfield. In *Cynthia*, the young poet recorded his imitativeness, and primarily the debt is to the *Faerie Queene*, especially its stanza form; but in *Lady Pecunia*, in which the reliance upon the poems of Spenser is everywhere evident and the levies are made from a wider body of Spenser's poems than merely the *Faerie Queene*, Barnfield has remained silent; and none of his editors or critics have realized the extent to which he travels under Spenser's aegis: the psuedo-encomion that may have been suggested by Spenser's version of *Virgil's Gnat*, the pastoral elegy that owed so much to the October and November eclogues, the *débat* that took its allegorical nature from Spenser's House of Alma, and the two tributes to Spenser in *Poems: In diuers humors* far outweigh the employment of verse form in *Cynthia*, the continued service to Elizabeth, which Barnfield seems to have copied from his master, and the general tone of many verses throughout "Cassandra" that echo the smooth metrics and linguistic ease of all the great poet's

---

[58]*The Complete Poems of Robert Southwell*, ed. A. B. Grosart (London, 1872), p. 84.

[59]See Christopher Devlin, *The Life of Robert Southwell: Poet and Martyr* (New York, 1956), pp. 110, 121, 248.

works. Only Drayton, equally early with Barnfield in imitation
of Spenser, owes possibly as much to him. Basse, Giles and Phineas
Fletcher, their lesser followers, and William Browne of Tavistock
are indebted for little more than the structure of the *Shepheardes
Calender* or the stanza of the *Faerie Queene* as well as some general tone and lyrical quality. But even as there is no slavishness in
Drayton, there is a quantity of originality, of newness, of inde-
pendence in Barnfield, especially in *Lady Pecunia*. Every line that
is taken from Spenser or from any other for that matter is en-
dowed with a uniqueness not often found in other poets of the
time. Barnfield's pseudo-encomion is not a translation like Spenser's
nor is it in prose like Nashe's *Lenten Stuffe*. The only thing close
to it in originality and verse is *The Metamorphosis of Ajax*, and
clearly there was no interplay between this work and Barnfield's.
The Complaint of Poetrie, though a pastoral elegy, is unique in
that the lament is not for a mortal but rather for the death of
patronage. I do not know of another piece like it in the entire
sweep of English literature. *The Combat, betweene Conscience and
Couetousnesse* is also unique in its age in that it combines the
debate with the allegory of the castle of the body. The shorter
poems of the fourth section are all conventional, but several of
these exhibit also a quality not usually met in Elizabethan poets,
that is the unselfish and wide praise of fellow poets. I do not think
another poet can be found whose list of colleagues praised will
equal Barnfield's in the few short pages of *Poems: In diuers
humors*: Spenser (twice), Dowland, R. L., Chaucer, Gower,
Surrey, Sidney (twice), Gascoigne, King James, Daniel, Drayton,
and Shakespeare. Generosity is not among the least of the virtues
in a poet.

CHAPTER V

DOUBTFUL PIECES

As for many poets, there is for Barnfield a body of poetry that has been ascribed to him doubtfully. In its entirety it is not a very large accumulation: twelve pieces in the Isham MS., printed by Grosart in his edition of the complete poems; six pieces in *The Passionate Pilgrim,* in addition to "If Musique and sweet Poetrie agree" and "As it fell vpon a Day," that have been claimed principally by Sidney Lee to come from Barnfield's pen; and a few scattered occasional pieces that one critic or another has fostered upon Barnfield. I exclude purposely from this consideration any mention of *Greenes Funeralls,* which is the subject of another chapter. Most of these pieces are held to be the work of Barnfield only upon the flimsiest evidence, and not even the most sanguine of the claimers for Barnfield belabor the case.

Perhaps the Isham MS. should be examined first. It contains the largest number of pieces and includes at least one to which the poet's name is appended. Charles Edmonds mentioned the discovery of the MS. among papers found at Lamport Hall in the nineteenth century. He called it "evidently the production of Barnfield, as his name, thus, *Richard Barnfild,* occurs on one of the pages."[1] Six years later, Grosart published the manuscript in its entirety, and it could be seen that Barnfield's name was appended to the verses that dedicated the 1605 *Lady Pecunia.* I have not seen the manuscript and must report it through the eyes of Grosart:

> It is a small paper book of eighteen leaves within a vellum skin, which seems a leaf of a Latin treatise. There is one leaf blank, and on the *verso* of the next the Latin lines on Tarquin and Lucrece begin; and so onward on other [*sic*] ten leaves—the last on one side only. The remainder is blank.
>
> . . . .
>
> The Isham MS. seems to us to vary in the dates of its handwriting, but to be all, or nearly all, from one. Yet there are carelessnesses of writing that make one doubt that it was a copyist following a somewhat puzzling original MS. rather than the Author himself. The Lines to Sir John Spenser have the name

---

[1]*The Passionate Pilgrim,* p. xxiv.

"Rich Barnfild" so very neatly executed that it seems no great risk to pronounce it his autograph.[2]

These assertions must seem very daring to the modern scholar. One would like all the newer techniques of watermark, ink, and handwriting analysis to be applied before making even the most general statements. No signature of Barnfield is extant; his will is subscribed with only a monogram, and its character is such that it tells us very little, if anything at all, of the poet's hand. Barnfield's name following the lines to Spencer may be only the copyist's indication of authorship *for that piece alone*. Three other pieces are variations of known works by Chidiock Tichbourne, Ben Jonson, and Ovid. Suspicion is cast therefore upon any theory of single authorship of the rest. Why are not the lines to Spencer the sole representation of Barnfield's work? Little in these pieces belongs to the realm of external evidence. Style and content, at times very untrustworthy yardsticks, are, most often, all we have to go by. Playing by ear then, at first, I feel that six of the eight pieces unaccounted for have no ring of Barnfield at all: two deal with love between woman and man, a topic he never wrote upon in his printed work; two comprise a poem in denigration of the office of wifehood and its answer, again a subject of no interest to the poet; the remaining two are comic pieces, one on a loose and diseased woman, the other on a secret ritual, both not Barnfield's usual concerns. Of the two pieces that coincide with his interests as well as his talents, one can be proved not his, the other suspected.

---

[2]*The Complete Poems*, pp. xxxiii-xxxiv, 200. Isham MS. is also described in Report No. 3 of The Historical Manuscript Commission (London, 1872), p. 253, by Alfred J. Horwood, whom Grosart chides for inaccuracy. Horwood claims that Barnfield's name appears at the end of the manuscript, certainly giving more support to an overall authorship than its appearance following the lines to Spencer; but since Grosart calls particular attention to this point, I believe that we can accept the critic's description as correct. I can wonder only then on what grounds Grosart is willing to give the entire volume, with the exception of the known poems of Tichbourne and Jonson, to Barnfield. Horwood begins his description of the MS. as follows: "A duodecimo volume, paper, c. 1600, contains extracts from the poems of Richard Barnfeld [*sic*] and other poets." On what authority Horwood uses the plural *poems* I do not know, but I suspect that he was familiar with the pronouncements of Edmonds who wrote two years earlier. Then, as in so many of these cases, a tradition had been started, and it was an easy thing for Grosart to perpetuate it.

But these initial impressions can be corroborated or corrected by more minute inspection.

First is a five-line piece in Latin, four lines of which come from Ovid's *Fasti*, II, 771-774. The fifth line I cannot identify:[3]

> Tarquinius viso Lucretiae gestu, haec secum absens reuoluit.
> Sic sedit, sic culta fuit: sic stamina mouit:
>   Neglectae collo sic iacuere comae,
> Has habuit vultus, haec illi verba fuerunt:
> Hic color, haec facies: hic decor oris erat.
>   (Grosart, p. 201)

The final four lines are perfectly accurate except in line two, where *mouit* should read *nevit* and line four, where *Has* should read *hos* and *vultus* should read *voltus*. The first line, which is not from Ovid at all, seems to be the transcriber's attempt to supply a reasonable introduction to the lines which follow. It is, in fact, a very loose paraphrase of Ovid's own introduction to the description of Lucrece:

> carpitur adtonitos absentis imagine sensus
> ille. recordanti plura magisque placent.[4]
>   (769-770)

Although the *Fasti* is not known to have been translated in any printed version during Shakespeare's lifetime, it is usually conceded that *The Rape of Lucrece* is indebted to lines 721-852 of Book II. Barnfield's knowledge of *The Rape of Lucrece* and even his imita-

---

[3]All quotations from the Isham MS. will come from Grosart's reprint in *The Complete Poems*, pp. 201-220. About the Latin lines Grosart wrote (p. xxiv), "It is impossible to say whether the Latin (incomplete) lines on Tarquin and Lucrece are original or extracted. Perchance he [Barnfield?] sought to celebrate the incident that Shakespeare had just made imperishable. There is a snatch of grace in the wording." Sir Sidney Lee identified the four lines from Ovid, although he gave the impression that four lines were the complete entry in the Isham MS.: "The first page gives, without indication of its source, a Latin quotation from Ovid's *Fasti*, ii. 771-4, which describes Tarquin's admiration of Lucrece's beauty. Shakespeare's poem of *Lucrece* no doubt suggested to Barnfield the transcription of these lines" (*The Passionate Pilgrim*, pp. 44-45). We can see that although Lee adds the source which Grosart did not know, yet he takes over completely Grosart's belief that the MS. is all Barnfield's work and the belief that Shakespeare's *Lucrece* prompted the copying.

[4]*Fasti*, ed. Sir James G. Frazer, Loeb Classical Library (London, 1931), p. 112.

tion of several lines has been documented amply. If Barnfield had copied this Latin, it may indeed have been because of interest in Shakespeare's poem, but he had a stake of his own in the works of Ovid. The prayer at the conclusion of *Lady Pecunia* intimates that Barnfield knew Ovid's *Nux*. The constant reference to Latin works, the claim that *The Affectionate Shepheard* imitated the Second Eclogue, the affixing of a Latin tag to the title page of every one of his works argues that he read widely in the classical writers. But all this is to play the devil's advocate. I do not believe that Barnfield transcribed the lines, and all the arguments that pertain to him might fit another as well. The owner of any commonplace book may have been moved by Shakespeare's *Lucrece* to seek out the source and copy a portion of it. Especially would this be true if he were a Latinist of Barnfield's quality.

The second piece, something of a shocker, is in prose. It is the longest inclusion, taking six pages in Grosart's edition. Whoever copied it was given to extreme abbreviation, in some places shortening words so greatly as to leave in doubt their meaning. It has the look of a piece never intended for general perusal, the transcriber expecting to be able to decipher his own speed-writing, while not caring particularly whether anyone else could. It is entitled "The Shepherdes Confession," and Grosart says of it that it "so runs parallel with 'The Affectionate Shepheard' and other pastoral pieces as to assert its originality. (Cf. The enumerated possible 'gifts," II. St. vii-xvii. &c.) There are regrettable touches in it."[5] I do not know whether Grosart understood fully what he was dealing with and mentioned the "regrettable touches" as a clue or whether his nineteenth-century Victorian mind was simply too pure to see that the entire work, from first to last, is an elaborately constructed piece of pornography. It is not direct, like Nashe's *Choice of Valentines,* but hidden behind many of the established Elizabethan subterfuges, the contemporary euphemisms and slang evasions that cover bawdy intent. I reproduce the work here, since Grosart's edition is rather hard to come by, in order that it may be compared to Barnfield's known work and a decision rendered upon its authorship:

The Shepherdes Confession.

To thy shrifte (greate chaplen of the familie of loue) coms yͤ passionat shephard of the westerne playnes to confes his faultes & to

---

[5] *The Complete Poems,* p. xxxiv.

offer sacrifice for his offences. I haue loud, a fool y^t I was & haue obtained. fy blab y^t I tell but trustinge to thy secresy let me open that thinge ye w'tting wherof is the greateste contente in loue. when in the blominge of my youth & in the florishinge time of the yere I first tooke vpō me ye charge of a shepherd, Phillis my fath^{rs} neighbo^{rs} Daughter draue likewise her fath^{rs} flocke. at noone time as it often happens a monge vs shepherds I to a void the heate of the sonne vsed to w^{t}hdraw my self to a foūtaine springinge in he^r sheepgate where beinge my custome to meete her as on[e] day vnder ye couerlet of a rocke wh're gazing on ye cristall streame, in the watry glas, she did see the shadowe of Bellin my rañe how he was moūted one the yeaw to p'forme the duty of marra^{d}g. She asked me what the rañe did. I said he got on the yeaws backe to discrie if on the the [sic] hedge were any better food (& holy preist let me confesse my faulte) I then spake as I thought but ye wily Phillis p'cevying my simplicity turnes her head and smiles as if her countenance should say what a foole is this. But longe she had not remaynd thus when on the leaues of a marygolde she saw a busy bee gathring hony. Willie saith shee for so am I cald, shall I be thy bee & sucke thy hony of thy lips? By the cleerenes of her posicons I hauinge my vnderstandinge now erected replied yee Phillis so y^t like ye marigold y^u wilt only to my bright beames ly open. O the crafte of women, how putly vpon my wordes did shee frowne & turne a way. I affeard of her displeasure said sweet Phil why looke yo^u from me? haue I offended. Dere then turne those eys nay fix them vpon me soe shall the flames thereof in burninge me be iust punishers of mine offence. Wth y^t I wold haue initated [sic] the gras where on we lay by clasping her in my armes but she t'ninge aside, espies my iuory pipe, and as women delight in faire thinges & yet through theire natures couetousnes doe rather take then giue, so now to make p'fit of her anger, she told me by no meanes I shoud enter acquaintance againe vnles franckly and freely I would giue her my white pipe. I made answer y^t giue it I could not but if she would lay the browne mazer her mother gaue her to my whistle vpon any wager I would try the venter. wee a greed & ye bargaine was who in runinge should firste come to the bush at ye bottom of the hill, he should haue the prize. we set forwarde & step for step, stroke for stroke she kept w^{t}h me nay was often times before me till drawinge neere y^e marke she begane to fainte & speechles fell downe. I whose mind was more on takinge her vp then on winninge the wager imployed my strength to y^e thrusting of her vp againe. This kindnes of mine in shewinge, I neglected my profit in comparisō of her suer footing did so deeply p'ce [=pierce] her as shee thought it not enough to giue me y^t curious wrought mazer confessinge it to be mine as woñe by maine speedines but w^{t}h all shee pñted it me replenished w^{t}h a most reviving liquo^r. I not to seeme defectiue in curteous bounty gaue her my pipe. She refusd the p'p'ty [=property] & only craued y^e vse of it to chere vp her spirites when she was in her melancholy dūps. Phi: said I if you returne me my pipe yet it is yo's at commaund and as for yor mazer since it is houshold stuf & y^t I am no huswif I p^r thee take it home againe but sweet Phi keepe it neatly. only I desire you woldst bringt a

feild adayes, y^t when through heat I shall grow thirsty w^{t}h the liquo^r
thereof I may 'alay my drought. Thus for y^t time we p'ted & often since
to ye high delightfull quenchinge of my most furious flames out of y^t
iolly polished mazor haue I caroused. But here is my misfortune, for this
offence I come now to aske p'done, my fair tressed Ph amonge other of
her delightes kept shut vp in a cage a bird called a wagtaile. him she fed
w^{t}h her owne hand, him she stroked, him she plaid w^{t}hall. I cominge on
a time to this cage & pittying to see y^t poore foule in capitiuitie wch was
free by the laws of kind vnpent the cage dore & out flue the bird. Ph:
findinge her play fellow gone & y^t through my falte, O hils O downs
into what arage was shee driuen. I was the man y^t invied her content,
twas I y^t had bereaud her of her morninges thought, he^r repose at euen
her make [=mate] by day and he^r valiant gûid by night, so y^t trans-
ported w^{t}h this tempestuos passion away she flinges from me & neu^r sinc
cold I regaine her fauo^r. how often sinc haue I sued for grace by crown-
inge those lañs w^{t}h garlandes wch I knew to be her fauorites. how often
haue I brought her a robbin^6 redbreste & told h^r y^t although he be sullẽ
[=sullen] & sollitary, yet is he a most kind & faithful bird, how often
haue I p^{r}sented her y^e nighting gale wth this commend'con y^t he vseth to
sleepe wth a pricke at his breste, and yet she scornes my guiftes & wth
despitfull thretninge makes answer to my passionat intreatinges y^t vnles
I find her lady bird againe I must neu^r vēter to come in her p'ñc. I haue
so wandered the woodes & made so many a tree brāchles for ye search of
this wagtaile as now beinge not able to wag any further, I am com vnto
thy shrine sinc she will not here me, to confes my greuos fault & offer
sacrifice for ye sinne. If my oblacon be of force to moue thy spirit, to
fore tell me I shall recou^r my La: bird againe who shalbe more bounde to
thy holynes then thy, poore shephard Willie? But if my offence haue
not merite[d] such fauo^r as to say ye truth what can he deserue in y^e
sight of loue, who hath wilfully lost his wagtaile yet accept this sacrifice
wch I bringe vnto thee. This viall wch I offer is a viall of teares wch I haue
wept for my los wch eydew being but small in quantity because ye glas
is but little & britel, may as a misticale relik be kept in thy temple to
shew maidens should not greue to much for the los of so brikle athinge
as is virgins maiden head. Holy father I haue cōfesse[d] all I attend
thine absolution.

(Grosart, pp. 203-208)

I do not see that this piece runs parallel to *The Affectionate
Shepheard* or any other pastoral piece by Barnfield. Grosart's
selection of stanzas 7-17 of the second day's lamentation as comparable to the gift offerings in "The Shepherdes Confession" is
far afield. Willie does not offer the pipe as a gift at all; he will

---

^{6}For the use of *Robin* as a phallic euphemism see Harry Morris,
"Ophelia's 'Bonny Sweet Robin,'" *PMLA*, LXXIII (Dec., 1958), 601-
603.

lend it only. In *The Affectionate Shepheard* a shepherd's pipe is
not one of the many gifts offered to Ganimede. Stanza 7 of Barnfield's poem and stanza 13 offer the boy a "Robbin red-brest" and
a "Nightingale" respectively; but these birds are selected in "The
Shepherdes Confession" for their bawdy connotations. They can
hardly be left out since the dominating pun is based on a bird
called a "wagtaile." Although Barnfield is perfectly capable of a
bawdy pun, and employs a bee-flower image in a pederastical
double-entendre,[7] the robin and the nightingale have no such
significance in the passages cited by Grosart. What makes it most
difficult to accept "The Shepherdes Confession" as Barnfield's is
its detailed interest in heterosexual love. Barnfield nowhere in
his known works shows the slightest interest in the ladies. Furthermore, the prose of "The Shepherdes Confession," while in some
places very vigorous and attractive, show a lack of continuity and
a logic that I find incompatible with Barnfield. Despite the lapses
in Barnfield's logic that I have demonstrated elsewhere, there is
nothing comparable to the confusion of pronoun, sex, ownership,
and situation as that which is found in "The Shepherdes Confession." Finally, although this may be a rather weak argument, the
naming of the shepherds is inconsistent with Barnfield's usual
practice. "The Shepherdes Confession," using the first person pronoun, seems like a private autobiographical pleasantry. Barnfield
throughout his work has identified himself as Daphnis. One would
expect that if he were the author of "The Shepherdes Confession,"
whether it were only for his own eyes or even for extremely private
circulation among his friends, he would continue under the pastoral name with which he was identified. Nashe did not hesitate
in the *Choice of Valentines* to call the hero Thomalin. Furthermore, for Barnfield to call the shepherdess Phillis, a very common
name in many of the pastoral productions of his age, is improbable. Where he had a choice to make, he selected the rather unlikely
Guendolena. Among his own friends, Phillis had been established
as the pastoral guise for Amyntas' lady, and in *Greenes Funeralls*
he followed the fashion. If he had any respect for Amyntas, and it
is clear that he had a great deal, he might have felt that to use
Phillis in a work such as "The Shepherdes Confession" would be
insulting.

    The third entry in the Isham MS. is prose also. Grosart sees

---

[7]See p. 40.

it as "satire on the ceremonial of contemporary knighthood, which was then venal honour."[8] Quite brief, it seems pointless enough without some larger ritual to which it may have been attached. There is a bare possibility, owing to the reference to a candle as a thief in the fourth, and to the nature of the piece which precedes it, that a bawdy double meaning was intended here also:

> Euery knight of ye order of ye Snuffe shall be well prouided in tearmes concerninge ye candle, as hauinge occasiō to bid one light ye candle he shall say incense ye candle, for puttinge him in to ye candle sticke, aduance him into his throwne, for snuffing of ye candle he shall say reforme ye candle, for takeinge away ye theefe, assiste ye candle, for fastninge him into ye socket establish ye candle, for stickinge of flowers adorne ye candle; and if he be taken a way by ratts or mice, he shall say, he is taken prisoner, if he be gnawne he shall say he is indented.
>
> (Grosart, p. 209)

Barnfield's authorship of this entirely pedestrian piece must be rejected. First it is to be doubted that the poet would be interested in this sort of ridicule, and second he has shown himself to be infinitely more clever than the handling of the above shows its author to be. There is no wit, no charm, no felicity to any part of "ye order of ye Snuffe," and Barnfield, whenever he writes light materials—the verse of "Hellens Rape" or *Lady Pecunia,* the prose addresses to the reader, prefacing his last two volumes—is witty, deft, and entertaining. I do not think even that the author of the second prose piece in the Isham MS. is the same as the author of the first. Spelling and punctuation are superior in the shorter entry; vigor, gaiety, and freshness mark the longer.

The fourth entry is Tichbourne's elegy and the fifth a heartless answer. Grosart writes about the elegy that there are "noticeable variations from the common text."[9] He was using Hannah's edition of the "Courtly Poets," which reprints the version found in *Reliquiae Wottonianae.* Both Hannah and Grosart were unaware apparently of the black-letter quarto, *Verses of Prayse and Ioye, written upon Her Maiesties Preseruation* (1586), published the year of Tichbourne's execution. If we compare the Isham elegy with the 1586 version, we find an amazing accuracy of transcription, with only spelling, punctuation, stanzaic separation, and

---

[8]*The Complete Poems,* p. xxxiv.
[9]*The Complete Poems,* p. xxxiv.

line indentation differing between the two.[10] Immediately following the elegy in *Verses of Prayse and Ioye* is a poem almost identical to the answer in the Isham MS. as Grosart prints it. Line five reads *shadowed* for Grosart's *shadow;* line nine *hath nipt* for Grosart's *haue impte;* line eleven *though* for *thowth.* I suspect that in every case, with the possible exception of *shadow* the difference can be explained by the difficulties of making out the Elizabethan hand. The replay in *Verses of Prayse and Ioye* carries the title "Hendecasyllabon T. K. in Cygneam Cantionem Chidiochi Tychbourne." Thomas Corser suggests that the initials may be Thomas Knell's, a quondam writer of attacks upon the Roman Catholics.[11] Beyond a reasonable doubt, Barnfield knew Tichbourne's poem. There are echoes of it in "The second Dayes Lamentation of the *Affectionate Shepheard*":

> Why is my Summer season almost done?
> My Spring-time past, and Ages Autumne gone?
> My Haruest's come, and yet I reapt no corne:
> My loue is great, and yet I am forlorne.
> (B₄ʳ)

And the tares-seed-garden-weed image is used in *Lady Pecunia* in a passage attacking papist infection of Protestant England:

> Some tares are sowne, amongst the choicest seed:
> No garden can be cleansd of euery Weede.
> (C₂ʳ)

Furthermore, an echo from Southwell in the "Comparison of the Life of Man" indicates that Barnfield was interested in the Catholic issue. But the appearance of the answer to Tichbourne in the 1586 pamphlet makes it impossible to attribute to Barnfield the Isham reply, even in the face of these correspondences; and a good object lesson is learned on attributing too facilely works to an author merely on the basis of recurrent imagery, phraseology, or structure patterns.

Some comment must be made upon Grosart's failure to mention that Hannah, immediately following Tichbourne's elegy, printed a reply that has so many features in common with the

---

[10]In line seven Grosart prints *harde* for *hearde*, which makes little sense and is unquestionably either a mistake in the Isham copyist or a mistake in Grosart's reading of his hand.

[11]*Collectanea Anglo-Poetica*, Part X (1880), pp. 336-338.

Isham reply that one must have come from the other or both must have had a common source. Hannah states that his text comes from a MS. which belonged to John Payne Collier, a fact disturbing in itself. Hannah's text is divided into three six-line stanzas, and the final stanza corresponds to the last six lines of the Isham poem, with only minor variations:

> Thou sought'st thy death, and found'st it in desert;
>   Thou look'dst for life, yet lewdly felt it fade;
> Thou trodd'st on earth, and now in earth thou art;
>   And men may wish that thou hadst ne'er been [made];
> Thy glory and thy glass are timeless run,
> Which, O unhappy! by thyself was done.[12]

While not one of the first twelve lines of Hannah's text is the same as its opposite number in the Isham MS., still it is apparent that one set of lines developed out of the other. Since the versions of both poems in the Isham MS. are identical with the 1586 printing in *Verses of Prayse and Ioye*, it is reasonable to assume that the versions in Hannah, both out of MS. collections, were later corruptions, altered during the passage of time. For Grosart not to cite the answer in Hannah argues that either his eagerness to attribute the poem to Barnfield made him blind to what was brief for Barnfield's authorship of all the pieces unattributed to before him or he suppressed the information as damaging to his others. Apparently Grosart must have been tried sorely in this decision, for he writes that the reply is "harder and harsher than at this softened distance we can approve." But desiring the MS. for Barnfield more than a gentle reputation for his poet, Grosart suggests that "The Author's patriotic love for the great Queen explains his passionate retort."[13]

At this point in the MS. the legend "Incerti Authoris" appears, and although Grosart prints it in his text, he calls no attention to, has no comment whatever upon it in his introduction or notes. Surely these words cast serious doubt on single authorship for the seven unidentified pieces. In this section the Jonson poem appears as well as the known Barnfield lines. But the first two entries constitute another poem-and-answer set:

---

[12]*The Poems of Sir Walter Raleigh, with Those of Sir Henry Wotton and Other Courtly Poets*, ed. J. Hannah (London, 1892), p. 116.
[13]*The Complete Poems*, p. xxxiv.

Wife.

The double V, is double woe
The I, is nought but ielosie
The F, is fawninge flatterie
The E is nought but enmitie.
Thus V wth I, wth f, wth E:
Brings nothinge els but miserie.

Answere.

Is double V such double woe
Speake of no more then that you knowe.
Tis weale, tis wealth, and nothing soe
I, Joye is, not iealosie.
F fauor is, not flattery.
E is true loues eternytie.
      Thus, V, wth I, wth F, wth E
      well consterd is felicitie.

                              (Grosart, pp. 213-214)

Grosart professes to have seen the "Wife" in several MSS., where it appears anonymously, "but nowhere it is believed the 'Answer.' "[14] Grosart thus would claim the "Answer" for Barnfield. I cannot imagine why he would want to do so, nor can I imagine Barnfield capable of the doggerel quality and the sentiment of these lines. Barnfield in defense of marriage is the poet in a role most unlikely.

The lines to Sir John Spencer create some insurmountable problems. I do not believe a single poem in the Isham MS., other than these lines, belongs to Barnfield. Where did these lines come from? They could not have come from the 1605 *Lady Pecunia* since there are not only several variations in the brief eight lines of the stanza but also the identification of the dedicatee is not to be found in the printed version. Whereas the copyist of "The Shepherdes Confession" seemed most careless, the copyist for all other pieces, illustrated by his perfect reproduction of Tichbourne's elegy and its answer, was a very accurate transcriber. In those two poems there is not a word altered probably in thirty-six lines. Why, in the brief eight lines of the dedication to Spencer should four words be changed? Does the printed poem come from the Isham MS., the altered words representing later revisions by the poet? Such is a possibility I cannot subscribe to, for I cannot see Barnfield composing this stanza in a commonplace book I take not to

---

[14]*The Complete Poems,* p. xxxiv.

be his own. Especially unlikely is the address to Spencer, for it
has no validity in a commonplace book. In fact, the whole stanza
is a strange inclusion:

> To the right Wor^{ll} Sir John Spenser Knighte
>   Alderman of the honnorable Citty of
> London and lorde treasurer of Lady pecunia.
> Led by the swifte reporte of winged fame,
>   with golden trumpet soundinge forth your name,
> To you I dedicate this merry Muse
> And for my Patron I your fauor chuse,
> She is a woman shee must be respected
>   Shee is a Queene she must not be reiected
> This is the shaddowe you the substance haue
>   Which substance nowe this shaddowe seems to craue.
>   Richard Barnfild
>   (Grosart, pp. 214-215)

It cannot be admired for its poetic value, although it may be said
that quite a few of the pieces in the Isham MS. can hardly have
been copied out for their beauty. It is the promise of a larger piece,
but what that piece may be is not very clear. Lady Pecunia is
mentioned in the address to Spencer, but not clearly as the subject
matter of a poem. The two feminine pronouns in lines five and
six must remain equally puzzling. The only reason a person might
have for copying it might be for its wit. If the copyist saw it in
conjunction with the poem it was meant to preface, he might
appreciate the humor of the final couplet. The conclusion to which
I come, although with considerable doubts and fears, is that both
the 1605 printed stanza and that in the Isham MS. come from a
common third source.

All this theorizing leads to the rejection of the name under
the poem as Barnfield's signature. I take it to be merely the copyist's identification of the author of some lines to which he took
a peculiar fancy; and I suspect that part of the fancy involved
the copyist's personal familiarity with Sir John Spencer, either
as an acquaintance or as a public figure well known to him through
municipal activities. Such familiarity would explain the inclusion
of the address, otherwise meaningless. If, therefore, Barnfield did
not enter the lines to Spencer in the Isham MS, we may not claim,
along with Grosart, that the alderman-knight is the dedicatee of
the 1605 *Lady Pecunia*. Barnfield's lines may have been intended
for almost anyone.

The ninth poem is the only other piece in the volume that, on the basis of its poetic qualities, is even faintly suggestive of Barnfield. Apart from Jonson's epitaph and Tichbourne's elegy, it is the only other accomplished poem in the manuscript. It has a certain subtlety of phrase, not unlike Barnfield's, and an evenness of meter that we have come to expect from this poet. The six-line stanza is his usual medium:

> There is a thing y^t much is vsd
> tis caulled loue, by men abusd:
> they write and sigh and sweare they die
> when all is done they know they lie,
>   but when they sweare by faith & troth
>   ile sweare they care not for an othe.
> They firste muste haue a mistress faire
> and then a fauor for to weare
> and then they go to flattries skoole
> and call her wise they knowe a foole
>   but let them sweare by faith and troth
>   ile sweare they care not for an othe.
> It is a practise in this age
> to lay theire creditts vnto gage,
> by wit by vowes by neate attire
> to conquer that they most desire
>   but let them sweare by faith and troth
>   ile sweare they care not for an othe.
>   (Grosart, p. 216)

Although he is fond of the sestet, Barnfield, with only one significant exception,[15] never uses the aa bb cc rime scheme employed here. Furthermore, despite Barnfield's addiction to the rhetoric of repetition, he does not employ refrain in any of his acknowledged volumes, although the third poem in *Greenes Funeralls* works upon a final couplet refrain in a manner not unlike the above. The poet here assumes the persona of a woman, something which, again, Barnfield never does; and the whole poem takes on an air of courtly love, a convention he eschews completely. In the final analysis, though the poem is good enough to be Barnfield's, though it has touches commensurate with his talents, I do not believe the poem to be his. Grosart writes that it "has a familiar sound; but just now we cannot recall any prior copy of it."[16] I suspect that if anyone ever traces it to its owner it will prove to be

---

[15]The dedicatory stanza to Nicholas Blackleech.
[16]*The Complete Poems*, p. xxxiv.

either from the first or second age of courtly makers, but from a group no later than Gascoigne. If it were not for the extreme regularity of its numbers, I would suggest Wyatt himself.

The tenth poem is headed simply "Epitaphium," but is immediately recognizable as Jonson's "Epitaph on S[alomon] P[avy] A Child of Q. El[izabeth's] Chappel." Grosart calls it a "not very correct copy."[17] There are considerable differences from the 1616 Folio and differences also, though fewer, from Ashmolean MS. 38, the only other text which the Herford and Simpson *Ben Jonson* collates. Since the child was buried on July 25, 1602,[18] the poem could not have been entered in the Isham MS. before that time. This date suits well with the dedication to *Lady Pecunia,* either as an entry immediately prior to publication in 1605 or at any time after. However, there is no necessity to assume that the epitaph was written into the Isham MS. before the appearance of the Jonson Folio in 1616. Apparently whoever kept the commonplace book was either captivated by pieces from the distant past, such as the Tichbourne poem (1586) or moved to make entries very sparingly, copying the Tichbourne poem and answer in 1586 but possibly not entering the Jonson epitaph until 1616 or even later. For our purposes this adequately brackets all possible dates and situations pursuant to the 1605 *Lady Pecunia* dedication.

Of the eleventh poem Grosart refuses to take notice, other than to print it as a responsible editor:

> A lustie nutt browne wench scant woorth ye naminge
> went downe a staier bearinge a candle flaming:
> A swagering gallant comming her t'encounter
> att first approache couragiously would mount her:
> Shee strongly made resistaunce and did sweare
> she would burne him by that candle she did beare:
> He blew ye candle out to breake her vowe
> she kept her promise still, immagine how.
> (Grosart, p. 219)

The subject matter of this poem, which was offensive apparently to Grosart, was unlikely to be of interest to Barnfield. Although the meter is smooth and regular, as Barnfield's would be, the narration moves forward much more directly than is usual in his

---

[17]*The Complete Poems*, p. xxxiv.

[18]*Ben Jonson,* ed. C. H. Herford and Percy and Evelyn Simpson (Oxford, 1952), VIII, 27.

hands. Comparing this piece to the lines to Spencer shows that in
the eight lines of Barnfield's known poem four of them, the second,
fourth, sixth, and eighth, are repetitions, variations, embellish-
ments, or flourishes appended to the lines they immediately follow;
this is Barnfield's method; it is his recognizable style; it can be
found on every page of his self-claimed work. The "lustie nutt
browne wenche" is not a meanly constructed poem; its meter,
imagery, and diction are appropriate to its matter; it is witty and
entertaining; but chiefly, and in this completely un-Barnfieldian,
it develops rapidly; and a full episode is told in eight lines, whereas
a much shorter tale would keep Barnfield busy for ten times that.

The final poem in the Isham MS. is a six-line stanza of riming
couplets about which Grosart writes that it is an epigram "of the
type of Sir John Davies' and Henry Hutton's":[19]

> Sweete hart to deale trewly I loue thee not much
>   disdaininge to serue thee thy kindness is such;
> For why thy demeanor commendeth thee not
>   thy bewty vnpleasing the better my lott:
> Then sweete I assure you ile loue you not more,
>   refusinge to loue you which loued you before.
>   (Grosart, p. 220)

Little need be said that has not been said already about the other
pieces. The matter is not of Barnfield's known concerns; the rime
scheme is one employed in only one stanza in his entire published
works; the general diction and handling are not his.

The arguments that I have marshalled poem by poem against
Barnfield's authorship of any piece in the Isham MS. other than
the lines to Spencer are admittedly all of a tenuous construction
and not to be given too heavy weight in the balance of acceptable
evidence. The correct question to be asked is by what right should
any of these poems even be considered as by Barnfield. Upon the
discovery of the MS. Charles Edmonds rashly put authorship upon
Barnfield merely because his name "occurs on one of the pages."
A. J. Horwood, in the Third Report of the Historical Manuscripts
Commission, perpetuated and added to the misconstruction by
stating that "at the end of the volume is written the name of Rd.
Barnfeld [sic]."[20] Grosart furthers these delusions by suggesting
authorship of individual pieces such as the Latin lines on Lucrece,

---

[19]The Complete Poems, p. xxxiv.
[20](London, 1872), p. 253.

"The Shepherdes Confession," the reply to Tichbourne, and others. All three accomplished this in six short years and so well established their beliefs that in 1905 Sidney Lee asserts confidently that the Isham MS. "contained some previously unprinted poems from Barnfield's pen."[21] And there the matter has stood, when in reality there is not only no shred of evidence to support Barnfield's authorship of the Isham MS. generally but also no good reason to accept the name under the lines to Spencer as an autograph, nor can Spencer be accepted as the dedicatee of the revised *Lady Pecunia*. Rather is it safer to believe that Barnfield had no hand in any of the poems found at Lamport Hall other than that printed over his name.

The second most notorious repository of supposed poems by Barnfield is *The Passionate Pilgrim*. Other than the two poems printed in *Lady Pecunia*—"If Musique and sweet Poetrie agree" and "As it fell vpon a Day"—Sidney Lee finds that six additional pieces may be possibly from Barnfield's pen. For one of these, "My flocks feede not," he has support from other writers. The theory that the author of "As it fell vpon a Day" may have written other poems in *The Passionate Pilgrim* is of reasonably modern invention. Surprisingly enough, although Edmonds, Grosart, and Arber fought generously for Barnfield's right to the sonnet and the ode, the thought that other pieces, unclaimed in *The Passionate Pilgrim*, might be his also never occurred to them. Sidney Lee is the chief architect of the theory, for in only one poem was he anticipated by Grosart. He is by no means forceful in the claim, but in making the suggestion he takes some unwarrantable liberties:

The authorship of these five poems VII, X, XIII, XIV, XVIII, which Jaggard first printed from manuscript, can in the present state of the evidence be matter for conjecture only. It is very possible that they are from Barnfield's pen. Barnfield was a voluminous writer, and not all his verse found its way to the printing press. Much of it circulated in manuscript only, and is still extant in that medium. It is probable, moreover, that much of it was entrusted to William Jaggard's brother John, who printed an ample but by no means exhaustive selection from it in 1598. Barnfield's imitative habit of mind rendered the six-lined stanza, which Shakespeare had glorified in his *Venus and Adonis*, a favorite instrument, and the internal quality of the many six-line stanzas in *The Passionate Pilgrim* justifies the theory that Barnfield was their author, at any rate of those of them that are in a serious vein.[22]

---

[21]*The Passionate Pilgrim*, p. 44.
[22]*The Passionate Pilgrim*, pp. 44-45.

These five poems do not include "My flocks feede not," about which Lee is more certain. They have never been printed elsewhere, although some of them have been found in various MSS., which may contain clues to their authorship.[23] However, Lee's claims must be questioned if only because of the terms with which he makes them. First, that "Barnfield was a voluminous writer" is simply not true. His three volumes, swelled with the additions entered into the 1605 *Lady Pecunia*, with *Greenes Funeralls*, with the Isham MS., were it his, with "My flocks feede not" and the five poems now under discussion, with the few scattered occasional pieces that at times have been suggested as his would not equal three-fourths the number of lines that there are in *Hamlet* alone. Second, that "not all his verse found its way to the printing-press" we do not know. Third, that "much of it circulated in manuscript only, and is still extant in that medium" is a statement based solely, as Lee himself shows in a footnote, upon the Isham MS. To say that "much" of a "voluminous" writer's work circulated in MS. on the basis of the twelve poems in the Isham MS. is less than innocent. Fourth, even if "much" of this verse were entrusted to John Jaggard, how can Lee assert that what was printed in 1598 was "by no means [an] exhaustive selection"? Fifth, the six-line stanza, while Barnfield's favorite vehicle, was probably one of the most common forms of the period. Sixth, the internal quality of these poems does not justify attributing them to Barnfield's authorship. And seventh, anyone familiar with Barnfield's work would not except the lighter poems.

These poems must be considered instead purely on the grounds of their own merit. Without any of the *desiderata* such as Lee has used, we must look at the poems closely and then decide for or against Barnfield's authorship; even then the best that we can say is that this "feels" like a Barnfield poem. Unquestioned acceptance into the Barnfield canon must wait until evidence of a more certain nature is unearthed, if it ever is. Of these five now up for judgment, the first (number VII under the standard editorial assignment, a method of designation I shall follow throughout this discussion) has as fair pretensions as any to be admitted:

---

[23]In Folger MS. 2071.7, once owned by Collier, VII and XVIII are undersigned "W. S."

Faire is my loue, but not so faire as fickle.
Milde as a Doue, but neither true nor trustie,
Brighter then glasse, and yet as glasse is brittle,
Softer then waxe, and yet as Iron rusty:
    A lilly pale, with damaske die to grace her,
    None fairer, nor none falser to deface her.

Her lips to mine how often hath she ioyned,[24]
Betweene each kisse her othes of true loue swearing:
How many tales to please me hath she coyned,
Dreading my loue, the losse whereof still fearing.
    Yet in the mids of all her pure protestings,
    Her faith, her othes, her teares, and all were ieastings.

She burnt with loue, and as straw with fire flameth,
She burnt out loue, as soone as straw out burneth:
She fram'd the loue, and yet she foyld the framing,
She bad loue last, and yet she fell a turning.
    Was this a louer, or a Letcher whether?
    Bad in the best, though excellent in neither.[25]

Only Lee has claimed this poem for Barnfield; only Montague
Summers has rejected it.[26] All other editors of Barnfield have
simply not considered the poems in *The Passionate Pilgrim* other
than to claim the two printed in *Lady Pecunia*. In addition to the
stanza form, which Lee has commented upon, the devices of
rhetoric which abound in this poem are among Barnfield's reper-
tory. The first stanza is constructed upon a series of antitheses,
wherein the first half line is opposed by the second half. No poet
delights in this sort of word play more than Barnfield (cf. especially stanzas 37-52 of "The second Dayes Lamentation of the
Affectionate Shepheard"). The entire poem employs feminine
rime, except for lines seven and nine, and this rime is, in lines five
and six, deployed over two words: *grace her, deface her*. Barnfield

---

[24]Compare this line to "Cassandra," Stz. 13, line 4: "Conioyning oft
her Corrall lips to his."

[25]*The Poems*, A New Variorum of Shakespeare, ed. Hyder Rollins
(Phila., 1938), p. 280. All citations from *The Passionate Pilgrim* come
from this edition.

[26]*The Poems of Richard Barnfield* (London, 1936), p. ix. A limited
edition of 500 numbered copies, Summers' text is virtually useless since
it was printed from Arber's edition, perpetuating the errors in that text
and compounding many new ones. His interest in the poems in *The
Passionate Pilgrim* is cursory only, obviously not including any real
concern over authorship. He states merely, "Number 7, 'Fair is my love,'
is of unknown authorship."

has exhibited great partiality to feminine rime, both when employing only a single word and also when using two. The first stanza
as well as the third is given to imperfect rime: *fickle, brittle;*
flameth, burneth; framing, turning, an irregularity that Barnfield
does not take particular pains to avoid. In the second stanza of
VII, still another rhetorical device favored by Barnfield is employed with somewhat less than his usual skill: the selection in a
single line of the key words of several preceding verses: *faith,*
othes, teares, which were the burden of lines six, seven, and eleven.
Compare with this stanza, both for style and for content, the
thirty-fourth of *The Affectionate Shepheard*:[27]

> But if thou wilt not pittie my Complaint,
> My Teares, nor Vowes, nor Oathes, made to thy Beautie;
> What shall I doo? But languish, die, or faint,
> Since thou dost scorne my Teares, and my Soules Duetie:
> And Teares contemned, Vowes and Oaths must faile;
> For where Teares cannot, nothing can preuaile.
>
> (B₃ʳ)

Finally, in the third stanza, Barnfield's inescapable anaphora is used
with great skill. External evidence in favor of Barnfield's authorship, for what it is worth, may include William Jaggard's publication of both *The Passionate Pilgrm* and the 1605 *Lady Pecunia*
and his brother's publication of the 1598 *Lady Pecunia,* giving the
family a chance, perhaps, to lay hands on Barnfield material.[28]
Also of interest is Lee's contention that a song by Greene in
Perimedes the Blacke-Smith (1588) "anticipates" VII both in its
first half line and in its content: "Faire is my loue for Aprill in

---

[27]See also for similar stanzaic rhetoric the sestet of "Loe here behold
these tributarie Teares," *Aff. Shep.,* Gʳ.

[28]E. E. Willoughby, *A Printer of Shakespeare,* p. 49, writes that
when William Jaggard published *Lady Pecunia* in 1605, possibly he left
out "As it fell vpon a Day" and "If Musique and sweet Poetrie agree"
because he had published them as Shakespeare's in 1599. Similarly, since
it is so clear that publishers frequently had more work belonging to an
author than they subsequently published, it is possible that when John
turned over to William the job of reprinting *Lady Pecunia,* he handed
over also several poems that had never made their way into the 1598
edition, and William, looking for materials to fill out *The Passionate*
Pilgrim seized upon unprinted work of Barnfield as readily as he had
appropriated the two printed pieces. But this is not to support Lee's
theory of voluminous productivity on Barnfield's part or widespread
circulation of unpublished works. No more than two poems to half a
dozen need be involved.

her face." Barnfield's interest in Greene and his indebtedness to an occasional lyric such as "Ah what is loue" has already been illustrated.[29] But the evidence against Barnfield's authorship is of equal weight. The poem celebrates heterosexual love, and I cannot stress too often that not once in this poet's acknowledged verse is there found such love. Barnfield is more careful with his rhetoric. In stanza two there is not an exact equivalence between *faith, othes*, and *teares* of the last line and the corresponding lines preceding. In stanza three the rime scheme alters to aa bb cc, a lapse that I have not found Barnfield guilty of elsewhere. With the exception of the subject matter, the other deficiencies might be accounted for by the nature of publication. Jaggard, who cared very little for the proprieties of the stationers' trade, his own calling, could hardly be expected to care for the accuracy of his galleys. Quite obviously no author got near any of the work published in *The Passionate Pilgrim*, and all the generally shady, corrupt, and conniving practices required to print such a book would hardly contribute to impeccable copy. When all is said, conjecture must leave the matter thus: no poem sounds or feels more like Barnfield, but Barnfield never dealt with such a love.

Again, X has only Lee's advocacy as Barnfield's, and only Summers rejects it, both operating on the same plan as for VII. It deserves serious consideration on the grounds that the sex of the beloved addressed is ambiguous:

> Sweet Rose, faire flower, vntimely pluckt, soon vaded,
> Pluckt in the bud, and vaded in the spring.
> Bright orient pearle, alacke too timely shaded,
> Faire creature kilde too soon by Deaths sharpe sting:
>   Like a greene plumbe that hangs vpon a tree:
>   And fals (through winde) before the fall should be.
>
> I weepe for thee, and yet no cause I haue,
> For why: thou lefts me nothing in thy will.
> And yet thou lefts me more then I did craue,
> For why: I craued nothing of thee still:
>   O yes (deare friend] I pardon craue of thee,
>   Thy discontent thou didst bequeath to me.
>   (Rollins, p. 286)

All commentators on this poem either imply tacitly or state explicitly that the beloved is a woman, but there is no clear evidence for such an assumption. On the contrary, the vocative "deare

---

[29]See Chapter II, p. 25.

friend" suggests otherwise. Another Barnfield touch is the use of parenthesis. As for the two Elizabethan usages of *vaded* and *For why*, Barnfield, in common, it is true, with many another writer, has used them at will, especially *for why*, which in a hasty perusal I came upon six times in the collected works. All in all, I do not think the evidence is strong enough for a decision either way. There is a general quality of delay, incremental repetition, and rhetoric about the lines that sounds like Barnfield; but when one moves back and reads them through, as a unit, any touch of Barnfield tends to lessen if not to disappear altogether.

Like VII, XIII has all the rhetorical devices of which Barnfield and, it must be admitted, many another Elizabethan are so fond. In XIII, however, the correspondences are kept more faithfully than in VII, a correctness which Barnfield is careful to observe:

> Beauty is but a vaine and doubtfull good,
> A shining glosse, that vadeth sodainly,
> A flower that dies, when first it gins to bud,
> A brittle glasse, that's broken presently.
>   A doubtfull good, a glosse, a glasse, a flower,
>   Lost, vaded, broken, dead within an houre.
>
> And as goods lost are seld or neuer found,
> As vaded glosse no rubbing will refresh:
> As flowers dead, lie withered on the ground,
> As broken glasse no symant can redresse.
>   So beauty blemisht once, for euer lost,
>   In spite of phisicke, painting, paine and cost.
>   (Rollins, p. 291)

There seems to be an alteration in the order in line five, but the change is maintained in line six. The correspondence to the first four lines is found in the initial four of the second stanza. The poem should be compared with the final stanza of "The Complaint of Chastitie":

> For what are Pleasures but still-vading ioyes?
> Fading as flowers, brittle as a glasse.
>   (G3^r)

Lee cites four possible analogues to XIII, which he finds in Greene's *Alcida*, in J. C.'s *Alcilia*, in a sonnet of Surrey's in Tottel, and in A. W.'s "An invective against love";[30] but none are in any way as close as these lines from Barnfield. Of the five poems in *The Passionate Pilgrim* which Lee alone gives to Barnfield, XIII seems to have the best claims, but it must be reaverred that none of these speculations can reach to certainty.

In XIV may be seen the dangers of arguments such as those gotten together for the analysis of VII, X, and XIII. Much of the rhetoric that I have used almost as touchstones for Barnfield is employed in XIV, although not so densely. Parentheses, feminine endings, and the lazy pace of Barnfield are all evident. But, in its entirety, the poem is so little like Barnfield that to reproduce it here would be to waste the space. Apart from tone, style, language, and spirit, which are not Barnfield's, the poet's eagerness to be with a woman is so great, so marked, that on such a score alone it may be rejected.

My feelings about XVII are much the same, but so much controversy has arisen over "My flocks feede not" that it cannot be dismissed summarily. Still I cannot understand how any student such as Grosart, who read Barnfield closely, could claim the poem for him. Excuse can be made for those editors of Shakespeare—Lee, Neilson, Porter, Brown, and Kittredge—who were led astray by the poem's appearance in *England's Helicon,* where it preceded "As it fell vpon a Day," which carried as a heading the legend, "Another of the same Sheepheards." But for Grosart to fall into the trap argues his eagerness to attribute poems he admires to poets he is attempting to rehabilitate. He prints it *"for the first time"* (p. 196 ff.) as Barnfield's, and he alone is responsible for the attribution. The pity is how many other commentators adopt Grosart's reasoning, which is this:

> Like "As it fell vpon a day," as it appears in E. H. "The Vnknowne Sheepheards Complaint" is signed Ignoto; but seeing that "As it fell vpon a day" is known from other sources to be Barnfield's, its heading, *"Another* of the same Sheepheards,"* enables us to redeem "The Vnknowne Sheepheards Complaint" for Barnfield. This is done *for the first time,* but it is clear that the somewhat ill-informed editor of "England's Helicon" (John Bodenham?), though for the moment unaware (or uncertain) of the authorship of either, did know that both belonged to the same Author.
>
> (*The Complete Poems,* p. 196)

The error in this reasoning has been pointed out by Rollins, who cites two other instances in *England's Helicon* (poems 121-122 and 145-146) in which *another* is used, but the works involved

---

[30]*The Passionate Pilgrim,* p. 41.

are known to be by different authors. Rollins concludes, "There is no reason whatever to assume that he [the editor of *England's Helicon*] knew anything about the author: by *the same shepherd* he meant, of course, not Barnfield but the anonymous author of the *Passionate Pilgrim* version."[31] I cannot see that this formalized and scholarly rejection is necessary. To my ear "My flocks feede not" is nothing like any Barnfield poem I know:

My flocks feede not, my Ewes breed not,
My Rams speed not, all is amis:
Loue is dying, Faithes defying,
Harts nenying [*sic*], causer of this.
All my merry Iigges are quite forgot,
All my Ladies loue is lost (god wot)
Where her faith was firmely fixt in loue,
There a nay is plac't without remoue.
  One silly crosse, wrought all my losse,
  O frowning fortune cursed fickle dame,
  For now I see, inconstancy,
  More in women then in men remaine.

In blacke morne I, all feares scorne I,
Loue hath forlorne me, liuing in thrall:
Hart is bleeding, all helpe needing,
O cruell speeding, fraughted with gall.
My shepheards pipe can sound no deale,
My weathers bell rings dolefull knell,
My curtaile dogge that wont to haue plaid,
Plaies not at all but seemes afraid.
  With sighes so deepe, procures to weepe,
  In howling wise, to see my dolefull plight,
  How sighes resound through hartles ground
  Like a thousand vanquisht men in blodie fight.

Cleare wels spring not, sweete birds sing not,
Greene plants bring not forth their die,
Heards stands weeping, flocks all sleeping,
Nimphes blacke peeping fearefully:
All our pleasures knowne to vs poore swaines:
All our merrie meetings on the plaines,
All our euening sport from vs is fled,
All our loue is lost, for loue is dead,
  Farewell sweet loue thy like nere was,
  For a sweet content the cause of all my woe,
  Poore Coridon must liue alone,
  Other helpe for him I see that there is none.
      (Rollins, p. 304)

---

[31]Variorum *Poems*, p. 552.

Metrically "My flocks feede not" is different from Barnfield's never varying practice; he is an iambic poet, except for the early experiments in hexameters. In addition there is an irregularity that is uncharacteristic of Barnfield, which cannot be charged solely to a corrupt text. Stanzaically the highly varied abcb ddee fghg[32] is a complex and lengthy form with which Barnfield never worked. He is drawn to the simpler couplet or six-line ababcc, although he often uses rime royal. The content is not Barnfield's usual offering despite the pastoralism; and the illogic of the second stanza is uncharacteristic. The shepherd calls himself Coridon, an improbable switch for the poet who always wrote under the name of Daphnis. This poem was very popular, having appeared in Thomas Weelkes' *Madrigals* (1597) and *England's Helicon* as well as *The Passionate Pilgrim* in printed versions and in at least one MS. (Harleian 6910, f. 156); Lee adds that it "was constantly copied in 'private' commonplace books."[33] It has many pleasantries as well as some really lovely lines such as the opening quatrain of the final stanza; and one feels that much of the confusion of the second stanza, which caused Swinburne to wonder whether the shepherd's affliction were "idiocy or lunacy"[34] would disappear if an authoritative text could be found. Grosart and Summers labored to claim the poem for Barnfield, and I can sympathize over some lines especially, but neither the felicities nor the drawbacks of a poem should influence the analyst unless these goods or evils are his man's trademarks. The poem simply does not belong to Barnfield.

The final poem under question in *The Passionate Pilgrim* is XVIII, and only Lee is its supporter. The difficulties in attributing this poem to Barnfield are so numerous as to make the task overwhelming. For a rehearsal of the features of the poem—its dating, its provenance, its relation to *Willobie his Auisa*—the student is directed to Rollins;[35] and since there is nothing about it that smacks of Barnfield—its content, its meter, its style, its tone—it will receive no further attention here.

Of the six poems in *The Passionate Pilgrim*, none can be given to Barnfield without danger: the first three—numbers VII, X,

---

[32]The third stanza varies in the final quatrain: fghh.
[33]*The Passionate Pilgrim*, p. 34.
[34]*Forum* (Oct., 1891), p. 173.
[35]Variorum *Poems*, pp. 308-315, 553-554.

XIII— remain distinct possibilities; the last three—numbers XIV,
XVII, XVIII—can be rejected with some degree of safety. A final
word about *The Passionate Pilgrim* problem may be said in rebuttal
of Montague Summers, who, though he claims no more than XVII
for the man he is editing, concludes that "much in *The Passionate
Pilgrim* shows the influence of Barnfield, and indeed is in no small
measure directly derived from him." Summers' purpose seems to
be to establish the "high esteem in which Barnfield was held by his
contemporaries."[36] But it is wrong to do so on invented grounds.
The poems in *The Passionate Pilgrim* are no more or no less imitated from Barnfield than Barnfield imitated others. He has been
charged with excessive borrowings, but he is no guiltier (if that
is the word) than his contemporaries. We are learning more and
more that, in respect to poetry, the Elizabethan age was an age of
convention, that there were source books of rhetoric and form,
that well-defined groups and movements organized themselves
about a few powerful literary personalities; these developments put
upon the entire body of Elizabethan lyric verse a shimmering
cloak of conformity, and it becomes impossible almost if not
gratuitous to find where poetic debts were owed, where literary
credits originated.

Barnfield, like many other writers, has had works attributed
to him merely because his initials corresponded with those subscribed to works identified in no greater measure. Concluding an
account of Barnfield in his *Bibliographia Poetica*, Joseph Ritson
directs us to an entry under "B. R.":

> B. R. wrote "An epitaph upon the death of the worshipfull
> maister Benedict Spinola, merchant of Genoa, and free denizen
> of England, who dyed on Tuesday the 12 of Julie 1580:" a
> broadside, in 22 four-line stanzas; printed by Thomas East: also
> "The plowmans complaint of sundry wicked liuers, and espe-
> cially of the bad bringing-vp of children:" printed for Hugh
> Corne, 1580, 8vo. See Barnfield.[37]

The implication that Ritson wants us to grasp without actually
committing himself is that Barnfield wrote these two pieces. This
mistake is not grotesque, as it might seem, when we learn from
the introduction to his book that Ritson did not see all the works
he wrote about and when it becomes clear that he did not know

[36]*The Poems*, pp. xi-xii.
[37](London, 1802), pp. 119, 124-125.

the date of Barnfield's birth.[38] Since the poet was only six years old at the time of publication of this trivia, we can reject them with good conscience.

In 1871, "the latest editor," as Grosart puts it, confused, as I am, over the editorial arrangement of Thomas Warton's *History of English Poetry,* revised that year by W. C. Hazlitt, tried to add to Barnfield's canon some encomiastic verses prefatory to Verstegan's *Restitution of Decayed Intelligence* (1605).[39] Grosart rejected the attempt as an outrage, and appends a retort that might serve in so many of these cases: "why single out one of at least half-a-dozen 'R. B.' contemporary pieces of the same kind that might be produced?"[40] Grosart could have explained also that Barnfield, whom he knew to be a strong anti-papist and whom he thought to be the author of a "hard and Harsh" response to Tichbourne, would never have supported the writings of a Catholic convert like Verstegan. In all probability the initials at the close of these very pedestrian verses belonged to the printer, Robert Bruney; it was a common practice for the shop owner to provide commendatory verse, especially when other writers were lacking: to wit, T. T.'s eulogies prefixing Barnfield's own *Cynthia.*

For all his warning against initial seeking, Grosart is the next scholar to do so. In his edition of Nicholas Breton (1879), he suggests that two four-line stanzas introducing the "Characters Vpon Essaies, Morall and Diuine" (1615) and signed "R. B." are by Barnfield. Sometime later, he appears to have gotten a different idea, for in his notes he thinks they belong to Richard Braith-

---

[38]But what excuse can be found for Bliss, the later editor of *Athenae Oxonienses* (London, 1813), I, 684, who perpetuates the suggestion in a similar manner, though well aware that Barnfield was born in 1574.

[39]Thomas Warton, *History of English Poetry,* ed. W. Carew Hazlitt (London, 1871), IV, 439-440. Although Hazlitt is the editor, he includes many notes and comments by a battery of scholars and critics; there is no adequate identification of many of the newly added materials.

[40]*The Complete Poems,* pp. iii-iv. This statement might bring in the whole issue of *Orpheus His Journey to Hell* (1595), which puts another R. B. on the scene, an R. B. whom no one has ever claimed to be Barnfield. Rather he is the still unknown author of a work which some scholars have identified as the book that Barnfield repudiated in the preface to *Cynthia.* It has since been shown that *Orpheus His Journey* was not entered in the Stationers' Register until after publication of *Cynthia.*

waite.[41] The stanzas awake no echoes of Barnfield, and it is to be doubted that he would have come out of literary retirement as late as 1615 only to comment on another poet, a man with whom, incidentally, there is no evidence he had any acquaintance whatever.

The last of these suggestions comes from Mr. Wilfred Paul James; in an unpublished dissertation he writes, "it is possible to suggest still another of Barnfield's friends—Robert Tofte."[42] This conjecture James bases on the letter appended to *Laura* (1597), which is signed R. B., and on the claim of Tofte that Thomas Watson was "a *quondam* kinde Acquaintance of mine."[43] But this evidence is so slight and the letter so unlike Barnfield's prose epistles prefacing *Cynthia* and *Lady Pecunia* that it is unwise to make so strong a statement as James's. I would think also that it is totally unlike the lackadaisical Barnfield to have gotten mixed up in a publishing venture such as the letter describes. Furthermore, *Laura* was printed by Valentine Simmes, a bookman with whom Barnfield never had the slightest dealings. If Barnfield had undertaken to get a friend's works published without that person's knowledge, it is to be expected that he would go to one of his own publishers or printers: Danter, Gubbin, Newman, Lownes, Shaw, or Jaggard.

Of all the doubtful works that have at one time or another been ascribed to Barnfield, then, it is safe to reject all but *Greenes Funeralls* and three poems from *The Passionate Pilgrim*: numbers VII, X, and XIII. Most other claims are extremely far-fetched; even these four pieces must remain under question.

It might be objected that I am implying little or no verse that Barnfield wrote was kept out of print entirely or failed ultimately to get into one of his collections. That is not my purpose. Actually there are several indications that he wrote other pieces which never saw print. The dedication to Blackleech which tells of "fruits of vnriper yeares" does not mean that all he had written before was going into *Poems: In diuers humors;* the eight poems

---

[41]*The Works in Verse and Prose of Nicholas Breton,* ed. A. B. Grosart, Chertsey Worthies' Library (Edinburgh, 1879), II, 2, 4, 54.

[42]*The Life and Works of Richard Barnfield: A Critical Study,* Dissertation, Northwestern University (Evanston, 1952), p. 30.

[43]See *The Works of Michael Drayton,* ed. J. W. Hebel (Oxford, 1941), V, 42.

have the flavor of being a selection from a larger body of diversi-
fied forms and subject matter. The two prose prefaces to *Cynthia*
and *Lady Pecunia* respectively print epigrams which Barnfield
tells us he had written at another time and in another place. Surely
there must be additional verse of this sort that failed to make its
way into a preface or some other form of print. And finally, in
the thirteenth stanza of "The second Dayes Lamentation of the
Affectionate Shepheard" Barnfield made this interesting claim:

> I haue a pleasant noted Nightingale,
> (That sings as sweetly as the siluer Swan)
> Kept in a Cage of bone; as white as Whale,
> Which I with singing of *Philemon* wan.
>   (C^v)

Is there anything autobiographical to this note? Such a possibility
exists, although no work on Philemon has been turned up. Thus
I do not mean to imply by rejecting the poems discussed in this
chapter that Barnfield never authored anything other than the
poems in his three volumes. Rather I strongly believe otherwise:
that there must be a large body of verse that he wrote but which
never saw print. It is difficult to believe that a young man who
had published three volumes by his twenty-fourth year wrote no
more, either in preparation for his public career or thereafter. I
want only to avoid careless attribution on flimsy evidence, and I
cannot go further than I have in the pages of this chapter.

CHAPTER VI

GREENES FUNERALLS

On February 1, 1593/4, there was entered in the Stationers' Register for John Danter a "Copie vnder thandes of bothe the wardens a booke intituled GREENE *his funeralles*."[1] It was published sometime during the same year as by "R. B. *Gent.*" The volume seems quickly to have disappeared from sight until 1802, when mention of it was made by Joseph Ritson in his frequently inaccurate *Bibliographia Poetica*. He attributed it to Richard Barnfield. In a paragraph that incorrectly describes and dates *The Affectionate Shepheard*, Ritson writes, "[Barnfield] is, likewise, suppose'd [*sic*] to be the 'R. B. gent.' who publish'd 'Greens funerals in xiv sonnets,' London, 1604, 4to. but of which there was probably an earlyer edition."[2] Since Ritson errs elsewhere, we can assume that he was wrong about the date. His speculation that there might have been an earlier edition was no doubt a belief that a defense of Greene in 1604 would have very little interest. But what provided Ritson with Barnfield's name as the author will, at this distance, no doubt never be ascertained. Was it a guess? Was there some now lost information (He uses the word *suppose'd*—his own supposition or someone else's)? Whatever the explanation, I find the matter a bit of uncanny magic, for it is certain that Ritson never had in his possession copies of *The Affectionate Shepheard* or *Cynthia* against which to compare the style and content of *Greenes Funeralls*.

Since Ritson's guess, only two other men have been put forward as possible authors of the pamphlet. In 1865 Collier conjectured that Barnabe Rich was the man, and in 1929 Charles Crawford maintained implausibly that the initials R. B. were the subterfuge of a very busy fellow named Nicholas Breton.[3] McKerrow, in the only edition of *Greenes Funeralls* since its publication, argues convincingly against Barnabe Rich on the three-fold

---

[1] *Transcript*, ed. Edward Arber (London, 1875), II, 644. The only copy extant is in the Bodleian.

[2] (London), pp. 124-125. He dates *The Affectionate Shepheard* 1596 and calls it a book of sonnets.

[3] *Bibliographical Account*, I, xvii; and "*Greenes Funeralls*, 1594, and Nicholas Breton," SP, Extra Series, I (1929), 1-39.

grounds that Rich's attitude towards Greene in another pamphlet was such that he was not likely to have defended him in *Greenes Funeralls*, that if Rich were a friend of Greene's, Nashe would not have mauled him as he did in *Haue with you to Saffron-Walden*, and that Rich, an ardent Protestant, would not have allowed the printer to insert in a volume of his two sonnets by the hated papist Stanyhurst.[4] Crawford's plea for Breton is so far-fetched as not to merit a rejoinder. The case for Barnfield, however, is not won by default. Several writers, though they offer no substitute, reject Barnfield because they find the pamphlet too poor for his skill.[5] There is also the serious impediment occasioned by Barnfield's renunciation of two unidentified works that some of his contemporaries tried to father upon him:

> vndeseruedly (I protest) I haue been thought (of some) to haue been the authour of two Bookes heretofore. I neede not to name them, because they are two-well knowne already: nor will I deny them, because they are dislik't; but because they are not mine. This protestation (I hope) will satisfie th'indifferent: & as for them that are maliciously enuious, as I cannot, so I care not to please.
>
> (*Cynthia*, A₈ʳ)

These are difficult words to get around, and yet I am convinced that Barnfield is the author of *Greenes Funeralls*. McKerrow supports a similar belief by arguing that Danter may have been responsible for affixing the initials, for expropriating a *few* pieces of Barnfield's and publishing them without the author's knowledge, and for eking out the rest of the pamphlet with other fugitive poems lying around his shop: Stanyhurst's and perhaps even Danter's own. McKerrow concludes that Barnfield "could hardly be blamed for attempting to dissociate himself altogether from the pamphlet, which was indeed a credit to no one concerned."[6] To this might be added the serious consideration that *Greenes Funeralls* was not one of the two books that Barnfield was repudiating. I have argued this elsewhere at length, but it bears repeating that Barnfield was not the kind of man who would

---

[4] *Greenes Newes*, etc., p. viii.

[5] These include Dyce, *The Dramatic Works of Robert Greene* (London, 1831), I, cxi; Collier, *The History of English Dramatic Poetry* (London, 1831), I, xxviii; and Charles Crawford, "*Greenes Funeralls*," p. 1.

[6] *Greenes News*, p. x.

deny a work that was "a loyal defense of a dead man calumniated."[7] The claim that *Cynthia* was his "second fruits, *The affectionate Shepheard* being the first" (*Cynthia*, A³ʳ) can be explained as his ignoring a work published "contrarie to the Authours expectation" (*Greenes Funeralls*, A³ʳ). It was a poor work, and as long as no one else brought it up, he would try to forget it; but if one of the two books charged to him was *Greenes Funeralls*, I cannot believe that he would so far disown a onetime loyalty as to reject it. It does not appear likely that we shall ever know the names of the two books disavowed.[8]

But these arguments are answers only to negative evidence without producing anything positive. The best way to establish Barnfield's authorship is through a study of each of the twelve unclaimed sonnets (numbers 13 and 14 being Stanyhurst's) and comparing them on the basis of style and content with the known works and with the poet's life. McKerrow's positive evidence consists solely of reemphasizing the initials, of calling attention to "the great similarity between the English hexameters of sonnet vii and the verses in the same meter entitled 'Helen's Rape,' " and of citing several instances of anaphora, a "figure of which Barnfield seems to have been particularly fond."[9] Only the second of these holds up when it is McKerrow himself who shows that the initials R. B. are also prefixed to *Orpheus his Journey to Hell* and when he gives only two instances of anaphora, hardly enough to prove a thesis. But the evidence can be added to on every page. The printer for *Greenes Funeralls*, John Danter, is the same man who printed *The Affectionate Shepheard* later the same year. It is not entirely impossible that Danter had on his hands a considerable number of Barnfield's poems. They may even have lain in his shop since sometime late in 1592, at which time *Greenes Funeralls* is thought by some scholars to have been written. Although any pamphlet that had to do with Greene at all was highly marketable, for some reason Danter did not cash in on *Greenes Funeralls* immediately after the poet's death. By early 1594, the interest in

---

[7]"Richard Barnfield, 'Amyntas,' and the Sidney Circle," *PMLA,* LXXIV (Sept., 1959), 323-324.

[8]*Orpheus his Journey to Hell,* once suggested along with *Greenes Funeralls,* has long been rejected since it was not entered in the Stationers' Register until six months after the publication of *Cynthia.*

[9]*Greenes Newes,* p. ix.

Greene had far from died down as the publication of *Greenes Newes both from Heauen and Hell* in 1593 and *Haue with you to Saffron-Walden* as late as 1596 show. Danter decided to risk still another pamphlet on Greene, and perhaps Barnfield's "reputation" was born. As McKerrow tells us, he must have been known in order for readers to ascribe to him books he had not written.[10] Danter may then have gone ahead with *The Affectionate Shepheard*, getting Thomas Gubbin and Edward Newman to go in with him on the basis of sales of *Greenes Funeralls*. Their faith in Barnfield was not misapplied since the preface to *Cynthia* establishes that "The Shepheards Content" was kindly received.

An address "To the Gentlemen Readers," signed by Danter, supplies little of help outside the statement that "contrarie to the Authours expectation I haue nowe published [the pamphlet], for it was his priuate study at idle times" (A3r). Enough has been made of the unauthorized issuance, which perhaps helps to explain Barnfield's refusal to claim it as his, but perhaps something of value can be found in the final clause. It carries the flavor of referring to something done in the past. The word *nowe* in the first clause helps support the contention that the book was written sometime before 1594, possibly in 1592 between Greene's death and Watson's. All fourteen poems are entitled sonnets and numbered consecutively. None are sonnets in our modern use of the term. The first poem begins with six lines of iambic pentameter, rimed in Barnfield's favorite arrangement: ababcc. The second six lines comprise three couplets of riming fourteeners, and the concluding couplet rimes a pentameter line with a hexameter. The first eleven poems were printed in italics, with various nouns altered to roman in direct opposition to ordinary practice. In quoting, I shall reverse this procedure:

> Why should my Pen presume to write his praise,
> And hee in perfect mould of *Vertue* framde?
> Why should my Muse sing of his happie daies,
> And he the marke, at which Dame *Nature* framde? [aimed?][11]
>   Why rather should I not such vertues show,
>   That such pure golde from drosse each man may know?

---

[10]*Greenes Newes,* p. x.

[11]*framde* should read undoubtedly *aimde;* the printer merely sighted upon the rime word above.

But cease my Muse, why dost thou take in hand so great a Taske:
Which to performe a greater wit, than *Mercuries* would aske?
For iudgement *Ioue*, for Learning deepe, he still *Apollo* seemde:
For floent Tongue, for eloquence, men *Mercury* him deemde.
For curtesie suppose him *Guy*, or *Guyons* somewhat lesse:
His life and manners though I would, I cannot halfe expresse.
    Nor *Mouth*, nor *Minde*, nor *Muse* can halfe declare,
    His *Life*, his *Loue*, his *Laude*, so excellent they were.
        (A4ʳ)

The meter is quite regular, a mark we expect his work to exhibit. General awkwardnesses indicate that the poem proceeded from a young craftsman or a beginner. The repetition of Mercury is not entirely felicitous, and the disturbing syntax of line eleven seems inept. This author's modesty parallels a similar component in Barnfield's verse. His dedicatory stanzas, epistles, and addresses almost always plead youth and lack of skill, and at the end of the sonnet sequence in *Cynthia,* he laments his shortcomings and wishes that Colin or Rowland could have written the praises of Ganimede in his stead. There is a play of rhetoric of the kind we know Barnfield to have delighted in, learning it steadily from the textbook of his early master, Abraham Fraunce. The illustrations of anaphora in Fraunce's *Arcadian Rhetorike* show that the preceptor would have considered lines nine through eleven good examples.[12] The revocation, first of his presumption to praise Greene (line five) and then of his decision to go ahead (line seven), a device called epanorthosis is found also in Fraunce.[13] In a section given over to a "number of conceited verses" we find this illustration of lines similar to Barnfield's concluding couplet:

> A goteheard, plowman, knight, my goates, my fields, my foes,
> I fed, I tild, I kild, with bowes, with plowes, with blowes.[14]

As for linking a pentameter line to hexameter, Fraunce gives specific examples from various classical writers.[15] *The Arcadian Rhetorike* appeared in 1588, and while most Elizabethan writers practiced many of the elaborate figures found in Fraunce's work, or in the works of predecessors like Puttenham, Wilson, and Ramus, none was so diligent as Fraunce himself. As I have shown in Chapter II, Barnfield was his close imitator.

---

[12]*The Arcadian Rhetorike*, pp. 40-42.
[13]*The Arcadian Rhetorike*, pp. 78-79.
[14]*The Arcadian Rhetorike*, p. 57.
[15]*The Arcadian Rhetorike*, pp. 31-32.

Perhaps the strongest link that can be wrought in the attempt
to tie *Greenes Funeralls* to Barnfield is cast of the same metal as
the link that attaches him to his master Spenser. Line eleven of
Sonnet I compares Greene's courtesy to that of Guy or Guyon.
When McKerrow glossed the line, he expressed uncertainty:

> The line is rather obscure, and I am not sure who are meant
> by Guy and Guyon . . . . Can guyon be Gawain? Guy and
> Gawain are mentioned together by Skelton twice . . . and the
> collocation of the names may have been customary.
> (p. 92)

McKerrow is searching too far afield. Had he been aware of Barnfield's tremendous indebtedness to Spenser, holding, as he does, the
suspicion that *Greenes Funeralls* might indeed be Barnfield's composition, he might have gone immediately to *The Fairie Queene* as
the source of the allusion.

Spenser's Guyon, it is true, exemplifies temperance and not
courtesy; furthermore Spenser provided a type for courtesy in
Sir Calidore of Book VI. But *Greenes Funeralls* was printed in
1594, when only the first three books of *The Fairie Queene* were
available. Of course, the absence of Sir Calidore does not turn
temperance into courtesy; but we have got to admit that whoever
was attributing courtesy to Robert Greene was not being very
careful with his virtues; and of the three presented by Spenser in
1590—holiness, temperance and chastity—it might be safest to
identify Greene with the representative of temperance: Guyon.
Some critics have found that even Spenser was not delineating very
carefully in the attributes given to Guyon and find him more a
type for continence than for temperance. Now while in one sense
it may seem as much folly to adjudge Greene either temperate or
continent as it is to call him holy or chaste, in another sense, the
sense Barnfield is reaching after, temperance may be just the thing.
Elsewhere in *Greenes Funeralls* its author attempts to show the
gentleness of Greene as opposed to the intemperance of his attackers, Harvey and Wolfe; and with no Sir Calidore, no Sir Courtesy
on the scene until 1596, what figure out of Spenser would serve
better than Guyon?

Finally, Book II of *The Fairie Queene* is the book to which
Barnfield, in his acknowledged work, owes most. As late as 1598
he was drawing on Spenser's episode of the House of Alma (Canto
IX) heavily for the framework to his allegory of the body in *The*

Combat, betweene Conscience and Couetousnesse, in the minde of Man.

Thus Sonnet I makes elaborate claims for Greene's virtues as well as his courtesy. Since what we know of Greene's life contradicts somewhat such a portrait, we see that Barnfield obviously was not attempting fidelity, but rather hyperbolic praise. Elsewhere he contradicts this pleasant picture of Greene. Sonnets II, IV, VII, VIII, XI, and XII call Greene foolish, "as bad or worse than a Hel-hound," lewd, sinful, abandoned. Through faulty logic, contradictions, and obvious exaggeration, the first poem as well as the entire sequence is weakened in content; through carelessness, immaturity, and lack of skill, it is marred in performance.

Sonnet II, in its first four lines, is one of the two illustrations of anaphora pointed out by McKerrow:

> *Fortune,* hates not, them that hate her:
> *Fortune,* loues not, them that loue her:
> *Fortune,* would, and cannot rate her:
> *Fortune,* shall, and must remoue her.
> And though fickle *Fortune* smile:
> It is but for a little while.
>
> *Greene* loude *Fortune* foolish Man,
> Foolish man, why loude he so?
> And her foolish race he ran,
> Foolish race thats run with woe.
> Who then (Alas) was lesse misused?
> Now (Alas) is more abused?
>
> But let *Fowles* and foolish fellowes,
> Barke and byte their belly fill:
> It is not spightfull Enuies bellowes,
> That can kindle fire still.
> No Booke pleases all that come:
> None so bad but pleases some.
> (A4ᵛ)

As the first stanza is a textbook exercise in anaphora, so the second is a conscientious student's attempts at anadiplosis, which Fraunce describes as "when the same sound is repeated in the ende of the sentence going before, and in the beginning of the sentence following after."[16] Though he uses the word *sentence*, the illustra-

---

[16]*The Arcadian Rhetorike*, pp. 36-37. Perhaps climax or gradation, "a reduplication continued by diuers degrees and steps, as it were, of the same word or sound" (p. 38), is involved also.

tions taken from Sidney show that in poetry it is *line* ending and *line* beginning where the repetition takes place. In the third stanza *"Fowles and foolish fellows"* is an illustration of paranomasia and agnominatio: "when a word is changed in signification by changing of a letter or a sillable."[17] Since we run into this sort of reliance upon Fraunce's *Rhetorike* throughout *Greene's Funeralls* and since to give further examples would be only a tedious multiplication of almost every figure of speech in the book, the relationship between these two works need be demonstrated no further.

With Sonnet II we get fully into the controversy that has raged about certain topical references in *Greenes Funeralls* and made it significant in literary history far out of proportion to its literary merit. The initial couplet of the third stanza has been taken by Charles Crawford to refer to the printer John Wolfe and the writers in his employ who boarded with him at his home.[18] These included Anthony Chute and Gabriel Harvey, but since Greene's quarrels were primarily with the latter, Harvey becomes the chief object of Barnfield's attack throughout the pamphlet. In the lines under examination, Wolfe is referred to, suggests Crawford, through the perfect anagram of his name in the word *Fowles*; Harvey is included among the "foolish fellowes." As a defender of Greene, Barnfield felt compelled to denounce the publisher and author of *Fovre Letters and certeine Sonnets*, which appeared shortly after Greene's death.[19] It is possible that "Barke and byte their belly fill" is an echo from Harvey's second letter, in which Greene is said to "most currishly snarle, & bite."[20]

Sonnet III, although somewhat different in form and content from the other pieces and somewhat different from usual techniques in Barnfield's undisputed works, includes just enough recognizable touches for us to be able to call it his. The burden of the poem is a defense against the charges of lewdness that Harvey, and perhaps others, had made against Greene:

---

[17]*The Arcadian Rhetorike*, pp. 49-51.

[18]*"Greenes Funeralls* . . . and Nicholas Breton," pp. 2, 32, and *passim*.

[19]*Fovre Letters* was entered in the Stationers' Register on Dec. 4, 1592, but recent investigations have shown publication of various parts to antedate registration. The significance of these dates will be discussed in the analysis of Sonnet VII.

[20]*Fovre Letters*, ed. G. B. Harrison (London, 1922), p. 16.

Yee dainty *Damsels* of *Dianes* Traine,
That long to dally, with your loued *Lords*:
And you braue Gallant, high resolued *Lords*.
That loue to gaze, vpon your stately *Starrs*.
    He he is dead, that kild you with disdaine:
    And often fedde your friendly hopes againe.

He he is dead, that wrote of your delights:
That wrote of *Ladies*, and of *Parramours*:
Of budding beautie, and hir branched leaues,
Of sweet content in royall Nuptialls.
    He he is dead, that kild you with disdaine:
    And often fed your friendly hopes againe.

His gadding Muse, although it ran of loue,
Yet did hee sweetly morralize, his songs:
Ne euer gaue the looser cause to laugh,
Ne men of Iudgment, for to be offended.
    But as he often kild them with disdaine:
    So did he often feede their hopes againe.

And though he often told of things to come,
In loue more like a Prophet than a Poet:
Yet did he wisely interlace the one,
With *Sages* sayings, euer mixt among.
    And though he often fedde their pleasing paine:
    Yet did he often kill them with disdaine.

Wherefore yee dainty *Damsels* of renowne,
That long to dallie, with your loued *Lords*:
And you braue Gallant, [*sic*] worthy noble *Lords,*
That loue to dandle in your *Ladies* lapps.
    Come hither come, and lend your mouths to **Fame**:
    That meanes to sound, his neuer dying name.
    (B^r-B^v)

The refrain, which is interestingly varied in the next to the last
stanza, is one of the more common devices of repetition that Barnfield ignores and that Fraunce does not illustrate in his *Rhetorike*.
In all, Sonnet III borrows sparingly from Fraunce's textbook,
but enough figures are used still to see the stylistic relationship of
this poem to the others. However, the strongest support to Barnfield's authorship is the similarity of the concluding couplet to
the ending of "A Remembrance of some English Poets": "Live
euer you, at least in Fame liue euer:/ Well may the Bodye dye, but
Fame dies neuer" (*Lady Pecunia*, E^{av}). Barnfield liked so well the
sentiment here expressed that he repeated it in at least two other

places: stanza 36 of "The second Dayes Lamentation of the *Affectionate Shepheard*" and the final lines of "The Complaint of Chastitie."[21]

Sonnet IIII puts us again into the contemporary conflict that occasioned *Greenes Funeralls.*

> Come from the Muses well *Minerua,*
>   Come and bring a Coronet:
> To crowne his head, that doth deserue,
>   A greater gift than *Colinet.*
>
> Come from *Bacchus* bowre *Silenus,*
>   Come and bring some good-ale grout:
> For to sprinkle *Vino-plenus*:
>   All his foolish face about.
>
> Come thou hither sweete *Amyntas*
>   All on a siluer sounding Swanne:
> Come and teach this fond *A-Mint-Asse,*
>   Leaue the game as hee began.
>
> Come thou hither my friend so pretty,
>   All riding on a Hobby-Horse:
> Either make thy selfe more witty:
>   Or againe renew thy force:
> { Come and decke his browes with baies, }
> { That deserues immortall praise. }
>
>   (B₂ʳ)

Crawford asserted that here we have "portraits . . . in little of Edmund Spenser, Thomas Watson, Anthony Chute, Abraham Fraunce, [and] Gabriel Harvey."[22] If Crawford was correct, and I believe that he was in at least two of these identifications, then we might say that Barnfield's defense of Greene must have been a mixture of sincere emotions and the hyperbole of heated rhetoric. I cannot believe that a man who thought so highly of Greene as to applaud him above Spenser in this poem could have forgotten

---

[21]"But Fame and Vertue neuer shall decay;
For Fame is toombles, Vertue liues for aye."
                (*Aff. Shep.,* C₄ᵛ)

"But Fame and Vertue neuer shall decay,
For Fame is Toomblesse, Vertue liues for aye."
                (*Aff. Shep.,* G₈ʳ)

[22]"*Greenes Funeralls* . . . and Nicholas Breton," p. 2.

him so completely as to omit him from the warm tributes bestowed upon Spenser, Sidney, Amyntas, and Drayton in *The Affectionate Shepheard* unless the initial puff was more an impassioned exaggeration, growing out of the zeal of the moment, rather than a considered appraisal. There is some, but by no means great, influence by Greene upon the early poems of Barnfield. Though personal sympathy — perhaps actual friendship — may have existed between Greene and Barnfield, the young poet more probably took up the cudgel for the unfortunate Greene either as an opportunist, which I doubt, or as one of a group of writers the other members of which were more intimately connected with the dead man than he was.

In Silenus, Crawford sees figured the poetaster and hack Anthony Chute, another of the boarders at Wolfe's. Chute was a drunkard as well as very corpulent according to Nashe; and on the basis of these characteristics, traditionally associated with Silenus, Crawford makes his identification. I doubt that Barnfield intended any such allusion. Silenus would appear here to be a friendly, convivial spirit, whereas Chute should be among the opposition. Silenus, in the second stanza, stands in the same relation to Greene that Minerva holds in the first. They are both gods, asked to bring recognition and comfort to Greene. The third stanza introduces Amyntas and along with him all the problems that associate with his name in the study of Barnfield. Crawford and Warren B. Austin[23] take him to be Thomas Watson and, on the basis of the identification, date the composition of *Greenes Funeralls* as having taken place between September 5, 1592, the date of Harvey's second letter, and September 26, the supposed date of Watson's burial. But the date of Watson's burial has never been authenticated. In 1866, Collier reported having come upon a burial notation in the register of St. Bartholomew the Less.[24] Crawford accepts apparently this finding as indisputable fact, but Mark Eccles finds Thomas Watson to be a common name in and around London in the 1590's, and has difficulty in linking various public records to the poet. He makes no attempt himself to date Watson's death.[25] However, I should think that those scholars who attempt to

[23]"A Supposed Contemporary Allusion to Shakespeare as a Plagiarist," *SQ*, VI (1955), 375.

[24]*Bibliographical Account*, IV, 221.

[25]*Christopher Marlowe in London*, pp. 60, 158.

identify Amyntas with Watson would rather have his death come somewhat later, although it would be difficult to push it beyond the 10th of November, when *Amintae Gaudia* was entered in the Stationers' Register, or at the very latest, to the end of the year in the case that C. M.'s dedication, mentioning Watson as dead, had been inserted after registration. Both Crawford and John Churton Collins believe that Sonnet XII of *Greenes Funeralls* echoes various parts of *The Repentance of Robert Greene*, which was not entered until October 6, 1592.[26] Sonnets IV and VII allude to a living Amyntas. If Watson died September 26, how could Barnfield borrow from a work not entered until ten days later and perhaps not published for some time after that? Crawford asserts that R. B. went to Greene's lodgings, just as Gabriel Harvey had, and saw manuscripts of both the *Groats-Worth* and *Repentance*.[27] G. B. Harrison and F. R. Johnson have shown that *Fovre Letters* was printed before being entered in the Stationers' Register,[28] a possible explanation for this difficulty with *The Repentance*. But these theories are far-fetched. Two other possibilities are much more reasonable. The first is that Watson did not die on September 26, as stated by Collier, but rather sometime between October 6, registration date for *The Repentance* and November 10, the date for *Amintae Gaudia*. The second is that Barnfield's appeal to Amyntas is not directed at Watson at all, but at Abraham Fraunce, who is not known to have died in 1592, although his last published work is dated that year, and who may have lived until 1633.[29] If the second of these hypotheses is correct, then *Greenes Funeralls* need not have been written until just before its entry in the Stationers' Register on February 1, 1594; but I do not believe that the work dates from any later than mid-1593. Stylistically it is more immature than *The Affectionate Shepheard*,

---

[26]*The Plays and Poems of Robert Greene*, I, 52; *Greenes Funeralls* . . . and Nicholas Breton," p. 12. Collins says that the prayer at the end is imitated in Sonnet XII, and Crawford believes that Cuthbert Burby's preface is echoed in the same Sonnet.

[27]*"Greenes Funeralls* . . . and Nicholas Breton," p. 11.

[28]See "Books and Readers, 1591-4," *The Library*, 4th Series, VIII (1927), 277; and "The First Edition of Gabriel Harvey's *Fovre Letters*," *The Library*, 4th Series, XV (1934), 219; 5th Series, I (1946), 135.

[29]For arguments concerning the death of Fraunce, see Chapter II as well as my article in *PMLA* and the controversy it occasioned: "Richard Barnfield, 'Amyntas,' and the Sidney Circle," *PMLA*, LXXIV (Sept.,

and the shift in the second work to a greater affection for Spenser must have had time to develop. An interesting sidelight of the third stanza involves its second line: "All on a siluer sounding Swanne." As early as 1590, William Vallans brought attention to Watson's description of swans, singing at their death, and appended Fraunce's translation of Watson's lines.[30] In *Greenes Funeralls,* Barnfield further establishes the practice of linking Amyntas to the swan. By 1595, Thomas Lodge refers perhaps to Watson and Fraunce as "the fore-bred brothers . . ./ Who in their swan-like songs Amintas wept." And the following year, William Smith, in *Chloris,* says of Amyntas that "Thy swan-like songs did show thy dying anguish."[31] Since both Watson and Fraunce were associated by Vallans and Lodge with the swan tradition, unfortunately we cannot use the reference to point exclusively to one or the other.

The second half of stanza three, with its reference to *A-Mint-Asse,* becomes very important. The vague reference in Sonnett II to Greene's attackers as *"Fowles* [Wolfe] and foolish fellowes" is here narrowed to a single person. Crawford's claim that A-Mint-

---

1959), esp. p. 321; and "Thomas Watson and Abraham Fraunce," *PMLA,* LXXVI (March, 1961), pp. 150-153. Some further evidence in the argument, not submitted previously, might be added here. The very preface that Professor Staton referred to in the controversy need not be read as he suggests. "Mutatus" refers perhaps to the alternation of Watson's *Amyntas* from the original Latin into the English translation by Fraunce, and thus Fraunce gets into the picture. In fact, in Grosart's edition of Dickenson (1878), a Latinist translates the appropriate passage as follows: "Amyntas pleased the god, in fashion new,/ Shining with English grace and Roman too" (p. xviii). I find of additional interest the stanza in which Dickenson bemoans the dead Amyntas; he calls upon the pastoral poets to honor the dead chief of shepherds: *"Acadians* doe him his deserued right,/ And on his Tombe greene Laurel-branches spread" (B₈ᵛ). I do not insist upon the significance of *Acadians* here, but its relationship to Fraunce's *Arcadian Rhetorike* might be pondered. If a link between Greene and Fraunce is needed, *Philomela; the Lady Fitzwaters Nightingale* will give it. In applying such a title, Greene claimed he was "imitating herein Master Abraham Fraunce, who titled the *Lamentations of Amintas,* under the name of the *Countess of Pembroke's Ivie-church"* (*Archaica,* ed. Sir E. Brydges, I, x).

[30] *A Tale of Two Swannes,* A₂ᵛ.

[31] Lodge's lines come from the Induction to *Phillis* and Smith's from Sonnet XIV of *Chloris.* Walter Staton has objected to my reading of Lodge's lines, rejuvenating Harold Littledale's theory that Lodge once wrote an Amyntas poem of his own and here refers to its unfortunate literary death (See *PMLA,* LXXVI [March, 1961], 150-152). To answer

Asse is Fraunce is illogical. The argument, as it has been developed through the first three poems, is a defense of Greene. There is no point in Barnfield's digressing here to call Fraunce a new-made ass, simply because, as Crawford would have it, he translated Watson's poem poorly. Especially is name-calling against Fraunce unlikely since it can be argued that Barnfield was heavily indebted to Fraunce's *Arcadian Rhetorike*. Instead, *A-Mint-Asse* must be looked upon as Greene's chief gadfly; he stands for Gabriel Harvey, as Warren Austin has suggested.[32] The final stanza reinforces this argument by its whimsical introduction of the Hobby-Horse. Crawford recognizes it as a variant of Hobbinol, which Spenser tacked onto Harvey in *The Shepheardes Calender* and which Harvey used himself in the commendatory verses to the *Faerie Queene*. Crawford reminds us that Nashe referred also, in *Haue with you to Saffron-Walden*, to Harvey and "his Hobby-horse revelling."[33] The concluding couplet of Sonnet IIII should be separated from the last stanza since it serves in the office of an envoi rather than as part of the stanza only. The request is to Minerva, to Silenus, to Amyntas, to Greene's friends to "decke his browes with baies" and certainly not to Harvey. The allusion to laurel bays both in the first stanza and this concluding couplet may owe something to Harvey's second letter:

Staton and Littledale at once, I should like to point out that Smith's borrowings from Lodge do not prove necessarily that it was from a now lost *Amintas* that the thefts came. All that Littledale succeeds in doing is to show that Smith borrowed from *Phillis*, which, says Littledale, is a sort of salvage from the storm-wrecked *Amintas*. But Lodge calls himself Damon in *Phillis*; why has he not continued the tradition of naming Phillis' lover Amyntas, especially when he must have done so in the hypothesized lost poem? Furthermore, it can be shown that Smith borrowed from many poets, Spenser and Watson included. See, for instance, L. A. Sasek, "William Smith and *The Shepheardes Calender*," PQ, XXXIX (1960), 251-253. Martha Crowe Foote, *Elizabethan Sonnet Cycles: Idea, Fidessa, Chloris* (London, 1897), p. 143, writes that "The melodies piped by other sonnet-shepherds re-echo with a great deal of distinctness in [Smith's] strains." And Sonnet XIV so closely retells the Amyntas story as it is in Watson and Fraunce, that if Lodge wrote one also, it is missing now because he hid it for shame.

[32]"A Supposed Contemporary Allusion," p. 378.

[33]*Works*, III, 73.

His sweete hostisse, for a tender farewell, crowned Greene with a Garland of Bayes: to shew, that a tenth Muse honoured him aliue. I know not, whether *Skelton, Elderton,* or some like flourishing Poet were so enterred: it was his owne request, and his Nurses deuotion: and happily some of his fauourites may imitate the example.[34]

Not only is the description of the crowning suggestive but also the information that Greene requested it and that Harvey hinted someone might imitate the hostess' act. The very verses of *Greenes Funeralls* are leaves of Bay, and the whole fourteen sonnets make the garland. Barnfield is honoring Greene's last wish.

Sonnet V presents problems of interpretation, although no additional problems of attribution. The man who wrote the poems preceding wrote Sonnet V as well. There are still the elaborate play of language and loyal defense of Greene at Harvey's expense. Rime is very irregular but lighthearted, showing immaturity in craftsmanship but also a delight in novelty, two characteristics of the early poems of Barnfield:

> Amend thy stile who can: who can amend thy stile?
>   For sweet conceit.
>   Alas the while,
> That euer any such, as thou shouldst die,
>   By fortunes guile,
>   Amids thy meate.
> Pardon (Oh pardon) me that cannot shew,
>   My zealous loue.
>   Yet shalt thou proue,
> That I will euer write in thy behoue:
>   Gainst any dare,
>   With thee compare.
> It is not *Hodge-poke* nor his fellow deare,
>   That I doe feare:
>   As shall appeare.
> But him alone that is the Muses owne,
>   And eke my friend,
>   Whome to the end,
> My muse must euer honor and adore:
>   Doe what I can.
>   To praise the man,
> It is impossible for me that am,
>   So far behinde.
>   Yet is my minde,

---

[34]*Fovre Letters,* p. 23.

As forward as the best, if wit so would
    With will agree.
      But since I see,
      It will not bee:
I am content, my folly to confesse:
    And pardon craue:
    Which if I haue,
My Fortunes greater than my former fall:
      I must confesse.

> But if he other wise esteeme of me,
> Than as a friend or one that honors thee:
> Then is my labor lost, my care consumde.
> Because I hate the hope, that so presumde
>   (B₂ʳ-B₃ʳ)

The first four tercets are not troublesome at all; but starting with the fifth, various nouns and pronouns create puzzling ambiguities. "*Hodge-poke*" has been taken by both Crawford and Austin as Gabriel Harvey, and with their reasoning I have no argument. Austin alone identifies "fellow deare" as Wolfe.[35] I do not think that we will ever identify Harvey's companion in this line, but I feel it cannot be Wolfe simply because the anagram *Fowle* is used to represent him elsewhere, and we expect it here too if Wolfe is our man. But the whole problem centers in *him* of the sixth tercet. Although none of the writers interested in *Greenes Funeralls* have commented on the pronoun, they apparently take *him* for Greene. Yet I suspect that Barnfield is referring to a living man. The present tense *is* which governs *Muse* and *friend* suggests someone other than Greene, and the pardon craved in the tenth tercet implies someone capable still of giving it. The reference to the improvement of Barnfield's fortunes if he gets his man's pardon opens all the probabilities of relationship that we find in *The Affectionate Shepheard*. And finally, the concluding quatrain indicates clearly that there is a pronominal use, at least in these last four lines if not in the last six stanzas above, that introduces a personage other than Greene: the "he" in the first line of the quatrain cannot be the same man as the "thee" of the second. If we read this as I outline it, much of the apparent strangeness of relationship between Barnfield and Greene that seems inherent in the pamphlet will disappear. Sonnet V tells us, I believe, that Barnfield has taken it upon himself to defend Greene's memory more to gain the friendship of one still living than to protect a

---

[35] "A Supposed Contemporary Allusion," p. 378.

dear friend already dead. The sometimes ungenerous references to
Greene as a foolish man, which do not square with such terms as
"honor and adore" and "my labor lost, my care consumde" are
explained by being statements addressed to different men. Barnfield desires someone living to esteem him highly, a hope he recognizes would prove presumptuous unless it is fulfilled. A new
problem raised by the solution of this old one is the identity of
the new man. He might be Amyntas, which presents two historical
possibilities: Watson and Fraunce. He might be Spenser, whom
we know Barnfield's muse has "euer honor[ed] and adore[d]."
Or it might be the man who is addressed as Ganimede in *The
Affectionate Shepheard*. My first choice would be Amyntas, standing for Abraham Fraunce.

Sonnet VI adds nothing new to our knowledge, either about
the authorship of *Greenes Funeralls* or its content. The *"Tel-tales"*
of the first line and the "wicked men" of the eleventh I take to
be Harvey and Wolfe, and the sonnet is merely an excoriation of
them, a suggested punishment, and a promise to write a different
kind of poem in the next sonnet. In this promise we are not misled,
for Sonnet VII manages some very singular hexameters as well
as multiple references to Amyntas:

> Though perchance it seeme to some but a toy and a trifle,
> Seeme to some in vaine, to bestowe but a part of an houre,
> In penning Poemes: in hon'ring him with a Poeme.
> Yet *I* appeale to the pen of pierelesse Poet *Amyntas*,
> Matchles *Amintas* minde, to the minde of Matchles *Amintas*,
> Sweete bonny *Phillis* loue, to the loue of sweete bonny *Phillis*,
> Whether pen, or minde, or loue, of *Phillis Amintas*
> Loue, or minde, or pen, of pen-loue-minder *Amintas*:
> Thinke of him (perhaps) as some doe thinke of *Amintas*:
> Oh that I might be loude, of *Phillis* louer: *Amintas*.
> Oh that I might be thought, as I thinke of *Phillis*: *Amintas*.
> Oh that *I* might be iudgde as *I* iudge of *Phillis*: *Amintas*:
> Then would *I* neuer care for such base beggarly make-bookes
> That in ueigh against the dead, like deadly maligners.
> What if he were a man, as bad or worse than a Hel-hound?
> As shall *I* thinke that he was as bad or worse than a Hel-hound?
> Yet it ill became sweete miudes [*sic*] to haunt in *Auernus*:
> Ill became such Cutes, to barke at a poore silly carcas
> Some had cause to mone, and mourne, & murmur against him:
> Others none at all, yet none at all, so against him.
> For my selfe I wish, that none had written against him
> But such men which had just cause t'haue wrtten [*sic*]
>   against him.   (B₄ʳ)

Nothing could be closer to Fraunce in style and preference for classical meters. The use in this poem, when he so passionately appeals to Amyntas, of Fraunce's rhetoric, of Fraunce's hexameters, even of Fraunce's words puts the identity of Amyntas in doubt.[36] Watson no longer holds the field alone. Compare those lines above in which the name Amyntas appears with these from Fraunce's translation of Watson's Latin:

> Loue did loue Phillis, Phillis was loud of Amintas,
> Phillis loues dearling, Phillis dearling of Amintas,
> Dearling, crowne, garland, hope, ioy, wealth, health
>   of Amintas,
> And what more shal I say? for I want words fit for *Amintas.*
>   (B₂ʳ)

Watson, although employing considerable rhetoric, is not so heavily burdened as this, nor does he drag in the name of Amyntas. What is striking is that for all Fraunce's repetition, his lines are not more bulky than Watson's:

> Chara tibi, mihi chara fuit formosula Phyllis:
> Nempe erat imperij notissima gloria vestri,
> Et ruris speculum, et solum solamen amantum:
> Et mea sola salus erat, et mea sola voluptas,
> Spes mea, vita mea, ac animae pars altera Phyllis.
> O quae sufficiant adiustas verba querelas?
>   (A₇ᵛ)

Sonnet VII is revealing in other ways as well. The *Funeralls* took "but part of an houre," hyperbole of course, but indicating its hasty composition. The speed cannot be associated with a publisher's desire to get something on the streets as soon as possible after Greene's death or Harvey's attack.[37] The pamphlet was probably a performance with the left hand, undertaken more to

---

[36]McKerrow, *Greenes Funeralls,* p. 92, has been struck also by such a possibility: "Presumably Thomas Watson, the author of the Latin poem *Amyntas,* is meant, and not Abraham Fraunce, the translator of that poem into English, though the fact that the author seems here to be imitating Fraunce's English hexameters may render the point a little uncertain."

[37]Warren B. Austin, "A Supposed Contemporary Allusion," p. 376, quotes Harvey's references in *Fovre Letters* to " 'Epitaphs and funerall devotions' being written on Greene within a week of his death . . . and the terms he uses suggest at least the possibility that it was *Greene's Funerals* written by a 'foe' of his that he had in mind." But elsewhere

enter the good graces of Amyntas or some other poet than anything else. Sonnet IV illustrates that at this time Spenser was not
yet the idol he became by late 1594. The reference therefore to
"pierelesse Poet *Amyntas*" may be an honest tribute. Barnfield
might well have considered Fraunce or Watson in 1592 the best
of poets. Such judgment seems to us absurd, and it is. Perhaps what
is fogging Barnfield's mind is some personal attachment or loyalty
to Amyntas, and the terms of lines 4-12 indicate such an interpretation. In fact lines 10-12, in which Barnfield would like to hold
the same relationship to Amyntas as Amyntas has to Phillis, suggest
the unnatural desires that Barnfield displays more openly in *The
Affectionate Shepheard* and the sonnets in *Cynthia*. I doubt that
the Amyntas of *Greenes Funeralls* became the Ganimede of *The
Affectionate Shepheard,* however, since there would be little cause
to alter the pastoral name. Also, Amyntas is referred to under
his own pastoral guise in poems where Ganimede appears. It is not
likely that the poet meant the same person to have two different
names. Lastly, we get the impression that Ganimede is a youth, and
both Watson and Fraunce were at least sixteen years Barnfield's
senior. Of course, if Watson is Amyntas, his death in 1592 puts
an end to all discussion. It is well known, through the report of
Nashe,[38] that Watson was no friend of Harvey, and I believe it
can be shown indirectly that Fraunce was no friend of his either.
Although Harvey includes Fraunce among those he recommends
"cordially . . . to the deere Louers of the Muses,"[39] we know
from the inclusion of Watson's name and Nashe's that the tribute
was an attempt to pacify friends of Greene and keep them from
entering the literary fray, or, as Nashe himself puts it,

(p. 375), Austin says that R. B. "seems to have read these writings by
Harvey very soon after they appeared." Austin cannot have it both ways;
but in any case, since *Greenes Funeralls* did not appear until 1594 and
since Amyntas just might be Fraunce, there is no necessity to attribute
haste of composition to the publisher's demands.

[38]Thomas Watson "those Hexameters made of him,

> *But, o, what newes of that good* Gabriell Haruey,
> *Known to the world for a foole and clapt in the* Fleet *for
> a Rimer?"*

Works, III, 126.

[39]*Fovre Letters*, p. 68.

Then thou [Harvey] goest about to bribe mee to giue ouer this quarrell, and saist, if I will holde my peace, thou wilt bestowe more complements of rare amplifications vpon mee, than euer thou bestowdst on Sir *Philip Sidney,* and gentle Maister *Spencer.*

Thou flatterst mee, and praisest mee.

To make mee a small seeming amendes for the iniuries thou hast done mee, thou reckonst mee vp *amongst the deare louers and professed sonnes of the Muses, Edmund Spencer, Abraham France, Thomas Watson, Samuell Daniell.*

With a hundred blessings, and many praiers, thou intreatst mee to loue thee.[40]

The inclusion of Fraunce's name, as well as Watson's, is for the same reason. Harvey is afraid of having too many adversaries, especially such learned men as he knew both Watson and Fraunce to be. I think the proof is in the Third Letter of Harvey's *Foure,* in which he hopes to be remembered as "The Inuentour of the English Hexameter." He praises Sidney and, of all people, Stanyhurst as great practitioners of the measure, but he excludes Fraunce, all of whose English verse was in that meter and who was a man praised largely by others: Nashe, Peele, Lodge, Greene, Vallans, etc. If Harvey had wanted to show the heights to which English hexameters had risen, he should have cited Fraunce, but this omission I take to be tacit corroboration that the men were not friendly.

Crawford and Austin see the "base beggarly make-bookes" again as Wolfe and his stable of writers. The two lines which query whether or not Greene was a "Hel-hound" I have noted previously as an example of Barnfield's fluctuating attitude toward the man's memory. But also, along with the line that names Avernus, they provide still another link with Amyntas, tellingly in favor of Fraunce rather than Watson. In *The Lamentations of Amyntas,* Fraunce associates Hell with Cerberus in two distinct passages:

Ouercome those hags and fiends of fearefull Auernus.

. . . .

Stay that bawling curre, that three throt horrible helhound.
(A_3^r-A_3^v)

darksome dens of Auernus,
Wher's no path to returne, no starting hole to be scaping,
Desteny, death, and Hell, and howling hydeus helhound.
(B_3^v)

---

[40] *Works,* I, 325.

Watson's Latin originals avoid the word *Avernus,* although *hell-hound* is suggested by the rather stiffly formal *Stygijque canis:*

> Threicei Vatis, Furias, Plutonaquetoruum
> Placato, Stygijque canis compesce furorem.
> (A₄ʳ)

> crudelia fata
> Immersas Erebo mentes hoc lucis ab orbe
> Detinet, ac nouiès Styx interfusa coërcet.
> (A₈ᵛ)

A certain native and colloquial charm must be granted in "Stay that bawling curre, that three throt horrible helhound" that is also a mark of Barnfield's diction.[41]

Crawford thinks line seventeen to be a glance at Spenser,[42] but "sweete mi[n]des" is merely another allusion to Harvey and his friends. Throughout the pamphlet Barnfield uses "sweet" or "dear" and similar epithets indiscriminately, friend as well as foe addressed affectionately or ironically as in "Come thou hither my friend so pretty," "Hodge-poke nor his fellow deare," and "sweet consent." Here he uses it didactically in the sense that no one claiming to a humane, sympathetic nature would treat a recently dead person as a hellhound. Spenser, of course, had never implied that he thought badly of Greene at all. The line is connected logically to the couplet that precedes it; the man (Harvey) who has referred to Greene as evil is exhibiting a mind as hunting in Avernus when it should display Christian (sweet) charity. Line eighteen denies any break in syntax, and thus the same minds that haunt Greene in Avernus are the *Cutes* (surely *currs* or *cures*) that "barke at a poore silly carcas." The poems, then, are directed more narrowly at Harvey as they progress. Along with his publisher, he becomes the sole object of Barnfield's scornful counter-attack. As we approach the now famous Sonnet IX, this realization becomes important. But first a look at the eighth, another poem in Fraunce-like hexameters, is in order.

The piece introduces the new figure of Meliboeus as well as other problems of identification in the cases of Pan, Marsyas, and the "Saint" of line eleven:

---

[41]For additional line by line comparisons between Barnfield, Fraunce, and Watson, see pp. 34-38. But not to be overlooked is the possibility that the phrase came from Barnfield's chief model, Spenser: "His [Orpheus'] musicks might the hellish hound did tame" (*Sh. Cal.* p. 96).

[42]"*Greenes Funeralls* . . . and Nicholas Breton," p. 37.

Mvse giue place to my mone, and mone giue place to my musing:
  One for an others cause, and one for cause of an other.
  First to behold him dead: last to behold him aliue.
And thou Shepheards Swaine, that keeps thy sheepe by the
  mountaines.
(Mountaines) of *Sicily,* and sweet *Arcadian* Iland,
Oh *Meliboeus*: leaue, Oh leaue any more to be mourning.
  For though his Art bee dead, yet shall it euer abide:
  Euer abide, to the end: light, as a light to the rest.
  Rest that haue wrot of loue: and the delights of a louer.
But by the sweete consent, of *Pan* and *Marsias* ofspringe.
Sweet consent of a *Saint* so sweet, of a *Fowle* an a foule one
  Greenes but a foolish man: and such as him doe defend.
Yet will I euer write both to defend and offend:
For to defend his friends, and to offend his foes.
                    (B₄ᵛ)

Crawford believes that Meliboeus is Watson,[43] since in 1590 that
poet wrote a Latin elegy mourning the death of Sir Francis Walsingham, in which the dead statesman is given the pastoral name
of Meliboeus. The poem itself goes by the same title. Crawford
is not disturbed at having Watson called Amyntas in Sonnet VII
and Meliboeus in VIII. I do not find it quite so easy to make this
jump and would like very much to urge that if Meliboeus is
Watson, it is all the easier for Amyntas to be Fraunce. But reluc-
tantly I must admit that it would be rather strange for Barnfield
to call Watson Meliboeus. In the elegy, Watson assumes the role
of Corydon. Crawford uses an argument based upon what he calls
"Antonomasia, or as Puttenham, in his *Arte of English Poesie* calls
it, the 'surnamer,' the authors being indicated by their composi-
tions."[44] My objection to this is that Watson had been too widely
and too successfully identified with Amyntas for any writer to
attempt a new mask for him. It would be about as difficult to
give Sidney any name other than Astrophel.[45] For Pan and Marsyas,

_____

[43]"*Greenes Funeralls* . . . and Nicholas Breton," p. 34.
[44]"*Greenes Funeralls* . . . and Nicholas Breton," p. 33.
[45]A possibility that has been overlooked, undoubtedly because of the
punctuation in the passage, is that "Shepheards Swaine" is Amyntas and
subject of the verbs "leaue, Oh leaue." Meliboeus would then be the
object of the verb. Since Fraunce never wrote a Meliboeus poem that we
know of, such an interpretation would be strong evidence for identifying
Watson as the elusive Amyntas. As for the punctuation which stands in
the way of such a reading, it may be dismissed as inconsequential argu-
mentation, pointing and compositing being what they were in the age.

Crawford calls upon the 'surnamer' again: "for 'Pan' means Spenser's *The Shepheardes Calender* and 'Marsias ofspringe' stands for *The Faerie Queene*."[46] Spenser is seen as the "Saint" of the following line. Austin would substitute Greene's attackers for "Marsias ofspringe"[47] and in this I believe he is correct. The two lines are set up in parallel structure, so that "Pan" corresponds to "Saint" and "Marsias ofspringe" to "*Fowle* and a foule one." As for identifying "Pan" and "Saint" with Spenser, I am somewhat dubious. Barnfield had already brought Spenser into the picture under the name of Colinet, his unmistakable signature from *The Shepheardes Calender*. I believe that Crawford and Austin are influenced in equating Spenser with "Pan" and "Saint" by first having identified him with the "sweet mindes" in Avernus, a conjecture unwarranted. They claim that Harvey, by using Spenser's name frequently in the Third Letter and by appending Spenser's commendatory poem at the end of the "certeine sonnets," implied Spenser's consent to the attack on Greene. But the references to Spenser in the letter are in no way ambiguous, and the poem at the end is dated clearly as having been written in 1586. Barnfield could much more damagingly have pointed out, on the basis of these non-committal items, that Spenser refused to support his friend in so disgraceful an enterprise. The question then becomes who is "Pan" and the "Saint"; for they are one and the same; and I have no satisfactory answer unless Francis Sabie will do, who published *Pans Pipe* not until 1595, but who may have had a manuscript circulating considerably before that time. Sabie is a very "sweet" or "Saintly" writer and seems well versed in the pastoral personalities of the nineties. In *The Fishermans Tale* (1595), he refers to Alexis, Amyntas, Corydon, and Meliboeus with some affection (D4ᵛ). If Barnfield knew him to admire Fraunce, Watson, Walsingham and their friends, he might have recorded an additional friendship with Harvey in

---

[46]"*Greenes Funeralls* . . . and Nicholas Breton," p. 37. Austin concurs with Crawford about "Saint" and Pan, but he sees "Marsias ofspringe" as a reference to Harvey and Wolfe. Austin seems to have read some version of Crawford's article which I have not seen, for he charges Crawford with emending "Marsias" to "Mars his." Austin also charges E. A. J. Honigmann in that scholar's "Shakespeare's 'Lost Source-Plays,'" *MLR*, XLIX (1954), with printing *Foule* for *Fowle* and thereby missing the Wolfe anagram, but I must be reading a different version of Honigmann's work also, for in my copy the author has it perfectly correct.

[47]"A Supposed Contemporary Allusion," p. 378.

just such terms as lines ten and eleven of Sonnet VIII. But the theory involves too many *ifs* and I have no more faith in it than I do in the Pan-Spenser arguments.

Sonnet IX is the center of the storm that continues to revolve violently about Greene's "vpstart Crow":

> *Greene,* is the pleasing Obiect of an eie:
> *Greene,* pleasde the eies of all that lookt vppon him.
> *Greene,* is the ground of euerie Painters die:
> *Greene,* gaue the ground, to all that wrote vpon him.
> Nay more the men, that so Eclipst his fame:
> Purloynde his Plumes, can they deny the same?
>
> Ah could my Muse, old Maltaes Poet passe,
> (If any Muse could passe, old Maltaes Poet)
> Then should his name be set in shining brasse,
> In shining brasse for all the world to show it.
> That little children, not as yet begotten
> Might royallize his fame when he is rotten.
>
> But since my Muse begins to vaile hir wings,
> And flutter low vpon the lowly Earth:
> As one that sugred Sonnets, seldome singes,
> Except the sound of sadnes, more than mirth,
> To tell the worth of such a worthy man:
> Ile leaue it vnto those, that better can.
>
> Now may thy soule againe, goe take his rest
> (His pleasant rest) in those eternall ioyes
> Where burning Tapers, still attend the blest
> To light, and lighten them from all annoyes.
> Goe then poore Poet, liue and neuer die:
> Euer, yet neuer but in miserie.
>
> And as I came into the world vnknowne,
> Moude with compassion, of thy piteous plaint:
> So will *I* now againe, my selfe goe mone,
> That durst presume, thy praise in verse to paint.
> And if the Muses pardon, mine so weake:
> I passe not of a pin, what others speake.
>   (C^r-C^v)

The earliest writer to mention Sonnet IX in connection with Greene's vehement outburst against the "vpstart Crow" was Dyce, who wrote in 1831 merely that the first six lines "seem to have

been suggested by the passage in [*Groats-Worth*]."[48] There is no
need to reproduce here Greene's famous attack; it is necessary only
to remind the reader of the phrase "beautified with our feathers";
for it is upon these words alone that any connection between IX
and the *Groats-Worth* must stand, accordingly as Barnfield's
"Purloynde his Plumes" are said to echo them. After Dyce, a
whole series of eminent Shakespearian and Elizabethan scholars
fell into line, either affirming that Barnfield's phrase was a verifi-
cation that Greene was indeed attacking Shakespeare or that contemporaries so understood the passage regardless of intention.[49]
Not until 1938 did any writer suggest that Sonnet IX might be
read differently.[50] René Pruvost, without suggesting the name
of a new culprit, militated against applying the lines to Shakespeare:

> Le but du poème est de protester contre les attaques dont
> Greene a été l'objet après sa mort, et dans une certaine mesure
> de leur répondre . . . . Les hommes qui ont "écrit sur Greene"
> et terni ou "éclipsé" sa gloire, ce sont les auteurs de ces attaques.
> Et ce sont eux que R. B. accuse d'avoir plagié celui que par
> surcroît ils ont diffamé. Aucune des allusions qu'il leur fait ne
> permet de dire qu'il soupçonnait Shakespeare d'être de leur
> nombre.[51]

In 1955, Warren B. Austin narrowed the theory to fit Harvey
and his friends and suggested that "there is good reason to believe
that, at the time he wrote *Greene's Funerals*, R. B. had not seen
the similar phrase in the attack on the 'upstart Crow.'" Austin's
argument rests on the belief that Thomas Watson died on September 26, 1592. Since *Groats-Worth* was entered on the 20th,

---

[48]*The Dramatic Works of Robert Greene*, I, lxxxi. J. O. Halliwell
saw these same six lines as an imitation of stanza 52 in "The second Dayes
Lamentation of the *Affectionate Shepheard*." See Halliwell's edition of
The Affectionate Shepheard for the Percy Society (London, 1845), XX,
51. Of course, the stanza in *The Affectionate Shepheard* would be the
imitation, but is not the correspondence another small link in the chain
of evidence that identifies Barnfield as the author of *Greenes Funeralls*?

[49]These include Halliwell (1843), John Churton Collins (1905),
A. W. Pollard (1929), Charles Crawford (1929), E. K. Chambers
(1930), J. Dover Wilson (1951), J. A. K. Thomson (1952), and E. A. J.
Honigmann (1954).

[50]McKerrow, it is true, had anticipated Pruvost at least to the extent
of writing in his edition of *Greenes Funeralls* that the passage was "possibly, but not certainly, an allusion" to the *Groats-Worth* charge (p. 81).

[51]*Robert Greene et ses romans* (1558-1592) (Paris, 1938), p. 520.

Greenes Funeralls, asking help from a living Amyntas (Watson), would then have had to be written during that period. Austin says, "Normally . . . such speed would be highly improbable." He offers, as a place where Barnfield might have found lines to imitate, a passage in the Third Letter, in which Harvey accuses Greene of stealing from the Italian romances: "Thanke other for thy borrowed & filched plumes of some little Italianated brauery."[52] Austin concludes, "here is Harvey accusing Greene of borrowing *his* tricks of style from others and yet himself filching from Greene the very figure of speech in which he makes the infamous charge." Thus R. B., as Austin calls him, exposes the immense heinousness of Harvey's actions by sending the iniquity home again.[53]

In general, I should like to agree with Austin's interpretation of the Sonnet as well as many other parts of the pamphlet. There are some holes in his arguments but not serious ones. For instance, Austin, who argues so eloquently for the fine scholarship that proved *Fovre Letters* was issued piecemeal, the first two epistles appearing unbelievably soon after Greene's death, can hardly hold that Barnfield probably did not see the *Groats-Worth.* Furthermore, there is no proof that Watson died on the 26th, and there is some doubt that Watson is Amyntas. But these facts do not damage the thesis that Sonnet IX is an integral part of a single statement, begun in Sonnet I and continuing logically through Sonnet XII. In all, where a sole opponent is indicated, the enemy is Harvey, and where several are mentioned, they are Harvey and his friends, especially Wolfe. In fact, Austin might have added to his argument, wherein he scrutinizes so minutely such words as *ground, wrot vpon him, Eclipst, fame, and Purloynde his Plumes,* that Barnfield uses the noun *men* and the pronoun *they,* whereas Greene's "vpstart Crow" is one man only. How can these plurals possibly be explained in terms of Greene's "onely Shakescene in a country"? Moreover, why must Barnfield's imitation of Greene's language here mean that he is using it for the same purposes as his model's? The history of borrowing or imitating in Elizabethan literature is often the history of pre-empting somebody else's words for use in an entirely different way. Greene's own re-employment of *"Tygers hart wrapt in a Players hyde"* is a case in point. Barnfield may well have seen *Groats-Worth* and may

---

[52]*Fovre Letters,* p. 37.
[53]"A Supposed Contemporary Allusion," pp. 379-380.

well be imitating Greene's passage, but not necessarily is he turning it upon the same man.

The remaining four stanzas of Sonnet IX have little more to offer to the larger concern of the authorship of the entire pamphlet. The second stanza is one of the best illustrations outside of Fraunce's own works of what is called in the *Arcadian Rhetorike* anadiplosis. The third stanza is a variation, combining two of Barnfield's frequently invoked admissions of inadequacy: first, his is a modest muse; and, second, other far-worthier men can do these things better.[54] The third stanza is interesting also for its use of "sugred sonnets." Not only has Barnfield employed similar diction in *The Affectionate Shepheard* ("Bath'd in a melting Sugar-Candie streame") and in *Cynthia* ("With sugred Noates of heauenly Harmonie") but also Meres, who made the phrase famous in its application to Shakespeare, may have borrowed it from his "friend master *Richard Barnefielde*."[55] The final couplet of the fourth stanza, in a somewhat garbled form, is still another variation of the sentiment found in at least three other places in Barnfield's acknowledged works.[56] The fifth and last stanza, if we take it literally, states that R. B. is unknown, in other words that he has not published anything; such, so far as we know, was true of Barnfield.

Sonnet X is a partial list of Greene's works and sheds little light on any of the matters with which we have been concerned. One item, however, which Barnfield entitles the *"Death of him"* and describes as causing "all *England* [to] shed so many teares" is identified by McKerrow as *A Maiden's Dream vpon the death of . . . Sir Christopher Hatton* (1591). If it can be shown that the *"Death of him"* alludes instead to *The Repentance,* the question of whether or not Barnfield saw that pamphlet before writing *Greenes Funeralls* will be settled. Since the *"Death of him"* is listed last, it might reasonably be regarded as Greene's final work. Hatton had died in 1591, and it may be presumed that tears still being shed in late 1592, possibly even 1593, would rather be for the more recently deceased Greene. *The Repentance* carried in its subtitle the legend "manner of his death," and Barnfield's cata-

---

[54]Compare, for instance, the entire third stanza with Sonnet XX in *Cynthia*, noting especially the similarity between the first two lines of each.

[55]*Palladis Tamia*, p. 284ᵛ.

[56]See p. 169 and footnote 21.

loguing elsewhere in the poem uses subtitles freely such as *Card of Fancie, Tullies loue, Nightingale, Metamorphosis,* etc. for *Gwydonius, Ciceronis Amor, Philomela,* and *Alcida.* The *"Death of him"* is a most natural substitute for *The Repentance.*

Greene, lodged in Hell, speaks Sonnet XI. If this should suggest to some that, though he authored the first ten, Barnfield did not write this one, five lines only need be produced from the middle of the poem to establish unmistakable stylistic links with the rest:

> For such foolish men, as *I* had neuer abused:
> Neuer abused alas, yet alas, had euer abused:
> Euer abused so, because so neuer abused.
>   Not onely seeke to quench my kindled glorie,
>   But also for to marre my *vertues* storie.
>   (C_2^v)

Extreme anadiplosis, epanalepsis, and *serpentina carmina,* as illustrated in the *Arcadian Rhetorike* (pp. 36, 45, 60) burden the first three lines. The next two refer to Harvey and are the basis of Austin's interpretation of Sonnet IX: "The paraphrase here of the same sentiment as in Sonnet IX defines beyond reasonable doubt the meaning of . . . 'Eclipst his fame' . . . . 'quench' and 'marre' take the place of 'eclipst'; and . . . 'kindled glorie' and '*vertues* storie' (*i.e.* Greene's literary repute and his good name, respectively) stand for 'fame.' "[57] As stated, I have no quarrel with this interpretation and believe it to be perfectly correct.

It might be said of XI, as well as of XII following, that Barnfield went to the *Arcadian Rhetorike* also for what is there termed "verse and meter." Pages 30-32 illustrate the *"Sapphike"* and *"Hexameters* ioyned with *Pentameters."* Sonnet XI practices the mixed meters and XII sapphics.[58] But apart from this further reliance on Fraunce, nothing can be gleaned from these, the last poems by Barnfield in *Greenes Funeralls.* Sonnets XIII and XIV have been recognized by McKerrow as the work of Richard

---

[57] "A Supposed Contemporary Allusion," pp. 378-379.

[58] John Churton Collins noticed the form of XII when attempting to establish Greene's authorship of *The Repentance*: The pamphlet "was accepted as genuine by the author of *Greenes Funeralls,* 1594, who translated into English Sapphics the prayer given at the end." *The Poems and Plays of Robert Greene,* I, 52. If Collins is correct, then Barnfield wrote his work after seeing *The Repentance,* which was not entered in the Stationers' Register until October 6.

Stanyhurst. They are reprinted with only a few minor variations. When arguing against Collier's thesis that R. B. is Barnabe Rich, McKerrow alleges that Rich disliked Stanyhurst primarily because of the hexametrist's Catholicism and that it would be unlikely for the militant Protestant to allow the poems in his pamphlet. The editor concludes, however, that "It is not certain that the two pieces in question were added to the book at R. B.'s desire."[59] A similar argument would be appropriate for Barnfield who fulminated against papists in *Lady Pecunia*. The entire production smacks so much of the publisher's hand, Barnfield so entirely divorced himself from it that no surprise is due if the poems turned out to be Gabriel Harvey's. An additional explanation for Barnfield's later repudiation of the work, if indeed *Greenes Funeralls* is one of the two he disclaimed, may be his unwillingness to be found in the company of Stanyhurst.

Everything points, then, to Barnfield's authorship. Style, content, and literary associations, even immaturity and ineptness mark the work as from the pen of a young man loyal to his friends, imitative of and indebted to Abraham Fraunce, and moving toward unnatural relations with men. He was developing an admiration for pastoral poetry, but had not yet cut any figure in the literary world of the 1590's. Amyntas, as alluded to in *Greenes Funeralls,* and even as in *The Affectionate Shepheard,* fits the accomplishments and outlines of Abraham Fraunce better than those of Thomas Watson, although I would not rule out the possibility that I am mistaken in this. The date of composition for *Greenes Funeralls* may be put back at least until after October 6, 1592 and possibly until early 1593. It should be remembered that Barnfield never thought to see the work in print and that therefore its unpolished quality, as well as its rejection in *Cynthia,* is not surprising. No work that the poet produced later ever reached the poetic depths to which the best of the pieces in *Greenes Funeralls* rose. We would hope, along with Barnfield, that, except for the gentility of soul and the loyalty of nature they display, these "Sonnets" will be forgotten as having come from the "pen of that pleasing poet."

---

[59]*Greenes Newes,* p. viii.

APPENDIX

BARNFIELD'S WILL

IN THE NAME OF GOD, AMEN, the 26th daye Februarie in the yeare of the Raigne of o^r Soveraigne Lord Charles by the Grace of God of England Scotland France & Ireland King Defender of the Faith &c. Anno Dm̄i 1626 [1627].

I RICHARD BARNFIELD of Dorlestone in the Countie of Stafford Esqre sick in bodie but of p̄fect remembrance make this my last Will and testament in manner and fforme ffollowinge. First I bequeath my soule to Almighty God my Creator and Maker and my Bodie to be buried in the p̄rshe church of Stone in the said Countie in full hope of salvation and of a ioyfull resurrection through Christ my onelie Saviour and as concerninge my worldly goods my will and mind is that Mr. John Skrimsher of Norburie Esquire his wife and sonne shall have iii 1. beinge equally divided betwixt them. Item I give to Mr. Henrie Hockenhull my purce Dagg one bedsteed one table my best saddle and bridle. Item I give to Mrs. Hockenhull xx s. Item I give to Charles Skrimsher and Gerrate Skrimsher either of them xx s. Item I give to m̄ris Elenor Skrimsher xx s. Item I give to Sarie Boeyer xx s. Item I give to Elizabeth Skrimsher xx s. and alsoe one goulde Ringe. Item I give to Martha xx s. and my gilte spoone. Item I give to Grisell Skrimsher xx s. Item I give my grandchilde Jane Barnfielde a gilte saulte which was Michill O'Ffley's if hee doe not redeeme the same in some shorte tyme. But if hee doe redeeme it she shall have the whole xi 1. that he doth owe mee. Item I give to Mr. Martin x s. Item I give to my man Richard Cotterall x s. my hare coulred sute and Cloake and x s. that I owe him. Item I give to Mrs. Doodie my truckle bedd. Item I give to my Cozen Ranforde my two best sutes. Item I give Margaret Richarsone my gonne and x s. It. I give George Hill my ould servant my other saddle and bridle. Item I give to everie servant in the house xii d. It. I leave v 1. to bestowe of a Dinner at my Buriall. Item I give to the poore of Darlestone xii d. a peece. It. I give to the poor of Stone xl s. Ite. I give to John Goodale of Waulton my blue breeches and first Jerkine. Ite. I give to my son Mr. Robert Barnefield xx s. Item the Residue of my goods being unbequeathed I give to Mr. Robert Barnefield and m̄ris Elinor Skrimsher whome I leave my sole Executors of this my last Will and Testament. In witness whereof the daie and yeare above written I have putt unto my hand and seale, R. B. [in monogram]

Sealed and published in p̄sence of us, Henry Hockenhull Thomas Daintrey, Richard Cotterall.

Probate was granted to Eleanor Skrymsher on April 7, 1627. The will was accompanied by the following inventory:

John Doodie
Richard Challenor
Thomas Daintrey
Peter Serisante
   his X mark.

A true and p̄fecte Inventorie of all the goodes of Richard Barnefeild Esqr diceased praysed the xxth daie of March Ann. Dom̄. 1626 [1627] by John Doodie Richard Challenor Thomas Daintrey Peter Serisante.

It̄m, tuw beddsteds		vi^s viii^d
item one flockbedd		iii^s iiii^d
item one bedd one boulster one pillowe one coverlid one cadwaw three blanketts	iii l.	
item nine Sheetes three pillowberes and one Towell		xxi^s
item fore Shirts		viii^s iiii^d
item sayd [=ditto]		iiii^s
item bandes ruffes handcarchyes and sockes		v^s
item stuckens garters & sockes		v^s
item gloves		ii^s vi^d
item all his waringe apperell	v l.	
item two saddes and bridlels		v^s
item his bookes		v^s
item one guilt sault 3 spoone	ii l.	
item all his glasses		iiii^s
item pewter		vii^s
item three chests one deske boxes and table		viii^s iiii^d
item warminge pan and one chest of toole		vi^s viii^d
item fire shovel tunges and grate		i^s

item bootes shooes and slippers		v^s	
item one locke and fetters		i^s	
item one goon and pistall		viii^s	iiii^d
item one brush and one cushen		i^s	vi^d
item in moneys	xl *l.*	xv^s	ii^d
Some	lxvi *l.*	xv^s	ll^d

This copy of Barnfield's will is taken from *The Complete Poems of Richard Barnfield*, ed. A. B. Grosart, pp. xiv-xvi. The sum of the moneys does not correctly total the items in the list. Grosart admits he may have made some errors in reading figures from the will.

BIBLIOGRAPHY OF WORKS CITED

A., T. *The Massacre of Money*. London, 1602.

Alexander, Peter. *Shakespeare's HENRY VI and RICHARD III.* Cambridge, England, 1929.

Archaica, ed. Sir Samuel Egerton Brydges, 2 vols. London, 1815.

B., R. *Greenes Funeralls*. London, 1594.

B., R. *Orpheus his Journey to Hell*. London, 1595.

Barnfield, Richard. *The Affectionate Shepheard*. London, 1594.

Barnfield, Richard. *The Affectionate Shepheard*, ed. J. O. Halliwell. London, 1845.

Barnfield, Richard. *The Complete Poems of Richard Barnfield*, ed. A. B. Grosart. London, 1876.

Barnfield, Richard. *Cynthia. With Certaine Sonnets*. London, 1595.

Barnfield, Richard. *The Encomion of Lady Pecunia*. London, 1598.

Barnfield, Richard. *Lady Pecunia*. London, 1605.

Barnfield, Richard. *The Poems of Richard Barnfield*, ed. Montague Summers. London, 1936.

Barnfield, Richard. *Richard Barnfield: Poems: 1594-1598*, ed. Edward Arber. London, 1896.

Baugh, A. C., *et al. A Literary History of England*. New York, 1948.

Beeching, H. C. "English Literature and American Professors." *Athenaeum* (1901), 661.

Breton, Nicholas. *The Works in Verse and Prose of Nicholas Breton*, ed. A. B. Grosart, 2 vols. Edinburgh, 1879.

Bush, Douglas. *Mythology and the Renaissance Tradition in English Poetry*. Minneapolis, 1932.

C., H. *Piers Plainnes Seauen Yeres Prentiship*, ed. H. Varnhagen. Erlangen, 1900.

Cavalier and Puritan, ed. Hyder Rollins. Cambridge, Mass., 1923.

Chambers, E. K. *English Pastorals*. London, 1895.

Chambers, E. K. *William Shakespeare*, 2 vols. Oxford, 1930.

Collections for a History of Staffordshire. Published by the William Salt Archaeological Society. London, 1900.

Collier, John Payne. *A Bibliographical and Critical Account of the Rarest Books in the English Language*, 4 vols. New York, 1866.

Collier, John Payne. *The History of English Dramatic Poetry*, 3 vols. London, 1831.

Collier, John Payne. "Shakespeare and Barnfield." *N&Q*, 2nd Series, II (1856), 8-9.

Collier, John Payne. "Shakespeare and THE PASSIONATE PILGRIM." *Athenaeum* (1856), 616-617.

Corser, Thomas. *Collectanea Anglo-Poetica*, Part X. Manchester, 1880.

Cory, H. E. "The Golden Age of the Spenserian Pastoral." *PMLA*, XXV (1910), 241-267.

Crawford, Charles. *Collectanea*. Stratford, 1906.

Crawford, Charles. "*Greenes Funeralls*, 1594, and Nicholas Breton." *SP*, Extra Series, I (1929), 1-39.

Crawford, Charles. "Richard Barnfield, Marlowe, and Shakespeare."
N&Q, 9th Series, VIII (1901), 217-219, 277-279.

Devlin, C. *The Life of Robert Southwell: Poet and Martyr.*
New York, 1956.

Dickenson, John. *Arisbas, Euphues Amidst his Slumbers.* London, 1594.

Dickenson, John. *Prose and Verse By John Dickenson,* ed. A. B. Grosart.
Manchester, 1878.

Dickenson, John. *The Shepheards Complaint.* London, 1596.

Drake, Nathan. *Shakespeare and His Times,* 2 vols. London, 1817.

Drayton, Michael. *The Works of Michael Drayton,* ed. J. W. Hebel,
et al., 5 vols. Oxford, 1931-1941.

Eccles, Mark. *Christopher Marlowe in London.* Cambridge, Mass., 1934.

Elizabethan Sonnet Cycles: Idea, Fidessa, Chloris, ed. Martha Crowe Foote.
London, 1897.

Elizabethan Sonnets, ed. Sidney Lee, 2 vols. Westminster, 1904.

England's Helicon, ed. Hyder Rollins, 2 vols. Cambridge, Mass., 1935.

Fleay, F. G. *Guide to Chaucer and Spenser.* London, 1877.

Forsythe, R. S. "The Passionate Shepherd; [*sic*] and English Poetry."
PMLA, XL (1925), 692-742.

Fraunce, Abraham. *The Arcadian Rhetorike,* ed. Ethel Seaton.
Oxford, 1950.

Fraunce, Abraham. *The Countesse of Pembrokes Emanuel.* London, 1591.

Fraunce, Abraham. *The Countesse of Pembrokes Yuychurch.*
London, 1591.

Fraunce, Abraham. *The Lamentations of Amyntas for the death of Phillis.*
London, 1587.

Fraunce, Abraham. *The Lawiers Logike.* London, 1588.

Fraunce, Abraham. *The Third part of the Countesse of Pembrokes
Yuychurch,* London, 1592.

Fraunce, Abraham. *Victoria,* ed. G. C. Moore Smith. Louvain, 1906.

Graves, T. S. "THE ARRAIGNMENT OF PARIS and
Sixteenth-Century Flattery." *MLN,* XXVIII (1913), 48-49.

Greene, Robert. *The Dramatic Works of Robert Greene,* ed. A. Dyce,
2 vols. London, 1831.

Greene, Robert. *The Plays and Poems of Robert Greene,* ed. John Churton
Collins, 2 vols. Oxford, 1905.

Greg, W. W. *Pastoral Poetry and Pastoral Drama.* London, 1906.

H., T. *Oenone and Paris,* ed. J. Q. Adams. Washington, 1943.

Hanford, James Holly. "The Pastoral Elegy and Milton's LYCIDAS."
PMLA, XXV (1910), 403-447.

Harington, Sir John. *Metamorphosis of Ajax.* London, 1596.

Harrison, G. B. "Books and Readers, 1591-4." *The Library,* 4th Series,
VIII (1927), 273-302.

Harvey, Gabriel, *Fovre Letters and Certeine Sonnets,* ed. G. B. Harrison.
London, 1922.

Henneman, J. B. "Barnfield's Ode: 'As It Fell Upon A Day.'"
An English Miscellany. Oxford, 1901.

Historical Manuscripts Commission, Report No. 3. London, 1872.

Honigmann, E. A. J. "Shakespeare's 'Lost Source-Plays.'" *MLR,* XLIX (1954), 293-307.

Hudson, H. H. "Penelope Devereux as Sidney's Stella." *HLB,* VII (1935), 89-129.

Hunter, Joseph. *Chorus Vatum Anglicanorum.* British Museum Add. MSS. 24487-24492.

Illustrations of Old English Literature, ed. John Payne Collier, 3 vols. London, 1866.

James, W. P. *The Life and Works of Richard Barnfield,* unpublished dissertation. Northwestern, 1952.

Johnson, F. R. "The First Edition of Gabriel Harvey's FOVRE LETTERS." *The Library,* 4th Series, XV (1934), 212-223.

Johnson, F. R. "Gabriel Harvey's THREE LETTERS: A First Issue of His FOVRE LETTERS." *The Library,* 5th Series, I (1946), 134-136.

Jonson, Ben. *Ben Jonson,* ed. C. H. Herford, *et al.,* 11 vols. Oxford, 1925-1952.

L., R. *Diella, certaine Sonnets.* London, 1596.

Leake, S. M. *Nummi Britannici Historia.* London, 1726.

Lewis, C. S. *English Literature in the Sixteenth Century.* Oxford, 1954.

Littledale, H. "Did Thomas Lodge Write a Poem about Amintas?" *Athenaeum* (1899), 82-83.

Lodge, Thomas. *A Fig for Momus.* London, 1595.

Lodge, Thomas. *Phillis.* London, 1593.

M., J. *A Health to the Gentlemanly Profession of Seruing-Men.* London, 1598.

Marlowe, Christopher. *Works and Life of Christopher Marlowe,* Gen. ed. R. H. Case, 6 vols. London, 1930-1933.

McNeir, W. F. "Barnfield's Borrowings From Spenser." *N&Q,* CC (1955), 510-511.

Meres, Francis. *Palladis Tamia,* ed. D. C. Allen. New York, 1938.

Miller, H. K. "The Paradoxical Encomium with Special Reference to Its Vogue in England, 1600-1800." *MP,* LIII (1956), 145-178.

Morris, Harry. "Ophelia's 'Bonny Sweet Robin.'" *PMLA,* LXXIII (1958), 601-603.

Morris, Harry. "Richard Barnfield, 'Amyntas,' and the Sidney Circle." *PMLA,* LXXIV (1959), 318-324.

Morris, Harry. "Richard Barnfield: THE AFFECTIONATE SHEPHEARD." *Tulane Studies in English,* X (1960), 13-38.

Morris, Harry. "Thomas Watson and Abraham Fraunce." *PMLA,* LXXVI (1961), 152-153.

Munro, John. *The Shakespeare Allusion Book.* London, 1909.

Mustard, W. P. "Later Echoes of the Greek Bucolic Poets." *AJP,* XXX (1909), 245-283.

Nashe, Thomas. *The Works of Thomas Nashe,* ed. R. B. McKerrow, 5 vols. London, 1910.

Nicholson, Samuel. *Acolastus His After-Witte,* ed. A. B. Grosart,

Ovid. *Fasti,* ed. Sir J. G. Frazer. London, 1931.

Paradise, N. B. *Thomas Lodge, The History of an Elizabethan.*
New Haven, 1931.

Pearson, L. E. *Elizabethan Love Conventions.* Berkeley, 1933.

Occasional Issues of Unique or Very Rare Books. Manchester, 1876.

Norlin, G. "Conventions of the Pastoral Elegy." *AJP,* XXXII (1911),
294-312.

Nugae Poeticae, ed. J. O. Halliwell. London, 1844.

Peele, George. *The Arraignment of Paris,* ed. H. H. Child. Oxford, 1910.

Pepys Ballads, The, ed. Hyder Rollins, 8 vols. Cambridge, Mass.,
1929-1932.

Phillips, Edward. *Theatrum Poetarum.* London, 1675.

Poirier, Michel. *Christopher Marlowe.* London, 1951.

Pollard, A. W. "Introduction," Peter Alexander, *Shakespeare's*
HENRY VI and RICHARD III. Cambridge, England, 1929.

Pruvost, R. *Robert Greene et ses romans (1558-1592).* Paris, 1938.

Puttenham, George. *The Arte of English Poesie,* ed. G. D. Willcock and
A. Walker. Cambridge, England, 1936.

R., B. *Greenes Newes both from Heauen and Hell by B. R. 1593 and*
Greenes Funeralls By R. B. 1594, ed. R. B. McKerrow.
Stratford-upon-Avon, 1922.

Ralegh, Sir Walter. *The Poems of Sir Walter Ralegh,* ed. Agnes Latham.
London, 1951.

Ralegh, Sir Walter. *The Poems of Sir Walter Raleigh, with Those of Sir*
Henry Wotton and Other Courtly Poets, ed. J. Hannah.
London, 1892.

Ritson, Joseph. *Bibliographia Poetica.* London, 1802.

Robinson, Robert. *The Phonetic Writings of Robert Robinson,*
ed. E. J. Dobson, *EETS,* No. 238. London, 1957.

Roxburghe Ballads, ed. John Payne Collier. London, 1847.

Sabie, Francis. *Pans Pipe.* London, 1595.

Saintsbury, G. *History of Elizabethan Literature.* London, 1887.

Sasek, L. A. "William Smith and THE SHEPHEARDES CALENDER."
PQ, XXXIX (1960), 251-253.

Scott, Janet. *Les Sonnets Élisabéthains.* Paris, 1929.

Seneca. *Seneca His Tenne Tragedies,* trans. Thomas Newton, *et al.* London,
1581.

Shakespeare, W. *The Complete Works of William Shakespeare,* ed. Sidney
Lee, 20 vols. New York, 1906-1908.

Shakespeare, W. *The First Sketches of the Second and Third Parts of*
King Henry the Sixth, ed. J. O. Halliwell. London, 1843.

Shakespeare, W. *Henry VI: Part II,* ed. John Dover Wilson. Cambridge,
England, 1952.

Shakespeare, W. *The Modern Readers' Shakespeare,* ed. H. N. Hudson,
et al., 10 vols. New York, 1909.

Shakespeare, W. *The Passionate Pilgrim,* ed. E. Dowden. London, n.d.

Shakespeare, W. *The Passionate Pilgrim,* ed. Sidney Lee. Oxford, 1905.

Shakespeare, W. *The Plays and Poems of William Shakespeare*, ed. John Payne Collier, 8 vols. London, 1878.

Shakespeare, W. *The Poems*, Variorum, ed. Hyder Rollins. Philadelphia, 1938.

Shakespeare, W. *Poems and Pericles*, ed. Sidney Lee. Oxford, 1905.

Shakespeare, W. *Shakespeare's Comedies, Histories, Tragedies, and Poems*, ed. John Payne Collier, 6 vols. London, 1858.

Shakespeare, W. *Shakespeare's Poems*, The Arden Shakespeare, ed. C. K. Pooler. London, 1911.

Shakespeare, W. *Shakespeare's Venus and Adonis*, ed. C. Edmonds. London, 1870.

Shakespeare, W. *Sonnets*, The Yale Shakespeare, ed. E. B. Reed. New Haven, 1923.

Shakespeare, W. *The Works of William Shakespeare*, ed. John Payne Collier, 9 vols. London, 1841-1853.

Sidney, Sir Philip. *The Complete Works of Sir Philip Sidney*, ed. A. Feuillerat, 4 vols. Cambridge, England, 1922.

Smith, Hallett. *Elizabethan Poetry*. Cambridge, Mass., 1952.

Southwell, Robert. *The Complete Poems of Robert Southwell*, ed. A. B. Grosart. London, 1872.

Spenser, Edmund. *The Works of Edmund Spenser*, A Variorum Edition, ed. E. Greenlaw, et al., 11 vols. Baltimore, 1932-1957.

Staton, W. F. Jr. "The Influence of Thomas Watson on Elizabethan Ovidian Poetry." *Studies in the Renaissance*, VI (1959), 243-250.

Staton, W. F. Jr. "Thomas Watson and Abraham Fraunce." *PMLA*, LXXVI (1961), 150-152.

Strode, William. *The Poetical Works of William Strode*, ed. B. Dobell. London, 1907.

Swinburne, A. C. "Social Verse." *The Forum*, XII (1891), 169-185.

Swinburne, A. C. *A Study of Shakespeare*. London, 1880.

Synesius. *A Paradoxe Prouing that Baldnesse Is Much Better Than Bushie Haire*, Englished by A. Fleming. London, 1579.

Thomson, J. A. K. *Shakespeare and the Classics*. London, 1952.

Transcript of the Registers of the Company of Stationers of London: 1554-1640 A. D., ed. Edward Arber, 5 vols. London, 1875-1894.

Tudor Poetry and Prose, ed. J. W. Hebel, et al. New York, 1953.

Vallans, William. *A Tale of Two Swannes*. London, 1590.

Verses of Prayse and Ioye, written upon Her Maiesties Preseruation. London, 1586.

Visitation of Shropshire, ed. G. Grazebrook and J. P. Rylands, 2 vols. London, 1889.

Warton, Thomas. *The History of English Poetry*. London, 1870.

Warton, Thomas. *The History of English Poetry*, ed. W. C. Hazlitt, 4 vols. London, 1871.

Watson, Thomas. *Amintae Gaudia*. London, 1592.

Watson, Thomas. *Amyntas*. London, 1585.

Watson, Thomas. *The first sett Of Italian Madrigalls Englished*. London, 1590.

Watson, Thomas. *Meliboeus*. London, 1590.

Watson, Thomas. *Thomas Watson: Poems*, ed. E. Arber. London, 1870.

Webbe, William. *A Discourse of English Poetrie*. London, 1586.

Whitney, Geffrey. *A Choice of Emblems*. London, 1586.

Willoughby, E. E. *A Printer of Shakespeare*. London, 1934.

Wilson, John Dover. "Malone and the Upstart Crow." *Shakespeare Survey*, IV (1951), 56-68.

Wilson, Mona. *Sir Philip Sidney*. New York, 1932.

Wood, Anthony. *Athenae Oxonienses*, 2 vols. London, 1721.

Wood, Anthony. *Athenae Oxonienses*, ed. Philip Bliss, 4 vols. London, 1813-1820.